Exploring the Financial Parables of Jesus

Exploring the Financial Parables of Jesus

The Economy of Grace and the Generosity of God

Keith Bodner

Baker Academic
a division of Baker Publishing Group
Grand Rapids, Michigan

Published by Baker Academic
a division of Baker Publishing Group
Grand Rapids, Michigan
BakerAcademic.com

Printed in the United States of America

Library of Congress Cataloging-in-Publication Data
Names: Bodner, Keith, 1967– author.
Title: Exploring the financial parables of Jesus : the economy of grace and the generosity of God / Keith Bodner.
Description: Grand Rapids, Michigan : Baker Academic, a division of Baker Publishing Group, [2025] | Includes bibliographical references and index.
Identifiers: LCCN 2024059584 | ISBN 9781540969323 (paperback) | ISBN 9781540969545 (casebound) | ISBN 9781493451609 (ebook) | ISBN 9781493451616 (pdf)
Subjects: LCSH: Jesus Christ—Parables. | Finance, Personal—Biblical teaching. | Finance, Personal—Religious aspects—Christianity. | Bible. Gospels—Criticism, interpretation, etc.
Classification: LCC BT375.3 .B63 2025 | DDC 226.8/06—dc23/eng/20250206
LC record available at https://lccn.loc.gov/2024059584

Unless otherwise indicated, translations of the Hebrew Bible (Old Testament) are the author's own.

In chapters 2 and 4, unless otherwise indicated, translations of the New Testament are from *The Bible for Everyone: A New Translation* by John Goldingay and Tom Wright. London: SPCK, 2018.

Cover design by Paula Gibson.

Baker Publishing Group publications use paper produced from sustainable forestry practices and postconsumer waste whenever possible.

25 26 27 28 29 30 31 7 6 5 4 3 2 1

Contents

Preface

Hidden Treasure

THE HIGHEST-RATED MOVIES, novels, plays, and TV shows all have some things in common. First, they have memorable characters. Whether heroes or villains, saints or sinners, tragically flawed or comically quirky, a great cast of relatable characters is paramount. Another factor is an interesting plot. The best storylines have a sequence of events that catches and holds the audience's attention. A third aspect is special effects. This is a reference not to CGI monsters or digital machines but, rather, to the powerful use of language and theme, with striking metaphors, stylish images, and evocative landscapes created with words (not just with software). When these elements are put together on a compact narrative canvas, all the raw materials are in place for a *parable*.

It could be that in our age of distraction the parable is an ideal genre. Some might even think of parables like the TikTok of the New Testament: short "videos" featuring everyday people rather than celebrities, with a grainy texture and spontaneous feel (and branded as dangerous in certain quarters). Parables are usually short—sometimes comical or sad, festive or serious—but always engaging and often ending with an M. Night Shyamalan surprising plot twist.[1] As we struggle to figure out the meaning of

1. For those who typically read footnotes like this, examples might include Kafka's *The Trial*, the writings of Kierkegaard, or some of the works of Charles Dickens; see, e.g., Linda M. Lewis, *Dickens, His Parables, and His Reader* (Columbia: University of Missouri Press, 2011); cf. Thomas C. Oden, ed., *Parables of Kierkegaard* (Princeton: Princeton University Press,

a parable, we are almost always challenged in the process. This book is an attempt to capture the joy of discovery that can accompany a fresh hearing of the parables that Jesus tells in the New Testament. More specifically, our primary focus will be on a portfolio of parables that have a financial angle or involve some facet of wealth. Here is a brief example:

> The kingdom of heaven is like treasure hidden in a field: someone found it, hid it again, and then in great joy went and sold everything and bought that field.

In roughly 147 characters or less, this is a valuable introduction to the world of parables. Found in Matthew 13:44, this short anecdote is part of a collection of seven parables in a row that Jesus shares in the region of the northern Sea of Galilee. At this stage in the narrative, there has been increasing suspicion and hostility from the religious authorities. In response to such opposition, Jesus wisely shifts to a different form of storytelling, making important points but with enough subtlety that the various authorities are unable to bring any formal legal charges against him.[2] Before long, these parables start to go viral and attract increasingly large crowds as Matthew's plotline continues.

Listening to the short parable quoted above, we can hear that Jesus is crafting a miniature portrait of the kingdom of God (or as Matthew calls it, "the kingdom of Heaven"). Jesus says that having a chance to enter this kingdom can be compared to someone making an unexpected discovery of a treasure of unimaginable worth. It is an encounter that prompts an abrupt shift in priorities and a life-altering change of direction. Whoever finds this new reality values it more than anything else and intends to cheerfully divest themselves of previous assets in order to enjoy its fullness.

It should be noted that the unnamed figure in the parable makes this discovery in a seemingly random way. Some readers might think that a similar situation happens to the main character in *Charlie and the Chocolate*

1978). On the plot twists in the Shyamalan film oeuvre, see Michael Bamberger, *The Man Who Heard Voices: Or, How M. Night Shyamalan Risked His Career on a Fairy Tale* (New York: Penguin Books, 2006).

2. Douglas D. Webster, *The Parables: Jesus's Friendly Subversive Speech* (Grand Rapids: Kregel Academic, 2021); Ian Boxall, *Matthew Through the Centuries*, WBBC (Oxford: Wiley-Blackwell, 2019), 204–5. See also Peter Yaw Oppong-Kumi, *Matthean Sets of Parables*, WUNT 2/340 (Tübingen: Mohr Siebeck, 2013), 73–76.

Factory, who is just walking along the street and alights upon some money that will buy the golden ticket, producing a seismic shift in his life. For Matthew's audience, the plot twist in the parable eventually sinks in: There are lots of people, so we are invited to consider, who discover the worth of the kingdom of God apparently by accident![3] In the routine of everyday life—whether laboring away or at school or in the library or at sports practice or at youth group—suddenly, in an unplanned way, a person stumbles upon a vast fortune.[4]

Does the parable suggest that everything is a sheer coincidence, or could there be another force and a larger design at work? It is left to the listener's imagination to wonder if the treasure, akin to Bilbo's discovery in *The Hobbit* and *The Lord of the Rings*, somehow was *meant* to be found. But perhaps the accidental nature of the discovery should be emphasized because, after all, people do not enter the kingdom of God because they deserve it, nor can it be earned.[5] Rather, one can enter this kingdom simply because they discover something priceless that has been concealed and they recognize its incomparable value. *The parable of the hidden treasure* is just a single example, and much more could be said. But it does give a flavor of what this book is about, as I aim to provide an *experience of Jesus's stories* and sample some colorful moments of interpretive history and scholarly opinion along the way.

GPS Overview

The objective of this book is to provide some concise explorations of the financial parables in the New Testament. My contention is that when we listen to all of them together, there is a message about how the economy of grace unfolds, along with examples of our optimal responses to divine

3. Barbara E. Reid, *The Gospel According to Matthew* (Collegeville, MN: Liturgical Press, 2005), 78–79; Michael Green, *The Message of Matthew* (Downers Grove, IL: InterVarsity, 2000), 153.

4. For the contrast in the next parable about the intentionality of the merchant and the pearl in Matt. 13:45–46, see Charles H. Talbert, *Matthew*, Paideia Commentaries on the New Testament (Grand Rapids: Baker Academic, 2010), 171; David E. Garland, *Reading Matthew: A Literary and Theological Commentary on the First Gospel*, Reading the New Testament (Macon, GA: Smyth & Helwys, 2001), 153.

5. Finding the treasure, as Ulrich Luz maintains, is *not* a reward bestowed for good behavior. Luz, *Matthew: A Commentary*, 3 vols., trans. James E. Crouch, Hermeneia (Minneapolis: Fortress, 2001–7), 2:277.

generosity. Of course, these parables may not provide the absolute entirety of the gospel message, but they do give insight about investing in the kingdom of God and offer an invitation to reappraise what is most valuable in life. Other scholars can further analyze the role of each of these parables within its particular context, and indeed, a larger biblical theology. The focus here, however, is on the overarching message and contribution of this unique group of stories told by Jesus.

By way of road map, chapter 1 sets the stage with an early parable from the Hebrew Bible, as Nathan the prophet confronts King David with a story about a stolen lamb in 2 Samuel 12:1–4. Remarks on Nathan's storytelling are followed by four general points about how parables are approached in this study: Parables can be less innocent than they sound; a parable can have more personal application than immediately meets the ear; parables might have several layers of meaning and resonate with images in or allusions to the Hebrew Bible; and the ultimate purpose of a parable is to challenge our perspective and shift the direction of our lives. After these comments, I briefly survey *the parable of the sower* in Mark 4:4–20, often referred to as a "master parable."[6] Our tour through the financial parables then begins by looking at a few scenes, including *the pearl of great price* in Matthew 13:45–46 and *the parable of the rich barn builder* in Luke 12:13–21.[7]

Chapter 2 undertakes a reading of *the shrewd manager* in Luke 16:1–9, often considered to be the most difficult or controversial of the parables. The problem revolves around the main character, and even the most charitable interpreters have to concede that he is a scoundrel. After this manager is dismissed for squandering his master's capital, he resorts to some very shady deals in order to secure his own future. It is notable that Jesus tells this story in a larger discussion about stewardship, so the audience can connect the parable with the issues of management theories and strategies

6. E.g., Frederick Houk Borsch, "Parables of Jesus: Told and Enacted," in *Earliest Christianity Within the Boundaries of Judaism: Essays in Honor of Bruce Chilton*, ed. Alan J. Avery-Peck, Craig A. Evans, and Jacob Neusner, BRLJ 49 (Leiden: Brill, 2016), 259–60.

7. The typical titles (The Lost Coin, The Prodigal Son, The Good Samaritan, etc.) were not originally included in the parables but added by later tradition. Sometimes these titles are helpful, but often they can be a bit misleading or a distraction. So I use them loosely and without much conviction throughout this book, trusting that the reader can follow along. For background and further discussion, see Lauri Thurén, *Parables Unplugged: Reading the Lukan Parables in Their Rhetorical Context* (Minneapolis: Fortress, 2014); David B. Gowler, *The Parables After Jesus: Their Imaginative Receptions Across Two Millenia* (Grand Rapids: Baker Academic, 2017).

within the kingdom of God. To be sure, the idea of a new kind of stewardship continues in chapter 3 when we turn to one of the most famous parables, *the good Samaritan* in Luke 10:25–37, with a surprising main character who is exceedingly generous with time and money.

Chapter 4 works through the account of *the rich man and Lazarus* in Luke 16:19–31, with two characters from opposite ends of the socioeconomic spectrum. Chapter 5 is the longest in this book because it tackles the epic *parable of the prodigal sons* (Luke 15:11–32), with its colorful shifts in spatial settings and open-ended conclusion. Chapter 6 studies two parables about fairness and justice: *the persistent widow* in Luke 18:1–8 and *the vineyard workers* found in Matthew 20:1–16. Chapter 7 focuses on three parables: *the Pharisee and the tax collector* in Luke 18:9–14, *the tower builder* in Luke 14:28–30, and *the parable of bags of gold* (also known as *the parable of the talents*) in Matthew 25:14–30. Finally, a short conclusion brings this book to a close with a reading of *the parable of the unmerciful servant* in Matthew 18:21–35, given in response to Peter's searching question about forgiveness and relationship meltdowns.

To reiterate, these parables with a financial edge are peppered throughout Matthew, Mark, and Luke. But when they are considered together, a larger theological plotline begins to emerge. As we noticed with *the parable of the hidden treasure*, these stories are intended to illustrate various angles of the kingdom of God. Most kingdoms have two things: a king and a group of citizens. Typically, kings are interested in keeping control over their citizens, and eventually many start hoarding all sorts of possessions (for example, stockpiling wealth and weapons).

But after listening to these parables, we discover that Jesus is announcing the kingdom of God, which operates according to a completely different kind of economy. In this kingdom, relationships are much more important than stuff, and love is preferable to fear. Resources are used to serve others, not just accumulated. Moreover, the citizens in the kingdom of God are not controlled through bribes or intimidation. Instead, they are partners in the same enterprise and shareholders in the company. We learn through these various parables that people are of immense value to God and are not mere commodities.

Financial parables can provide fresh insight on familiar ideas. Someone could, theoretically, march up to you and say, "Quit sinning!" Alternatively, someone might share an illustration of what sin can be compared to. Through these parables that summarize all sorts of biblical teaching, it becomes clear that sin is like a bad debt. Imagine you were given money to invest and yet you squandered it with all sorts of useless (even self-destructive) purchases, and now you are facing a mountain of debt. Forgiveness is experienced when another person is willing to pay that debt for you. Why would someone do that? As will be suggested, the kingdom of God works on *the economy of grace*. Rather than having to earn God's favor, grace is offered as a gift and ought to be received with gratitude. Moreover, grace is the most prized asset in this kingdom, and miraculously, there is no scarcity as there is with other resources.

The Write Stuff

This book was written in the middle of a global crisis. It started with various lectures given to university and seminary students and a teaching series at the church where I serve every weekend. The various chapters flow out of classroom notes, chapel talks, podcasts, pandemic preaching, and Zoom sessions. Experts are not the intended audience for this book, and plenty of such large volumes exist already.[8] Alternatively, this short book is directed toward students and general readers who are less acquainted with biblical studies. Such readers might really want to learn more about the Bible but aren't sure where to start. Left to our own voracious devices, we might be tempted to drift toward Netflix and other attention-grabbing escapes. This book intends to point us in a different direction, and in my view, parables are an excellent point of entry into the larger biblical story.[9]

8. One could usefully cite the prefatory remark of Simon Gathercole in *Defending Substitution: An Essay on Atonement in Paul*, ASBT (Grand Rapids: Baker Academic, 2015): "On Callimachus's principle that 'a big book is a big evil' (μέγα βιβλίον μέγα κακόν), I hope that the brevity of this book is more an advantage than a disadvantage."

9. For general overviews of parables and their contribution to biblical literature, the following works (in addition to citations throughout this book) can be consulted: Craig L. Blomberg, "Interpreting the Parables: Where Do We Go from Here?," *CBQ* 53 (1991): 50–78; Klyne R. Snodgrass, "From Allegorizing to Allegorizing: A History of the Interpretation of the Parables of Jesus," in R. Longenecker, *Challenge of Jesus' Parables*, 3–29; I. Howard Marshall, *New Testament Theology: Many Witnesses, One Gospel* (Downers Grove, IL: InterVarsity, 2004); Thomas R. Schreiner, *New Testament Theology: Magnifying God in Christ* (Grand Rapids: Baker Academic, 2008), 59–64; Raymond E. Brown, *An Introduction to the New Testament: The Abridged Edition*, ed. Marion L. Soards, AYBRL (New Haven: Yale University Press, 2016), 47–48, 64–65, 84–85; Eckhard J. Schnabel, *Mark*, TNTC (Downers Grove, IL: InterVarsity, 2017); Peter Stuhlmacher, *Biblical Theology of the New Testament*, trans. and ed. Daniel P.

Translations of Scripture can be tricky, and the market is presently flooded with versions. One of the most frequent questions I get is "What translation is the best?" Unless otherwise indicated, the renderings of the Hebrew Bible are my own, and for the New Testament I use the NIV (sometimes slightly adjusted). The exceptions are chapters 2 and 4, where I have adopted the fairly recent translation produced by Tom Wright.[10] Having used this translation in lectures and sermons, I found that it worked well for these chapters. The reader doesn't need to agree with every word choice made by Wright, but overall his translation is a user-friendly rendering of the Greek New Testament, and one of its strengths is the colloquial feel of the parables. Only punctuation and a few very trivial things are occasionally altered. It would be a good idea for readers to have another standard version at hand (such as the NRSV or ESV), for ease of reference and to gain a larger sense of the surrounding context.

If parables are like buried treasure, then I should admit that I stumbled into this book project without the typical kinds of planning or foresight. Consequently, I am grateful to a number of people who have offered roadside assistance along the way, not least my academic colleagues, scholarly friends, and longsuffering parishioners at Brunswick Street Baptist Church in Fredericton, New Brunswick, who endured *all* of these chapters in verbal form (with way too much detail). A hearty word of thanks to all my students in those pandemic years—from first-semester undergraduates to seasoned PhD thesis writers—who have listened patiently and happily discussed the extraordinary literary power of parables. I have learned much more from you than the other way around.

Bailey (Grand Rapids: Eerdmans, 2018); N. T. Wright and Michael F. Bird, *The New Testament in Its World: An Introduction to the History, Literature, and Theology of the First Christians* (Grand Rapids: Zondervan, 2019), 204–5.

10. John Goldingay and Tom Wright, *The Bible for Everyone: A New Translation* (London: SPCK, 2018).

1 The World Wide Web of Parables

Two men lived in the same city—
one was very rich, but the other was really poor.
The rich man had vast holdings of flocks and herds,
but the poor man had nothing,
except for one little ewe lamb that he had bought.
He raised the lamb, and it grew up with him and his children together.
From his own plate the lamb ate, and it drank from his own cup,
sleeping soundly in his arms, and it was like a daughter to him.
One day a traveler stopped by to see the rich man.
But instead of taking something from his own flock or herd
to prepare as a meal for the wayfarer who arrived at his house,
he went and took the poor man's little lamb.
The rich man slaughtered it,
and then he prepared it for the visitor who had arrived.

THIS SHOCKING EPISODE of greed and cruelty is found deep in the Old Testament, at the beginning of 2 Samuel 12. As we will see in a moment, the story is used to unmask a royal crime, and it is a classic example of a *parable*. We might not use the word "parable" very often, but it is a genre of storytelling with a long history. The ancient philosopher Plato wrote a parable about a cave, and it is still discussed in college courses today.[1] Contemporary writers also use the genre, as in the recent book *The Nutmeg's Curse: Parables for a Planet in Crisis*.[2] At first glance, we might see parables as unassuming stories that usually involve characters or situations from our everyday routine. Yet they can also be quite deceptive and can disarm the reader in order to make a point that is not quickly forgotten. A typical definition is something like this: "At its simplest the parable is a metaphor or simile drawn from nature or common life, arresting the hearer by its vividness or strangeness, and leaving the mind in sufficient doubt about its precise application to tease it into active thought."[3]

Parables are often strategically employed to break down a reader's wall of defense. The following analogy might be helpful: When the Greek army was unable to conquer the city of Troy, they resorted to a different tactic. The wily Odysseus and a group of soldiers hid inside a wooden horse left outside the city gate. With a fatal underestimation, the Trojans themselves brought the horse through the gate and into the city, to their lasting regret. Indeed, too many modern citizens in our day have unwittingly allowed a Trojan virus to infect their computer terminal and have lost their hard drives, much as the Trojans lost their city. Similarly, the rustic charm or subject matter of a parable catches the listener's attention and enables the story to gain a hearing. In many cases it can be hard to grasp the meaning of a parable right away, and it becomes clear only after some reflection or explanation. When finishing *The Nutmeg's Curse*, for instance, the reader eventually realizes that the book is not so much about the planet's crisis as it is about our own: How are we living our lives, and is it possible to change our ways?

Returning to the parable of 2 Samuel 12 quoted above, we should note that it occurs at a crucial time in the career of Israel's most famous king.

1. Gregory L. Ulmer, "Post-Criticism: Conceptual Takes," in *The Routledge Companion to Experimental Literature*, ed. Joe Bray, Alison Gibbons, and Brian McHale (New York: Routledge, 2012), 269.

2. Amitav Ghosh, *The Nutmeg's Curse: Parables for a Planet in Crisis* (Chicago: University of Chicago Press, 2021).

3. C. H. Dodd, *The Parables of the Kingdom* (London: Collins, 1961), 16. Note also Ruben Zimmermann, *Puzzling the Parables of Jesus: Methods and Interpretation* (Minneapolis: Fortress, 2015), 137: "A *parable* is a short narratival (1) fictional (2) text that is related in the narrated world to known reality (3) but, by way of implicit or explicit transfer signals, makes it understood that the meaning of the narration must be differentiated from the literal words of the text (4). In its appeal dimension (5) it challenges the reader to carry out a metaphoric transfer of meaning that is steered by contextual information (6)."

David is well known for some brave exploits in his younger days, such as the victory over the Philistine Goliath and the later conquest of Jerusalem (which he turns into his capital city after he becomes king of all Israel). But the events of 2 Samuel 11 are catastrophic, as the king first impregnates Bathsheba—the wife of one of his top generals—and then orders the secret death of her husband, Uriah. There are some sordid deeds earlier in David's career, but these brazen acts of adultery and murder are a new low. Lest the reader think that David gets away with it, in the very next chapter (2 Sam. 12) God sends the prophet Nathan. We first meet Nathan earlier in the narrative when he announces an astonishing promise to David in 2 Samuel 7 about a lasting dynasty and an enduring house. But now Nathan arrives and confronts the guilty king with his parable about the wealthy man's rapacious behavior. In 2 Samuel 12, David's reaction after he hears Nathan's parable sounds loud and aggressive:

> [5]David's wrath was greatly kindled against the man, and he said to Nathan, "As the LORD lives, surely the man who did this is a son of death! [6]The ewe-lamb he'll repay fourfold, on account of the fact that he did this thing, and had no compassion!"
> [7]But then Nathan said to David, "You are the man!"

Instead of a direct accusation, Nathan unfolds a story designed to catch the king's interest, a story about a merciless rich character seizing something that does not belong to him. There are good reasons why Nathan might use a parable here. In most ancient Near Eastern countries, the king was essentially the chair of the supreme court. Nathan's parable is so effective that it generates a judgment from the king on the spot.[4] For all David knows, he thinks he's hearing a report from the nightly news: In his anger over the rich man's conduct, he is quick to render a verdict.[5] But as

4. For an overview of the genre of parables in the Old Testament, see Jeremy Schipper, *Parables and Conflict in the Hebrew Bible* (New York: Cambridge University Press, 2007). Cf. Susan Niditch, *Ethics in the Hebrew Bible and Beyond* (New York: Oxford University Press, 2024), 88: "The *mashal*, sometimes translated parable or fable, is rooted in the drawing of comparisons, of 'being like.' The weaver of a *mashal* creates a metaphor, a comparison among a story, characters, a description, or a more telegraphic piece of content, and a current situation."

5. On the juridical parable specifically, see Chaya Halberstam, "Law in Biblical Israel," in *The Cambridge Companion to Judaism and Law*, ed. Christine Hayes (New York: Cambridge University Press, 2017), 38–40. Such a parable has "the effect of bringing the hearers

Nathan soon makes clear, when the king pronounces a punishment, *it's on himself*. Recalling the above definition, a parable is the kind of story that can be arresting through its vividness. The combination of recognizable images and earthy realism causes David to be bamboozled by the story. Only in retrospect does it become clear that Nathan has recounted a veiled account of the king's own malevolent conduct.

Of course, not every parable works exactly like Nathan's. But based on this example, we can make four general points by way of introduction. First, *parables can be less innocent than they sound*. Confronting kings and rulers is often a dangerous business, as Saul's spear (see 1 Sam. 20:33) and Jehoiakim's scribal knife (Jer. 36:22–26) graphically illustrate. Instead of speaking a direct accusation, Nathan guides David's attention toward another set of characters. The parable is an *indirect* strategy for condemning the king's corruption. Moreover, long before becoming king, David was a shepherd. The tender language of "lamb" and "flock"—when addressing a former shepherd—surely evokes a sentimental feeling in the hearer that pulls on the heartstrings. Ingenuity is certainly at work, and Nathan is able to elicit sympathy and kindle the royal wrath with just a handful of carefully chosen words about a character who has been behaving very badly.

Second, *a parable can have more personal application than immediately meets the ear*. Shakespeare applied this idea to great effect back in the days of Elizabethan theater. There is a famous scene in *Hamlet* (act 3, scene 2) where the protagonist hosts an evening of festivities: His uncle Claudius arrives expecting a pleasant production by some visiting entertainers, but the actions on stage increasingly resemble his own actions in usurping the throne of Denmark. Hamlet calls it *The Mousetrap*, and the young prince is quite sure that his ruse will be successful: "The play's the thing," says Hamlet, "wherein I'll catch the conscience of the king." Similarly, Nathan's parable is directed toward a guilty king, and the action in the parable resembles David's conduct in 2 Samuel 11. As it turns out, Nathan's account of exploitation and trampling on the poor is *all about David*, and he belatedly discovers that parables have the ability to become much more personal than the listener initially thinks they will be.

---

to self-condemnation." Craig A. Evans, *Jesus and His Contemporaries: Comparative Studies*, AGJU 25 (Leiden: Brill, 1995), 395.

Third, *a parable might have several layers of meaning*. For instance, when Nathan says to David "You are the man!," the most natural interpretation is that David is the rich man of the parable. But in fact there is more going on. Earlier in his career David was a poor man, and he was also a "traveler," spending a long time as a fugitive in the wilderness on the run from Saul. Of course, he is the rich man at present, and he is at fault for abusing his royal position. He will also soon be, as Nathan later explains, a poor man again and will nearly have the kingdom stolen from him by his own son as a measure-for-measure punishment.[6] At various points in his career, David has been (or will be) all three characters in the parable. Furthermore, the *city* might be a significant spatial setting. Although only mentioned once, the urban landscape might be a subtle part of the accusation against David. Perhaps this urban environment is intended to evoke a contrast with David's shepherding youth, recalling memories of better days undefiled by adultery in the city. The image of the lamb sitting at the poor man's table represents a child, and later in 2 Samuel 12 David's own child will die because of his coldheartedness, confirming the multiple levels of meaning in the parable.

Fourth, *the ultimate purpose of a parable is to challenge our perspective and shift the direction of our lives*.[7] It cannot be a coincidence that a *prophet* is sent to David. Throughout the history of Israel, a variety of prophetic figures addressed the people of God with messages, poetry, oracles, and on occasion, parables. In every case the prophets were aiming to persuade the people to think differently and used vivid images and stories to influence actions and attitudes. This continues into the New Testament era, as one scholar remarks: "Religion has been defined as designed to comfort the afflicted and to afflict the comfortable. We do

6. Robert Polzin, *David and the Deuteronomist* (Bloomington: Indiana University Press, 1993), 126. For the dynamic of double meanings, see Lieve M. Teugels, "Talking Animals in Parables: A *Contradictio in terminis*?," in *Parables in Changing Contexts: Essays on the Study of Parables in Christianity, Judaism, Islam, and Buddhism*, ed. Eric Ottenheijm and Marcel Poorthuis, JCPS 35 (Leiden: Brill, 2020), 134–36.

7. Cf. M. Eugene Boring, *Mark: A Commentary*, NTL (Louisville: Westminster John Knox, 2006), 122: "Parables are polysemic; that is, they generate new meaning in new situations. While a parable cannot 'mean' simply anything (it is not a Rorschach blot), it has no one meaning that can be ferreted out by objective methods. It takes on meaning as it gently forces the hearer/reader to participate in the construction of meaning. This process can subvert the life-world of the hearer, opening up a new vision of reality. Parables thus often function by beginning in the familiar world of the hearer, but then they present a different vision of the world that challenges the everyday expectations of the hearer."

well to think of the parables of Jesus as doing the afflicting. Therefore, if we hear a parable and think, 'I really like that' or, worse, fail to take any challenge, we are not listening well enough."[8]

At this point in his midlife crisis, David is going off the rails and is in desperate need of an intervention. After hearing these words from the prophet, David confesses his sin. It is entirely possible that Nathan's parable rescues David from even worse disaster. David's actions still have enormous consequences at both the personal level and the national level, but the king is shocked to his senses through Nathan's story, which is part of a larger prophetic confrontation. This could have been the end for David, but it is not, and God's promise remains as David receives undeserved forgiveness.

Parables in the New Testament

As hinted at earlier, the greatest exponent of the parable genre is Jesus in the Gospels. In church circles Jesus is often underrated as a storyteller, and since many of these parables are familiar, their edginess has perhaps worn off over the years. We could use a reminder that "a typical Jesus story or parable was atypical for his day. It didn't leave people with a conclusion but made them draw one on their own. And it would never be the obvious one. A parable by definition undermines the status quo; it doesn't reinforce it."[9] Huge crowds gathered to hear these stories; if Jesus were speaking nowadays, we might imagine selfies and other social media posts as reports of the parables start trending. Under the shadow of occupation by the fearsome Roman Empire, the masses in ancient Judea and Samaria heard stories about an entirely different kind of freedom, stories with the potential to transform their worldview.

A textbook example is *the parable of the sower* at the beginning of Mark 4: "Again Jesus began to teach by the sea. The crowd that gathered around him was so large that he got into a boat and sat in it out on the sea,

8. Amy-Jill Levine, *Short Stories by Jesus: The Enigmatic Parables of a Controversial Rabbi* (San Francisco: HarperOne, 2014), 9. Similarly, note Craig L. Blomberg, "Poetic Fiction, Subversive Speech, and Proportional Analogy in the Parables," *HBT* 18 (1996): 115–32.

9. Leonard Sweet, *The Bad Habits of Jesus: Showing Us the Way to Live Right in a World Gone Wrong* (Carol Stream, IL: Tyndale, 2016), 59. For an extended application, see Heidi Jokinen, "New Wineskin of Conflict Resolution: Conditions of Change in the Parable on Wineskin," *BTB* 50 (2020): 22–34.

while all the people were along the shore at the water's edge. He taught them many things by parables." Just like Nathan told a story about a lamb when he addressed a former shepherd, so Jesus uses the same tactic: The assembled crowd would have immediately connected with the planting and landscape images used in this parable. Notice that Jesus starts with the verb "listen."[10] Hundreds of times the prophets of Israel used the same imperative, so this might be the first clue that something important is about to unfold. I will also suggest below that this parable is essentially about listening and hearing:

> [3]"Listen! A farmer went out to sow his seed. [4]As he was scattering the seed, some fell along the path, and the birds came and ate it up. [5]Some fell on rocky places, where it did not have much soil. It sprang up quickly, because the soil was shallow. [6]But when the sun came up, the plants were scorched, and they withered because they had no root. [7]Other seed fell among thorns, which grew up and choked the plants, so that they did not bear grain. [8]Still other seed fell on good soil. It came up, grew and produced a crop, some multiplying thirty, some sixty, some a hundred times."
>
> [9]Then Jesus said, "Whoever has ears to hear, let them hear."

Instead of the typical word for "farmer," another clue that something more is going on is signaled through the term "sower." It seems odd that the seed is randomly scattered, including on pathways or in thornbushes where there is less chance of the seed taking root. But perhaps this shifts the focus to the seeds and to the best opportunity for their growth. The most alert listeners might catch an allusion here to Isaiah 55:10–11, a lyrical prophetic word that celebrates God's word going forth, growing into a bumper crop, and accomplishing its intended purpose.

Periodically in the Gospels, Jesus gives further details about a parable.[11] In this case he explains that careful listening is a key to understanding his message, and the best soil of the parable is a receptive heart that strains

10. For the notion of Mark 4 as a master parable, see Frederick Houk Borsch, "Parables of Jesus: Told and Enacted," in *Earliest Christianity Within the Boundaries of Judaism: Essays in Honor of Bruce Chilton*, ed. Alan J. Avery-Peck, Craig A. Evans, and Jacob Neusner, BRLJ 49 (Leiden: Brill, 2016), 259–60.

11. Evan Hershman, *Jesus as Teacher in the Gospel of Mark: The Function of a Motif*, LNTS 626 (London: T&T Clark, 2021), 112–13. Some common problems when interpreting rhetorical figures are further elucidated by Jonathan Culler, *Literary Theory: A Very Short Introduction* (Oxford: Oxford University Press, 1997), 70–72.

to hear to his words.[12] By contrast, "ears distracted, inattentive, casual, or diffused in concentration are the several unfruitful soils of the parable. The key attitude in life—spiritually and socially—is the attitude of active listening."[13] Nathan pointed to the personal application of his parable to the life of David, and Jesus explains the parable to the disciples in Mark 4:

> 13Then Jesus said to them, "Don't you understand this parable? How then
> will you understand any parable? 14The farmer sows the word. 15Some people
> are like seed along the path, where the word is sown. As soon as they hear
> it, Satan comes and takes away the word that was sown in them. 16Others,
> like seed sown on rocky places, hear the word and at once receive it with
> joy. 17But since they have no root, they last only a short time. When trouble
> or persecution comes because of the word, they quickly fall away. 18Still
> others, like seed sown among thorns, hear the word; 19but the worries of
> this life, the deceitfulness of wealth and the desires for other things come
> in and choke the word, making it unfruitful. 20Others, like seed sown on
> good soil, hear the word, accept it, and produce a crop—some thirty, some
> sixty, some a hundred times what was sown."

The Greek term for "parable" means "to throw or place alongside," and involves a comparison.[14] As we notice in the above example, everyday images of seeds and soil are used to explore and illustrate the larger story of the good news that Jesus is announcing. The many parables in the Gospels use

12. On the role(s) of Isa. 6:9–10 (And he said, "Go, and say to this people: / 'Keep on hearing, but do not understand; / keep on seeing, but do not perceive.' / Make the heart of this people dull, / and their ears heavy, / and blind their eyes; / lest they see with their eyes, / and hear with their ears, / and understand with their hearts, / and turn and be healed" [ESV]) in Mark 4:11–12, see Craig A. Evans, *To See and Not Perceive: Isaiah 6:9–10 in Early Jewish and Christian Interpretation*, JSOTSup 64 (Sheffield: Sheffield Academic Press, 1989); Joel Marcus, *Mark 1–8: A New Translation with Introduction and Commentary*, AB 27 (New York: Doubleday, 2000), 299–306.

13. Frederick Dale Bruner, *Matthew: A Commentary*, rev. ed., 2 vols. (Grand Rapids: Eerdmans, 2004), 2:46. For the importance of hearing and the pattern of listening, see Thomas E. Boomershine, "Audience Address and Purpose in the Performance of Mark," in *Mark as Story: Retrospect and Prospect*, ed. Kelly R. Iverson and Christopher W. Skinner (Atlanta: Society of Biblical Literature, 2011), 133–34.

14. E.g., Adela Yarbro Collins, *Mark*, Hermeneia (Minneapolis: Fortress, 2007), 231: "According to Aristotle, the 'comparison' (παραβολή) is one of the proofs common to all branches of rhetoric. It belongs to the category of the example, which has two kinds, historical and fictional. The comparison is a fictional argument but, unlike the fable, one that is based on a plausible situation in daily life. In a rhetorical situation, the speaker makes a point by a simple, clear illustration. If the metaphorical meaning is not clear, the argument is not effective." For a brief overview of the literary turn in the interpretation of parables, see Michal Beth Dinkler, *Literary Theory and the New Testament*, AYBRL (New Haven: Yale University Press, 2019), 49–50.

all kinds of subject matter and a diversity of images and characters. There are fishing nets and wedding celebrations, along with children making requests of their parents and kings counting their soldiers before going into battle. Strange things can happen in these parables: A friend gets angry after being disturbed at midnight, a fig tree becomes a sign of the future, yeast and lamps are used as hidden or illuminating symbols, and unlikely guests are invited to a lavish banquet. But there is also a series of parables with a financial or an investment theme, and it is to this category that our attention now turns.

Pearl Jam

At the very outset of this book we drew attention to *the parable of the hidden treasure* in Matthew 13:44. Using just a handful of words, it tells a compelling story: Evidently in the course of an ordinary day, someone unexpectedly encounters a cache of treasure and promptly goes off to do everything possible to secure this field of dreams. In light of the discovery, whatever the person owned previously now diminishes in value. Encountering the treasure brings great joy, and this joy is the catalyst for a complete overhaul in the person's life and perceptions of what is truly important. When the kingdom is discovered, the audience is invited to imagine how priorities are completely recalibrated.

Let's pause for a moment to consider what is not said in this parable. Key questions linger, such as, "Who concealed the treasure, and why was it hidden?" Instead of giving us an easy answer, Jesus follows up with another parable, one that is closely related but with a different emphasis. In the first one, the person in the field wins the lottery. The finder simply stumbles upon the treasure, though this person had no prior awareness of such treasure and certainly wasn't seeking it. In fact, the person's actions after the discovery are highlighted in the parable: first reburying the treasure, then planning the sale of all other possessions in order to go all-in on the field. The finder secretly knows that the field has skyrocketed in price and reacts quickly on the basis of this inside information. But a more deliberate algorithm is at work in the gem of a parable that follows in Matthew 13:

> [45]Again, the kingdom of heaven is like a merchant looking for fine pearls.
> [46]When he found one of great value, he went away and sold everything he had and bought it.

Buried in 2 Kings 7 is an episode with several points of resemblance to this scene in Matthew 13. It takes place at a dark time in the history of God's people—with frequent wars and invasions—and during this period the capital city of Samaria is under siege by the more powerful Arameans. At the gate of the city, four men with leprosy are lamenting their particularly dismal fate. After some debate, they decide that the best option is to surrender to the marauding army and hope for mercy. But as they arrive at the edge of enemy's camp, they are startled to find out that the camp is empty! So "they entered one of the tents, and ate, and drank, and carried off from there silver, gold, and clothing, and buried them. Then they came back and entered another tent, carried stuff away from there, and buried it" (2 Kings 7:8). Eventually they report this good news, and the city is relieved because the siege is over. We can easily visualize the eruption of surprise when the lepers—who may well have believed that they were walking their last mile—stumble into an empty camp. That feeling is mirrored in *the parable of the hidden treasure*, as similarly great wealth is found suddenly without any planning or foresight.

But the short parable in Matthew 13:45–46 about the pearl is also a bit different. This scene involves more calculation, and the main character has a vocational identity as *a business trader*. "Merchant" is a fairly neutral term nowadays, but "trader" is more ambiguous. The trader in this story is not on a spiritual quest but, rather, is keeping an eye out for fine pearls in the marketplaces. Since Israel has very little waterfront property, pearls are mentioned infrequently in the Bible, in keeping with their exotic quality. Historians tell us that pearls were among the most valuable objects in the ancient world: "For example, we know that Caesar presented Brutus's mother with a pearl then worth $400,000 and Cleopatra was said to have one worth $4 million."[15] In the book of Revelation, pearls are a crown jewel: "The twelve gates" of the New Jerusalem, we are told, "were twelve pearls, each gate made of a single pearl" (Rev. 21:21). Mention of pearls in this parable, then, evoke images of fabulous wealth.

True to form, when catching a glimpse of the inestimable pearl, the trader takes a risk by selling everything he owns in order to acquire it:

15. Ben Witherington III, *Matthew* (Macon, GA: Smyth & Helwys, 2006), 272. On the relationship with the preceding parable of the hidden treasure, see David E. Garland, *Reading Matthew: A Literary and Theological Commentary on the First Gospel*, Reading the New Testament (Macon, GA: Smyth & Helwys, 2001), 153: "The pearl merchant did not discover the magnificent pearl simply by chance; he had a skilled eye and was looking deliberately for pearls to buy. Both parables make the point that the kingdom comes as a chance of a lifetime."

After discerning its worth, the trader does what is necessary to secure the pearl. With that sale, we see how *the parable of the pearl of great price* and *the parable of the hidden treasure* together give us insight on the kingdom of heaven: "When people truly encounter it and realize what it is, it enters their hearts, seizes their imaginations, and overwhelms them with its precious value. No price is too great; nothing that they own can rival its value. Everything they possess goes on the auction block for the sake of possessing the kingdom."[16] *The parable of the sower* discussed earlier uses agricultural images to give insight on how the gospel is received by the human heart. By shifting to economic parables, the *value* of the kingdom, the worth of every life, and the quality of our response to the gospel are underscored. Indeed, economic parables have great currency for explaining the kingdom in memorable ways, which we can further discern through the examples that follow.

Bitcoin Lost

From *The Hunt for Red October* to *Finding Nemo*, stories of "lost and found" often connect with the general public. The despair caused by losing something costly is then eclipsed by the exhilaration of recovery, providing lots of raw material for a novel or a screenplay. Our next parable may have cost less to produce than most Hollywood ventures, but it does capture the frantic desperation of searching for a missing object of value: *the parable of the lost coin* in Luke 15:8–10. But first we need to pay attention to the audience and another parable in the buildup: *the parable of the lost sheep*. These days, a typical evening in a modern sports stadium—or at a political event or even a church gathering—includes all kinds of different people in attendance, and a similarly eclectic crowd can be seen at the beginning of Luke 15:

> [1]Now the tax collectors and sinners were all gathering around to hear Jesus.
> [2]But the Pharisees and the teachers of the law muttered, "This man welcomes sinners and eats with them."

16. Thomas G. Long, *Matthew* (Louisville: Westminster John Knox, 1997), 156. On the question of demands, see Stanley Hauerwas, *Matthew*, BTCB (Grand Rapids: Brazos, 2006), 134: "The parable of treasure in the field and the parable of the precious pearl make clear that much is required if we are possessed by the joy of the kingdom, for it seems that the discovery of the kingdom of heaven requires the selling of all we have in order to buy the field that contains the treasure of the kingdom or the pearl of great value."

Evidently Jesus does not shun those with a bad reputation or wastrels with dubious backgrounds. Within this crowd, it is notable that the seedy people are *listening*, whereas the religious leaders are *grumbling*. The idea of grumbling goes all the way back to the exodus, where the Israelites complain about God not meeting all their needs or performing according to their expectations (e.g., Exod. 15:24; 16:7–8; 17:3).[17] To these authorities, who object to a more hospitable approach, Jesus responds with a parable about how God views sinners and outcasts. Nathan's parable, we recall, featured a little lamb as a main character, loved and nurtured by the poor man. But in this parable that Jesus shares in response to the grumbling, there is nothing remarkable about the lost sheep except that this creature has wandered away and is the object of the shepherd's concern:

> [4]Suppose one of you has a hundred sheep and loses one of them. Doesn't he leave the ninety-nine in the open country and go after the lost sheep
> until he finds it? [5]And when he finds it, he joyfully puts it on his shoulders
> [6]and goes home. Then he calls his friends and neighbors together and says, "Rejoice with me; I have found my lost sheep." [7]I tell you that in the same way there will be more rejoicing in heaven over one sinner who repents than over ninety-nine righteous persons who do not need to repent.

It would be tempting for any shepherd to be content with ninety-nine sheep and not worry about only one that is missing. But that's not the mindset at work in this parable. As Jesus tacitly explains at the end, this is a picture of the character of God. Shockingly, God responds to a lost soul with an almost reckless pursuit. The legal experts should recognize an allusion here to Ezekiel 34, a chapter where the prophet has a vision of the arrival of the ultimate shepherd, who launches a search and rescue operation. Ezekiel lives during a chaotic time—dislocated in exile, far from home—but this vision anticipates a day when those who have strayed can be reconnected with God.[18] Reading Ezekiel's word alongside the parable of Jesus here, the listener is further invited to imagine God's

17. R. Alan Culpepper, "The Gospel of Luke," in *NIB* 8:295. On the contrasting reactions of the undesirables and the legal experts in Luke 15:1–2, see François Bovon, *Luke 2: A Commentary on the Gospel of Luke 9:51–19:27*, Hermeneia (Minneapolis: Fortress, 2013), 404: "On their lips 'this fellow' (οὗτος) is pejorative, just as 'him' (αὐτός) is complimentary from the point of view of the tax collectors and sinners."

18. Darrell L. Bock, *Luke*, 2 vols. (Grand Rapids: Baker, 1994–96), 1302.

celebration when the lost are recovered. Earlier there was joy when the hidden treasure was discovered, and now there is joy when someone lost has been brought back to the community. In fact, there is a noisy contrast between the grumbling of the Pharisees and the out-of-this-world raucous celebration of God and the angels in heavenly places.

The concluding term that Jesus uses in the parable's explanation is "to repent," and the underlying Greek term involves a change of mind. There may be a jab at the legal experts when Jesus refers to the "righteous persons who do not need to repent," as though their lives are exemplary.[19] But for others in the audience, this is mind-blowing. If you are lost and know the feeling of alienation and darkness, the idea that God is *actively pursuing you* would surely catch your attention. And if God searches for you when you least deserve it, your response might be to change your mind about the character of God: The notion that God celebrates after finding you is a potentially life-altering belief. But even as we linger on that radical idea, Jesus immediately follows up with another parable about God's relentless search for the lost:

> [8]Or suppose a woman has ten drachmas and loses one. Doesn't she light
> a lamp, sweep the house and search carefully until she finds it? [9]And when
> she finds it, she calls her friends and neighbors together and says, "Rejoice
> with me; I have found my lost coin." [10]In the same way, I tell you, there is
> rejoicing in the presence of the angels of God over one sinner who repents.

While *drachma* may sound like some sort of cryptocurrency, in the ancient world it is the equivalent of a day's wage.[20] The woman in the parable does not appear to be wealthy, so losing even one coin would be quite serious. This parable allows us to think of our spiritual state in terms of a financial crisis. As a result, other aspects of the character of God are revealed here.[21] The focus is on the enormity of the woman's efforts to

19. Greg W. Forbes, *The God of Old: The Role of the Lukan Parables in the Purpose of Luke's Gospel*, JSNTSup 198 (Sheffield: Sheffield Academic Press, 2000), 117–18.

20. David H. Wenkel, *Coins as Cultural Texts in the World of the New Testament* (London: T&T Clark, 2017), 40–41. Cf. the response of Anthony Giambrone, "A Note on Luke's Parable of the Minas and the Ancient Practice of Burying Coin Hoards," *NTS* 65 (2019): 589–97.

21. Linda Maloney, "'Swept Under the Rug': Feminist Homiletical Reflections on the Parable of the Lost Coin (Lk. 15.8–9)," in *The Lost Coin: Parables of Women, Work and Wisdom*, ed. Mary Ann Beavis, The Biblical Seminar 86 (London: Sheffield Academic Press, 2002), 37: "But many people of faith are not as comfortable with the metaphor of God the anxious woman,

recover the lost object of value, as she makes a very careful and comprehensive search. Like the frantic shepherd who rejoices after finding the lost sheep, so the woman rejoices upon finding the drachma. Maybe there is irony at work with the *money* in the parable. Lots of people are trying to earn God's favor or blessing, but these two parables show us another side of the coin: God is searching for us even when we are not searching for God. Repentance is mentioned again, reinforcing the idea of cosmic celebration when one lost soul arrives at this transforming reality.[22] And as we will see in our next example, the *actions* of repentance may well speak louder than words.

Debt Ceiling

The Mentalist, a popular TV series that ran from 2008 to 2015, features a charming and well-trained main character who could almost read someone's mind. In this next example, there actually *is* mind reading, and the episode starts with an unexpected invitation. We have already seen some hostility between Jesus and the Pharisees, but in Luke 7:36 a Pharisee named Simon invites him over for a meal. Lest all Pharisees be painted with the same brush, it is best to keep an open mind here, even though Simon's motive for the invitation is not stated.[23] Earlier in Luke 7 there is an incredible resurrection, and in verse 21 we hear how Jesus cures diseases, casts out demons, and gives sight to the blind. It is quite possible that Simon has heard these reports and wants to check it out himself. So we find ourselves reclining around a table with Jesus, although there is no indication that Simon's hospitality is particularly lavish.[24]

---

the poor woman laboriously seeking in the dark for the tiny, precious thing she has lost. This parable says that God is *like* that woman, just as God is *like* that shepherd."

22. On the high cost of throwing the celebration party, see James R. Edwards, *The Gospel According to Luke*, PNTC (Grand Rapids: Eerdmans, 2015), 81: "From an economic point of view the woman's response is folly. The parable is not about economics, however. It is about God's grace, perhaps the folly of God's grace, that seeks the lost until they are found and, once found, celebrates their recovery in abandon. The joy of God has no price tag."

23. See, e.g., Hermut Löhr, "Luke-Acts as a Source for the History of the Pharisees," in *The Pharisees*, ed. Joseph Sievers and Amy-Jill Levine (Grand Rapids: Eerdmans, 2021), 170–84. On Simon in particular, see Robert C. Tannehill, *The Shape of Luke's Story: Essays on Luke-Acts* (Eugene, OR: Wipf & Stock, 2005), 277.

24. Patrick E. Spencer, *Rhetorical Texture and Narrative Trajectories of the Lukan Galilean Ministry Speeches: Hermeneutical Appropriation by Authorial Readers of Luke-Acts*, LNTS 341 (London: T&T Clark, 2007), 112: "While Simon certainly abrogates normal hospitality

But then the real action begins, and instead of a wedding crasher, there is a Pharisee-party crasher as Luke 7 continues:

> [37]A woman in that town who lived a sinful life learned that Jesus was eating at the Pharisee's house, so she came there with an alabaster jar of perfume. [38]As she stood behind him at his feet weeping, she began to wet his feet with her tears. Then she wiped them with her hair, kissed them and poured perfume on them.

Simon the Pharisee has evidently heard reports about Jesus previously. This unnamed woman with a scandalous reputation must also have been following the news. Maybe she has listened to accounts of healing and deliverance, prompting this risky visit and her extraordinary response to Jesus. Her teardrops resonate with the poetic lyrics of Psalm 126, which celebrate the renewal and restoration of those who were once far from God.[25]

Such an outpouring of emotion is liable to be misunderstood in this gathering at the Pharisee's house. When Jesus tells *the parable of the lost sheep*, the Pharisees had been grumbling that Jesus is not socially distanced from tax collectors and outcasts, as though anyone disreputable has a contagious virus. Simon's reaction here is unveiled though an internal soliloquy. He observes the woman's apparent violation of boundaries and his guest's lack of concern. Both disturb him, and he is skeptical: "If this man were a prophet," Simon says to himself, "he would know who is touching him and what kind of woman she is—that she is a sinner" (7:39). With some rich irony, Jesus can read Simon's mind better than any TV show detective. A prophetic tradition of related mind reading is seen in 2 Kings 5–9, as Elisha is variously pictured as gazing upon the furtive actions of his servant Gehazi, the troop movements of the Arameans, and the havoc that will come from Hazael of Damascus. In response to Simon's inner monologue, Jesus shares a short parable in Luke 7 about insolvency. The story seems designed to give Simon a more

---

protocol, which is fulfilled by the actions of the woman, he is not presented by the narrator as attempting to entrap Jesus in a premeditated plot (in contrast to the Pharisees in the episodes contained in 5:17–26; 6:6–11)."

25. For the Psalms connection and references to other related passages, see Joel B. Green, *The Gospel of Luke*, NICNT (Grand Rapids: Eerdmans, 1997), 310.

acute experience of what forgiveness might feel like, and it may give rise to a different kind of internal conviction:

> [40]Jesus answered him, "Simon, I have something to tell you."
> "Tell me, teacher," he said.
> [41]"Two people owed money to a certain moneylender. One owed him five hundred denarii, and the other fifty. [42]Neither of them had the money to pay him back, so he forgave the debts of both. Now which of them will love him more?"
> [43]Simon replied, "I suppose the one who had the bigger debt forgiven."
> "You have judged correctly," Jesus said.

Perhaps there is a measure of cold formality when Simon says, "Tell me, teacher." But judging from his correct response to Jesus's question, it is clear that he was listening carefully. *The parable of the moneylender*, as Simon correctly discerns, features a creditor who does something utterly mystifying: He cancels the debts rather than opting for a more natural and severe alternative. Neither of the debtors can pay, but Simon adduces that the one with the larger amount of debt canceled will have a greater sense of relief. Along the same lines as David's case, here Simon has been drawn into a prophetic web that is about to elicit a self-judgment. When Nathan follows up his parable of the stolen lamb with a stinging rebuke of the king, David realizes the parable was actually about him.[26] Simon now hears a follow-up speech that has way more personal application than he realizes, as Jesus compares the extravagance of the woman with the lack of various courtesies extended by Simon:

> [44]Then he turned toward the woman and said to Simon, "Do you see this woman? I came into your house. You did not give me any water for my feet, but she wet my feet with her tears and wiped them with her hair.

26. On the notion of rhetorical entrapment at work in this scene, see John R. Donahue, S. J., *The Gospel in Parable: Metaphor, Narrative, and Theology in the Synoptic Gospels* (Philadelphia: Fortress, 1988), 34; James L. Resseguie, "The Woman Who Crashed Simon's Party: A Reader-Response Approach to Luke 7:36–50," in *Characters and Characterization in Luke-Acts*, ed. Frank E. Dicken and Julia A. Snyder, LNTS 548 (London: T&T Clark, 2016), 16: "Entrapment is a surprise attack on a character who makes a premature judgment—as Simon has in verse 39—who then is forced to abandon that assumption and revise his conclusion. Jesus catches Simon off-guard by posing a question that he cannot get wrong, which forces him to reconsider his point of view. His hesitation ('I suppose') is a faint attempt to make the trap more bearable or to lessen the damage to his own perspective."

[45]You did not give me a kiss, but this woman, from the time I entered, has
not stopped kissing my feet. [46]You did not put oil on my head, but she has
poured perfume on my feet. [47]Therefore, I tell you, her many sins have been
forgiven—as her great love has shown. But whoever has been forgiven little
loves little."
[48]Then Jesus said to her, "Your sins are forgiven."
[49]The other guests began to say among themselves, "Who is this who even
forgives sins?"
[50]Jesus said to the woman, "Your faith has saved you; go in peace."

Unique contours of God's character can be perceived through this short parable at the end of Luke 7, as the listener discovers that God somehow holds vast quantities of mercy in reserve.

In whatever ways it might be expressed, those who receive such divine grace should no doubt respond with extravagant gratitude and will gain a quite different view of themselves: "It is not what the sinner *is* that Jesus sees, but what the sinner could be through God's love. It is Jesus's awareness of how God can transform people that makes him, rather than dwell on their past, look forward to what God can make of them."[27] In the parable told to Simon, both debtors are *graciously granted* (ἐχαρίσατο) release in the same way, even though the amounts differ.[28] The plot twist in the parable does not lie so much in the story itself as in its point of reference. Simon is closer to the five-hundred-denarii club than he might have previously believed, and the open-ended conclusion to the episode leaves the reader wondering how Simon will respond.[29] When Jesus raises the issue of *faith* at the end of the episode, it would seem that faith is the willingness to believe that God can and does extend astonishing grace toward the undeserving.[30] It might further be noted that the name Simon is the Greek form of the Hebrew name Simeon. Curiously enough, the

27. Bock, *Luke*, 763.

28. David E. Garland, *Luke*, ZECNT (Grand Rapids: Zondervan, 2011), 604.

29. As one scholar writes, "The threat of the parable is that it subverts the myths that sustain our world." Bernard Brandon Scott, *Hear Then the Parable: A Commentary on the Parables of Jesus* (Minneapolis: Fortress, 1989), 424, cited in Matthew S. Rindge, "Luke's Artistic Parables: Narratives of Subversion, Imagination, and Transformation," *Int* 68, no. 4 (2014): 404.

30. For a preliminary probing of what faith might illustrate in this parable, note the remarks of Robert W. Jenson, *Systematic Theology*, vol. 1, *The Triune God* (New York: Oxford University Press, 1997), 167: "Rudolf Bultmann's own greatest single systematic contribution was the strictness with which he held to the correlation between faith and the actual proclamatory speaking of the gospel. Faith, his exegetical work on John taught him, is not general trust in

name Simeon means "to hear," and we might agree that Simon has heard about the deal of a lifetime from his guest on this evening.

No Time to Die

Our next example concludes this introductory chapter and builds a bridge to the next chapters of this book. *The parable of the rich barn builder* is found in Luke 12:16–21, and it occurs in the context of a larger discussion about our ultimate sources of security. There is a sizable crowd, and one member steps forth to ask a question about *inheritance*. In the absence of any background details about the dispute, our attention is drawn to the root of the problem. The guy in the crowd wants an independent voice to justify his claim, thus giving him what he perceives to be his right. In other words, he wants Jesus to force his brother to give him what he wants. The issue of inheritance is creating a stressful situation, and it appears to be fracturing a relationship. Keep in mind that the quarrel over inheritance revolves around wealth that is not earned but, rather, is a gift, presumably from their father.

> 13Someone in the crowd said to him, "Teacher, tell my brother to divide the inheritance with me."
> 14Jesus replied, "Man, who appointed me a judge or an arbiter between you?" 15Then he said to them, "Watch out! Be on your guard against all kinds of greed; life does not consist in an abundance of possessions."

The speaker who steps out from the crowd might deserve some credit for recognizing the significance of Jesus as a wise teacher. But in making his demand, it is clear that he has his own agenda. In the previous episode at Simon's house, we saw tears of repentance from someone who was in need of forgiveness. Now we have a case where Jesus is being used to justify acquiring stuff. Although the speaker is expecting Jesus to provide a decision about this inheritance, Jesus instead gives a twofold warning starting with "be on your guard against all kinds of greed." We should note that greed involves more than just money, as it also includes other lusts and desires. In *the parable of the sower*, recall that some seed fell

an entity called God, but what happens when the gospel is spoken and heard as an address that can only be God's own speech."

among thorns, a picture of those who hear the word "but the worries of this life, the deceitfulness of wealth and the desires for other things come in and choke the word, making it unfruitful" (Mark 4:19). The listener is invited to wonder if the enticement of riches might be a trap that can suffocate the work of divine forgiveness in our lives.

Moments before Jesus dramatizes his warning with a parable, he also tells the speaker that "life does not consist in an abundance of possessions." So, the question becomes, "What *does* define you? Is it what you can get, or is it what God has done for you (and can do through you)?" Back in *the parable of the moneylender* above, the audience was invited to rethink some serious matters about what is of lasting value and what is fleeting or temporary. In *the parable of the hidden treasure*, the issue is raised about how one's life should be invested. Notably, we now have a parable of a rich man, and keep in mind, it is a response to someone who is keen to receive an inheritance. As we see in the parable, the rich man's possessions begin to possess his thoughts and dictate his long-term priorities. He won't be able to think of anything except through the filter of his material security, *which will not be as secure as he thinks*! So far, we have seen characters who find lost coins or are released from crushing debts. This rich man in Luke 12 has some new money but will face a day of accountability much sooner than he anticipates. Jesus told them this parable:

> 16The land of a certain rich man yielded an abundant harvest. 17He thought
> to himself, "What shall I do? I have no place to store my crops."
> 18Then he said, "This is what I'll do. I will tear down my barns and build
> bigger ones, and there I will store my surplus grain. 19And I'll say to myself,
> 'You have plenty of grain laid up for many years. Take life easy; eat, drink
> and be merry.'"
> 20But God said to him, "You fool! This very night your life will be demanded
> from you. Then who will get what you have prepared for yourself?"
> 21This is how it will be with whoever stores up things for themselves but is
> not rich toward God.

We have no exact indication of how much money the main character in this parable has prior to the bumper crop described here, but he is certainly more wealthy now. The first clue that all is not right, however, comes early in the story: We are told that "the ground . . . yielded an abundant harvest" (12:16). It is almost like the land is personified and is responsible for generating the man's wealth. But there is no acknowledgment or obvious gratitude in the lengthy series of soliloquies in which the rich man has an inner dialogue. The multiple uses of "my" (*my* crops, *my* barns, *my* surplus, *my* self) indicates a self-centeredness with not much room for anything else.[31] Responsible stewardship is expected in the Bible, and greed and hoarding are equally frowned upon. It is evident from his soliloquy that the rich man is motivated by anxiety at first, but he then entertains fantasies about a life of luxury and pleasure. Jesus is telling this parable because someone in the crowd is concerned about inheritance. Ironically, the rich man is preoccupied with building bigger barns that someone else is going to inherit very soon!

In fact, that very night the rich barn builder has to stand before God, and like a CEO answering to the board of directors, he is called to give an account. In the parable, the rich man doesn't seem to have contemplated the notion that his collection of bigger barns actually has all the stability of a house of cards. Lots of careful planning has taken place, but the inevitability of death didn't enter into the equation. While it might sound abrupt that God labels him a "fool," it is conceivably a reference to Psalm 14:1: "The fool says in his heart, 'There is no God!'"[32] This is not an expression of atheism, but rather, an assertion that God has no relevance, and thus the fool is someone who does not account for God in daily decisions. The absence of any generosity or gratitude is no doubt cause for regret, as is the lack of attention to the real estate of his soul.

The closing words of Jesus—"This is how it will be with whoever stores up things for themselves but is not rich toward God"—are spoken to the crowd that includes a guy who is keen to acquire an inheritance.[33] After

31. Culpepper, "Gospel of Luke," 8:256.

32. Alternatively, Matthew S. Rindge, *Jesus' Parable of the Rich Fool: Luke 12:13–34 Among Ancient Conversations on Death and Possessions*, ECL (Atlanta: Society of Biblical Literature, 2011), 224, proposes that "the man's folly is best understood in terms of his limited imagination (in failing to practice any sapiential recommendations for the use of possessions in light of death's inevitability), the selfish and socially isolating nature of his greed, his saving for the future (and underlying assumption regarding the control he wields over his future), and the neglect of his own mortality." Among the numerous wisdom texts cited in Rindge's helpful study, one might also consider the speech of regret in Prov. 5:12–14, "How I hated discipline! / How my heart spurned correction! / I would not obey my teachers / or turn my ear to my instructors. / And I was soon in serious trouble / in the assembly of God's people" (NIV).

33. Cornelis Bennema, "The Rich Are the Bad Guys: Lukan Characters and Wealth Ethics," in *Characters and Characterization in Luke-Acts*, ed. Frank E. Dicken and Julia A. Snyder, LNTS

hearing the parable, how is he going to live, and is he willing to change his ultimate investment strategy? Near the beginning of this chapter we noted that parables both challenge our perspective and can have more personal application than immediately meets the ear. *The parable of the rich barn builder*, we assume, becomes a cautionary tale for the individual who wants his sibling to divide their inheritance. When Jesus talks about being rich toward God, we suspect that he is referring to relational capital. The idea of living in relational connection with God is a key pillar in the economy of grace, and we will have opportunity to discuss this further as our journey continues through some other financially oriented parables.

548 (London: T&T Clark, 2016), 98: "In 12:33–34, Jesus provides the antidote to both anxiety about daily existence and the foolishness of πλεονεξία. Instead of selfishly amassing wealth on earth, Jesus's followers are to use their earthly possessions to alleviate need, an act that will result in amassing wealth in heaven. The locus of one's treasure (earth or heaven) corresponds to the focus of one's life (καρδία denotes the center of one's life)."

An Oil Baron and an Embezzler

OUR FIRST EXTENDED EXAMPLE of a financial parable is often considered the most difficult. It is certainly among the most controversial of the parables because it revolves around a highly suspicious main character and some dubious scheming.[1] This parable is located in Luke 16:1–9, and part of the larger context is *stewardship*—that is, how we handle the resources we've been given.[2] Jesus shares a parable with his disciples about a manager who gets called in by his boss because he is accused of blowing money, and promptly loses his job. The manager panics because he doesn't have any other marketable skills. But suddenly he has a light-bulb moment: He quickly arranges meetings with his clients and offers to lower their bills if they pay right then. The clients are more than happy to do so. We should expect that when the boss finds out about this racket, he'll go completely ballistic. But instead, *he praises the dishonest manager because he acted wisely*.

Do you see the problem, and why interpreters are confused? If the main character is a shady business dealer who profits through dishonesty, then what on earth is the message of this parable? Our goal is to carefully move

1. "By anybody's reckoning," writes Douglas M. Parrott, "the Parable of the Dishonest Steward in Luke 16.1–8a is a problem. Here Jesus seems to be holding up a criminal act as an example to be emulated." Parrott, "The Dishonest Steward (Luke 16:1–8a) and Luke's Special Parable Collection," *NTS* 37 (1991), 499.

2. E.g., Rachel L. Coleman, *The Lukan Lens on Wealth and Possessions: A Perspective Shaped by the Themes of Reversal and Right Response*, BIS 180 (Leiden: Brill, 2019).

through each line, and in the end some insight might emerge about how the parable can make a difference in a disciple's life. But before we do that, we are going to press rewind. Back in 1 Kings 18, there's a story that might provide us with an interesting comparison as we proceed. That story is also about a shrewd manager but one in a different kind of situation. In 1 Kings 18, we gain some insight into the kinds of decisions and stresses faced by such an employee. After reading this much older story, we will have a good frame of reference for returning to Jesus's parable about a scoundrel who needs to hastily devise a plan after getting the axe.

Horrible Boss

Of all the kings of Israel, Ahab ranks among the worst. There are over forty kings, all with flaws. They are variously guilty of murder, adultery, usurping the throne, idol worship, child sacrifice, fraud, and every kind of corruption. One king named Abijah—whose name means "the Lord is my father"—apparently marries his own mother (2 Chron. 13; 15) in a desperate bid to keep his power. Another king named Zimri reigns for seven days, then burns down the royal palace. An obvious difficulty is that Zimri remains inside the palace when he torches it.

But it is hard to find a more loathsome resumé than Ahab's. He rules in northern Samaria along with his wife, Jezebel, and it is a bleak time in national history. His nemesis is the prophet Elijah, who calls him to account for turning the people away from God and opting for a deviant route to prosperity. The watershed moment occurs at the beginning of 1 Kings 17, when Elijah confronts Ahab with an announcement: "As the Lord God of Israel lives, whom I stand before, there will not be any rain or dew in these next few years except at my word." After this, Elijah hides from Ahab and manages to stay alive while the famine gets worse. Here is how the story begins in 1 Kings 18:

> 1After many days the word of the Lord came to Elijah, in the third year,
> saying, "Go, present yourself to Ahab, and I will send rain upon the face of
> the earth." 2So Elijah went to present himself before Ahab, and the famine
> was severe in Samaria. 3At that time, Ahab summoned Obadiah, who was
> the manager of his household. 4(Obadiah, though, greatly feared the Lord,
> 4because when Jezebel cut off the prophets of the Lord, Obadiah took one

hundred prophets and hid them in groups of fifty in caves and kept them alive with food and water.) [5]Ahab said to Obadiah, "Walk throughout the land, to every spring of water and every valley, perhaps we can find pasture so our horses and mules can live, and we will not have to cut off any animals." [6]They divided the land between them so they could pass through it all. Ahab went in one direction by himself, and Obadiah went in the other direction by himself.

As Elijah is preparing to meet the king, we overhear a conversation between Ahab and the manager of his property, Obadiah. Even though he works for the king, Obadiah follows the ways of God while his employer does not. Consequently, Obadiah is forced to lead a double life: He acts in secret to save the lives of the prophets, even as Queen Jezebel is trying to destroy them. Such actions show us the massive risk Obadiah takes and how precarious his position is. He works for Ahab, but he is part of a rebel alliance working to keep the worship of God alive in dark times. Obadiah has a certain amount of latitude in his position over Ahab's house, which allows him to operate in a strategic way, and he is somehow able to pull off the feat of hiding the prophets in caves. Meanwhile, we also see that Ahab's priorities are warped: While his wife is killing prophets, he is more concerned about finding grass for his mules. In this scene Ahab and Obadiah split the duties of searching the land for any kind of pasture. This means that Obadiah is alone, and the leader of Israel's prophetic movement makes an unscheduled appearance:

[7]When Obadiah was on the road, look, Elijah was there to meet him! He recognized him, fell down on his face, and said, "Is this you, my lord Elijah?"
[8]He said to him, "Yes. Go, say to your lord, 'Elijah is here!'"

Arguably the most gruff of Israel's prophets, Elijah hails from the outback with wild hair and clothes. Such an outward appearance means that he is instantly recognizable. So whether they have met before or not, Obadiah—the steward of Ahab's house—bows down and pays respect to the very person whom his employer is hunting down! But when Elijah tells Obadiah to deliver a message to Ahab, Obadiah is scared that his true loyalties will be revealed to Ahab. As we will hear in his very long complaint in verses 9–16, Elijah has put even more pressure on Obadiah. His response has a frantic tone as he pleads and protests, telling Elijah of his brave deeds. Obadiah also fears that Elijah will teleport somewhere, a mode of transport that must have been invented long before *Star Trek*:

> [9]He said, "How have I sinned, that you are simply giving your servant into
> the hand of Ahab to kill me? [10]As the LORD your God lives, there is not a
> nation or kingdom where my lord has not been looking for you. If they
> said, 'He's not here,' he made that kingdom or nation swear an oath that
> they could not find you. [11]So now you are saying, 'Go, tell your master,
> "Behold Elijah is here!"' [12]Here's what will happen: when I leave you, the
> Spirit of the LORD will carry you off—I have no idea where—then I will
> come to Ahab, he won't find you, and he'll kill me! But your servant has
> feared the LORD from my youth. [13]Has anyone told you, sir, what I did
> when Jezebel was killing the prophets of the LORD? I hid one hundred of
> the LORD's prophets in groups of fifty in a cave and kept them alive with
> food and water. [14]But now you're saying, 'Go, say to your master, "Behold,
> here's Elijah!"' He *will* kill me!"
>
> [15]Elijah said to him, "As the LORD of Hosts lives, before whom I stand,
> indeed today I will present myself to him."
>
> [16]So Obadiah went to meet Ahab, and told him, and Ahab went to meet
> Elijah.

This is the one and only scene featuring Obadiah. He takes the message to Ahab, and he is not heard from again. Maybe that doesn't bode well for his future, or maybe it is his fifteen minutes of biblical fame. Most readers of Kings would certainly view Obadiah in a heroic light, as a person who keeps hope alive by hiding prophets and sustaining them with food during a period of turbulence and raging culture wars. We will return to Obadiah and his stewardship at several points below. But for our immediate purposes, we get a few scenes that show a real steward in action. As the manager of a large household, Obadiah gives us a sense of an employer's expectations and how a steward might fall out of favor if there is any hint of backroom scheming. Of course, for Obadiah the stakes are high, and he risks certain death if Ahab finds out. But Obadiah also provides a concrete example of a steward acting *shrewdly*. He is clearly aware of his master's movements, as well as his strengths and weaknesses, and Obadiah leverages this access and awareness in a clever way.

Unsavory Allegations

Returning now to Luke 16:1–9, the parable begins with a rich man who hears some rumblings about his steward. Jesus is addressing his disciples here, although the parable may well have been spoken within earshot of the Pharisees. Since later in the chapter we are told that the Pharisees are lovers of money, no doubt they would be wise to attend to the issues raised in this story. But our primary attention should be on the disciples, and the words of Jesus at the end of the parable seem to have them in mind. The use of money and stewardship of resources is therefore a topic that the group of disciples needs to think about, and this parable is a vehicle for doing so.

> [1]Jesus said to his disciples, "Once there was a rich man who had a steward, and charges were laid against him that he was squandering his property."

The first character in this parable is another rich man, eliciting a comparison with the barn builder whom we met earlier in Luke 12:16–21.[3] Does this rich man have similarly misplaced priorities? Does he also put too much stock into things that don't have enduring significance? The barn builder was called a fool, but no equivalent term is used here. However, we do know how the barn builder gets his wealth: The land produces a good harvest. We find out that the rich man here owns real estate, and he evidently takes rent in the form of produce. He takes wheat as payment, and also (olive) oil. Perhaps he can be called "the Oil Baron," and it can be surmised that he too gets wealthy because the land is fruitful. But the focus in this parable isn't primarily on the Oil Baron's possessions; rather, attention focuses on the manager of his property.

In Luke 16:1 the term for "steward" implies someone who is placed over the house and manages its affairs.[4] Obadiah, as discussed above, is a good example, and there are a number of others in the Bible. The overseer of

3. See further R. Daniel Schumacher, "Saving Like a Fool and Spending Like It Isn't Yours: Reading the Parable of the Unjust Steward (Luke 16:1–8a) in Light of the Parable of the Rich Fool (Luke 12:16–20)," *RevExp* 109 (2012): 269–76.

4. For the use of οἰκονόμος, note Ryan S. Schellenberg, "Which Master? Whose Steward? Metalepsis and Lordship in the Parable of the Prudent Steward (Lk. 16.1–13)," *JSNT* 30, no. 3 (2008): 277. On scholarly opinions about the meaning of "steward" ranging from someone who has the status of a slave to someone who is practically a free agent, see Fabian E. Udoh, "The Tale of an Unrighteous Slave (Luke 16:1–8 [13])," *JBL* 128 (2009): 311–35.

Abraham's household appears to be Eliezer of Damascus, and Joseph's steward is an important minor character in Genesis 43–44. In fact, Joseph himself is placed in charge of Potiphar's household in Genesis 39, and before he gets thrown in prison because of a false accusation, there is substantial blessing on the house and fields of his master. From these other texts we can conclude that stewards are entrusted with considerable responsibility and are expected to operate in the best interests of their employers. More subtly, we can also see that stewards are given some latitude to exercise sound judgment when necessary, but they always work for the interests of the household rather than their own personal gain.

Abrupt Dismissal

Joseph is sent to prison in Genesis 39 because his master's wife spreads some fake news about his conduct. Here in Luke 16:1 there are rumors, but these allegations of the steward's wrongdoing seem to be more authentic than claims made against Joseph. Are the accusations against the steward in this parable coming from multiple sources? We should underline that these are not formal *legal* charges—that is, the FBI isn't arriving at the Oil Baron's door with a warrant for the steward's arrest. Rather, it sounds more like the reports of misconduct are coming from clients or others involved in business. The reports imply a pattern of conduct over a length of time, giving us a sense of how the steward has been operating. It is these fairly aggressive complaints that induce the boss to call his employee for a meeting of accountability. If you've ever experienced this kind of judgment before—with a parent, teacher, employer, or even a spouse—then you can relate to how the steward is feeling here. They meet not in a courtroom but, rather, in the equivalent of the rich man's corner office:

> 2So he called him and said to him, "What's all this I hear about you? Present an account of your stewardship; I'm not going to have you as my steward anymore!"

In 1 Kings 18, Obadiah was scared that Ahab would find out about his secret activities, and that he was working behind his back to protect the prophets of the Lord even as Jezebel was on a rampage trying to destroy them. Joseph worked his way up the ladder and became head of an Egyptian household but was then accused of a making an unwanted advance on his master's wife. The situation of the steward in Luke 16 is a bit different: He is charged with money squandering. More precisely, the Greek term has a root meaning "to scatter," and it conjures an image of wasteful irresponsibility.[5] Keep this in mind, because the exact same word is used in *the parable of the prodigal sons*, which will be discussed later. In that parable, an entitled younger son squanders his inheritance with wild parties and (presumably) an entourage of friends.

Instead of incompetence in running the master's affairs and mismanagement of the property, the allegations brought against the steward hint at wasteful activities. Perhaps the steward's mismanagement is along the lines of Jordan Belfort's in *The Wolf of Wall Street* when he uses the company credit card for various kinds of purchases that have less to do with the firm's bottom line and more to do with personal indulgence.[6] Is it possible that the Oil Baron at some point had suspicions about his employee? Going back to the barn builder of Luke 12, it certainly seems like he's the kind of rich guy who knows every single possession in his garage(s) and probably has a sixth sense if anything is missing. Either way, on the basis of these allegations of improper conduct, the steward hears the dreaded catchphrase, "You're fired!" But we are not told if the boss gives him two weeks' notice or if he's planning on announcing this termination on social media at some point down the road.

Pivot

During the tense interview between the Oil Baron and his sneaky manager, we notice that there is no reply to question "What's all this I hear about you?" (Luke 16:2). Such silence from the steward might be a virtual admission of guilt, or perhaps the rich man is in no mood for an appeal. Equally vague are the steward's motives. In the case of Obadiah, it is very clear

5. E.g., Luke Timothy Johnson, *The Gospel of Luke* (Collegeville, MN: Liturgical Press, 1991), 243: "The term *diaskorpizein* is the same one used of the younger son in Luke 15:13. As in the previous story as well, the crisis and need for decision are created by the mismanagement of possessions."

6. Eugene H. Peterson, *Tell It Slant: A Conversation on the Language of Jesus in His Stories and Prayers* (Grand Rapids: Eerdmans, 2008), 99–100. Note also the remarks of Parrott, "Dishonest Steward," 504; and Delbert Burkett, "The Parable of the Unrighteous Steward (Luke 16.1–9): A Prudent Use of Mammon," *NTS* 64 (2018): 329.

from his interaction with Elijah that he is motivated by his commitment to God, and hence he aims to undermine the heterodox conduct of King Ahab. But the steward here in Luke 16 does not plead his case or offer any kind of defense for his behavior (e.g., "My parents never bought me a new Tesla," or "I was infrequently applauded in kindergarten"). But maybe the wheels of the steward's mind are already turning even as he receives his pink slip. Like a quarterback facing a linebacker or an emergency room physician during a pandemic, he has to start evaluating his options, and do so in a hurry. Fortunately for the listener, we next have a soliloquy that gives us some inside information on the steward. Just like the barn builder's monologue reveals his priorities, we now see how the manager reacts to the announcement of his sudden termination:

> [3]At this, the steward said to himself, "What shall I do? My master is taking away my stewardship from me! I can't do manual work, and I'd be ashamed to beg . . ."

In this soliloquy we don't hear any protest from the fired steward, nor is there a loud declaration of his innocence. Whether or not this is basically an admission of guilt, the steward doesn't complain about being treated unfairly or maligned by his critics, so perhaps we can assume that the allegations are correct. Such considerations are important, because we are *not* dealing with a paragon of moral virtue in this story. At the same time, the steward might lament his predicament, but he doesn't spend long wallowing in self-pity or remorse. Instead, he seems to get to work right away, asking how he should respond to this adversity of unemployment and looming penury. After a quick review of his skill set, however, he realizes that his choices are limited. Manual labor is out of the question, and panhandling outside of the liquor store likewise seems unattractive. Is there any other solution?

More recently, books about reinventing one's career in an uncertain global situation have been advertised on such platforms as *Forbes* or *Fast Company*. One such is example is Jenny Blake's *Pivot: The Only Move That Matters Is Your Next One*.[7] Career shifts are more common in the New Testament than we might think. In Acts 9, for example, young Saul

7. For the motif of the trickster, see Fergus J. King, "A Funny Thing Happened on the Way to the Parable: The Steward, Tricksters and (Non)sense in Luke 16:1–8," *BTB* 48 (2018): 18–25.

of Tarsus is a sworn enemy of the emerging Christian movement. But in a startling upheaval, as he is on the road to Damascus to round up the usual suspects and bring them back to Jerusalem to face the consequences, he has a dramatic encounter with the risen Jesus. Almost overnight, the most vicious and hostile opponent of the Christian faith becomes its most articulate defender. The guilty manager here in Luke 16 isn't going to have any kind of spiritual awakening, but he certainly appears to pivot in the next section of the parable.

The Big Short

From the outset it is quite certain that the steward's strategy is *not* to get his old job back. Sometimes when we offend our employer, we need to both apologize and make amends for our error(s). But the steward here recognizes that he's been fired, and there is no going back. He is, therefore, planning for an entirely different kind of future. Professional traders in the financial world often hedge their bets when forecasting the direction in which a given market will move. Such decisions are surely based on algorithms and related mathematical models. But we also suspect, deep down, that there is always a bit of a gamble involved, and that factor appears to be in play with the manager's next move in Luke 16:

> 4"I have an idea what to do!—so that people will welcome me into their households when I am fired from being steward."
> 5So he called his master's debtors to him, one by one. "How much," he asked the first, "do you owe my master?"
> 6"A hundred measures of olive oil," he replied.
> "Take your bill," he said to him, "sit down quickly, and make it fifty."
> 7To another he said, "And how much do you owe?"
> "A hundred measures of wheat," he replied.
> "Take your bill," he said, "and make it eighty."

Desperate for new prospects, the manager's endgame is to forge alliances with his master's debtors and be warmly received into their homes. This mischievous plan takes advantage of the fact that the Oil Baron didn't take him to court. Because nobody yet knows that he's been sacked, he runs around offering sizable price cuts, for what better way to receive a salutary handshake than to offer someone a discount between 20 and 50 percent of their debt? It has been estimated that one hundred liquid measures (*baths*) of oil would be worth one thousand denarii, and if a denarius (like a drachma) is roughly one day's wage, then a 50 percent price cut is a very substantial liquidation indeed.[8]

On that calculating note, scholars have offered no shortage of complex theories about the crafty steward's plan. Some rely on reconstructing ancient Near Eastern interest rates, and then suggest that the steward slashed those rates. Other theories rest on the assumption that commission rates were charged but then deducted by the (now unemployed) steward.[9] Although these are interesting speculations, the most plausible explanation is that the manager is a bold and blatant cheater. "By reducing the amounts of the debts while he is still in the service of the rich man, or at least while the debtors still assume that he is the rich man's steward, he will gain their favor," argues one commentator. The Oil Baron "will not be able to reverse his actions later without losing face with his debtors, and the steward will have acquired a debt of honor and gratitude from each debtor that will ensure their goodwill toward him in the future."[10] Having concocted the plan, the steward then executes it quickly.

Checkmate

We already mentioned that *the parable of the shrewd manager* is the most misunderstood of Jesus's stories. It is perhaps the hardest to interpret, and, statistically, it has a high number of detractors. For instance, the fourth-century Roman emperor Julian the Apostate "used the parable to assert the inferiority of the Christian faith and its founder," while the influential twentieth-century German New Testament scholar Rudolf Bultmann decided that the episode was incomprehensible.[11] To hazard a

8. Darrell L. Bock, *Luke*, 2 vols. (Grand Rapids: Baker, 1994–96), 1329–32. Cf. Thomas R. Schreiner, "Luke," in *ESV Expository Commentary*, vol. 8, *Matthew–Luke*, ed. Iain M. Duguid, James M. Hamilton Jr., and Jay Sklar (Wheaton: Crossway, 2021), 965.

9. Douglas D. Webster, *The Parables: Jesus's Friendly Subversive Speech* (Grand Rapids: Kregel Academic, 2021), 134.

10. R. Alan Culpepper, "The Gospel of Luke," in *NIB* 8:308.

11. See Anna Wierzbicka, *What Did Jesus Mean? Explaining the Sermon on the Mount and the Parables in Simple and Universal Human Concepts* (New York: Oxford University Press, 2001), 415: "The seeming incongruity of a story that praises a scoundrel has been an embarrassment to the Church at least since Julian the Apostate used the parable to assert the

guess, such dim views of the parable most likely come from the plot twist at the end. There have been some surprises in the parables we have seen so far. Our shepherd leaves ninety-nine sheep in the wilderness to go off on a search-and-rescue mission for the single lost sheep. The barn builder had just told his "soul" to get ready for a lifetime of luxury, but he wasn't banking on his death that very same night. Such surprises, however, might be exceeded by the Oil Baron's flabbergasting compliment of his former manager's subversive behavior. We are not sure how he finds out about the steward's actions, but there is no doubt about his response:

> [8]And the master praised the dishonest steward because he had acted wisely. The children of this world, you see, are wiser than the children of light when it comes to dealing with their own generation.

Without any sarcasm, the unrighteous steward receives the praise of his (former) master. There is no conversion or flash of spiritual spark, just a commendation because he acted intelligently—that is, the steward saw the situation and reacted adroitly. At a corporate meeting in the grim 1980s, he might have been referred to as the smartest guy in the room. Like a chess player, the Oil Baron has been rooked by his new opponent, and he admits it. Of course, the steward isn't hired back; all the master does is give a compliment along these lines: Good for you for getting ahead in this corrupt world. You outflanked me and won, because I can hardly go back to my clients and explain how you shafted me, so well played. Who is the master talking to? It is uncertain if this is a public utterance or a private thought. Maybe it is a refraction of his inner thought process, as most likely this worldly oil executive would have done the same thing in his manager's place. Perhaps he wistfully regrets not throwing the manager in jail (with other financial-criminal types of the same ilk as Gordon Gekko) when he had the chance.

Honest Brokers

With respect to Julian the Apostate and others who follow in his wake, parables are designed to challenge our perspective. There can often be a

---

inferiority of the Christian faith and its founder" (quoting Kenneth E. Bailey, *Poet and Peasant: A Literary-Cultural Approach to the Parables in Luke* [Grand Rapids: Eerdmans, 1976], 86). On the citation from Bultmann, see Peterson, *Tell It Slant*, 99.

plot twist, but such an unusual ending aims to take the listener to unfamiliar territory in order to consider what is really important. After mentioning the Oil Baron's begrudging praise, Jesus immediately provides an illuminating transition: "The children of this world, you see, are wiser than the children of light when it comes to dealing with their own generation" (Luke 16:8 AT). Based on what we have heard in the parables so far, someone who is "in the light" has probably been rescued, much like a lost sheep wandering in the darkness and brought home to a great celebration. These words of Jesus, then, sound like a wake-up call or a reminder to live according to this paradigm-shifting enlightenment.

Given that transition, the larger implications of the parable gradually move into focus. On one level, the main character squanders his master's money and then gets caught, but he is willing to pivot and cleverly uses his skills and experience in order to succeed in a changed economic landscape. The point is not just some happy ending but, rather, an ironic challenge through this unexpected yarn about a rogue who plays by the world's rules and earns some kudos in the process. Despite blatant underhandedness, the Oil Baron praises the manager because he *acted* shrewdly.[12] And considering this rich man is now *less rich* than he was at the start of this short parable, that's quite a compliment indeed.

A scene in Genesis 41 uses similar kinds of ideas and gives us some insight here. Joseph is a former steward who has been serving a prison sentence, but he is called to a meeting with Pharaoh. After interpreting the king's dream, Joseph suggests that Pharaoh find someone with *shrewdness* to manage the land of Egypt, and he gets hired (Gen. 41:33).[13] In the last lines of this episode in Luke 16, then, we wonder if Jesus is going to turn to the disciples and address them more personally. They have just been engaged by this story of a rascal, and now Jesus might well encourage them to apply their minds and energy toward the kind of projects that are worthwhile in the kingdom of God:

12. Adjectives such as "crafty" or "shrewd," Rachel Coleman notes, "are sometimes applied to the man's *character*, although φρονίμως is an adverb that qualifies his *actions* ('he *did* wisely,' φρονίμως ἐποίησεν). Jesus provides the actual character description, calling him 'the *dishonest* manager' (οἰκονόμον τῆς ἀδικίας, 16:8a). The man's action is praised by his master within the parable, but his character is not applauded by Jesus the story-teller." Coleman, *Lukan Lens on Wealth*, 75.

13. Elements of Israel's wisdom tradition in the Joseph narrative are discussed, among others, by Michael V. Fox, "Wisdom in the Joseph Story," *VT* 51 (2001): 26–41; R. W. L. Moberly, *The Theology of the Book of Genesis*, OTT (Cambridge: Cambridge University Press, 2009), 225–46.

> [9]So let me tell you this: use that dishonest stuff called money to make yourselves friends! Then, when it gives out, they will welcome you into homes that will last.

Periodically, Jesus uses the phrase "how much more" to express the worth of an object. For example, in Luke 12:24 the audience is invited to consider the ravens: They are not farmers and have no storage facilities, yet God feeds them. *How much more valuable are you than birds*? By analogy, the story of the shrewd manager is a *how much more* parable. Here is a shady character who operates by the principles of the world: But if you are a steward of the kingdom of God, then *how much more* do you have the opportunity to live with wisdom and operate according to the economy of grace?[14] The explanation of Jesus in these closing lines also takes us back to *the parable of the moneylender*, as heard by Simon the Pharisee in Luke 7:41–42. If you have been forgiven a great deal, *how much more* are you invited to live in light of this new reality of lavish debt cancellation? To reinforce the point, it might be an idea to glance through *The Message* paraphrase of the last verses in Luke 16:

> [8–9]Now here's a surprise: The master praised the crooked manager! And why? Because he knew how to look after himself. Streetwise people are smarter in this regard than law-abiding citizens. They are on constant alert, looking for angles, surviving by their wits. I want you to be smart in the same way—but for what is *right*—using every adversity to stimulate you to creative survival, to concentrate your attention on the bare essentials, so you'll live, really live, and not complacently just get by on good behavior.

On this score, Obadiah might serve as an innovative example of a shrewd manager. In the turbulent world of Ahab's reign, here is a steward who takes a risk and invests his spare time toward a much more valuable enterprise: preserving the prophetic word. Hiding prophets in caves is an extreme situation, to be sure, but the principle nonetheless emerges: The disciples should be alert for every chance to live wisely and effectively in whatever time and circumstances they find themselves. As the early history

14. Cf. the same use of the term "manager" (οἰκονόμος) in Luke 12:42 after parables about a wedding banquet and a thief in the night: "Who then is the faithful and wise manager [οἰκονόμος], whom his master will set over his household, to give them their portion of food at the proper time?" (ESV).

of the Christian movement in the book of Acts indicates, there will be ample adversity in the days ahead. But through this surprising parable the disciples are invited to use their resources in creative ways that express the values of God's kingdom. This is not just money, but also time and resources. Disciples don't have to hoard like the barn builder, but are given the freedom to be generous, rich toward the priorities of God, and stewards of the grace poured out on them. The system of *kingdom values* will be apparent in our next extended example where money is spent on someone with *no* expectation of any kind of return.[15] That someone, in an equally shocking twist, happens to be a despised enemy, so the audience hearing this parable would wisely be prepared to pivot.

15. For preliminary definitions, see Michael F. Bird, *Evangelical Theology: A Biblical and Systematic Introduction*, 2nd ed. (Grand Rapids: Zondervan, 2020), 305–17.

3

A Solicitor and a Samaritan

IN OUR JOURNEY through the parables so far, we have seen a range of characters and several surprising plot twists. The examples we have focused on have a financial edge, and they collectively draw us into a larger discussion about what is truly valuable in life and what is really worthy of our biggest investments. Among other things, we have noticed that the kingdom of God ushers in a new economy of grace, and this set of countercultural values invites us to completely rethink the enterprise of our lives. On the surface, *the parable of the shrewd manager* is about a Wall Street wheeler-dealer who outmaneuvers his rich boss. But after further reflection we gradually realize that the parable is a clever way of challenging any disciple to live with energy and vitality for something that endures.[1] Why does Jesus use this kind of artistic strategy? A leading scholar reminds us, "Jesus knew that the best teaching concerning how to live, and live abundantly, comes not from spoon-fed data or an answer sheet. Instead," this scholar continues, "it comes from stories that prompt us to draw our own conclusions and at the same time force us to realize that our answers may well be contingent, or leaps of faith, or traps. It

1. Arland J. Hultgren (*The Parables of Jesus: A Commentary* [Grand Rapids: Eerdmans, 2000], 154) suggests that "Paul's message to the Thessalonians relates beautifully and appropriately to the parable. He addresses his readers as 'children of light,' assures them that they are 'destined for salvation,' and exhorts them to encourage one another and to build each other up in faith and love (1 Thess. 5:5–11). Such is the way of life of those who seek to be as wise in spiritual matters as others are in the normal transactions of this world."

comes from stories that community members can share with each other, with each of us assessing the conclusions others draw, and so reassessing our own. The parables, if we take them seriously not as answers but as invitations, can continue to inform our lives, even as our lives continue to open up the parables to new readings."[2]

Our next installment features another select cast of characters and a plot with an astounding conclusion. In this chapter we explore *the parable of the good Samaritan* found in Luke 10:25–37. Even in the language of popular culture we often hear about an act of random kindness ("ARK"). As explained in movies like *Evan Almighty*, such acts include helping someone in need or responding to an emergency with generosity (and not expecting to be repaid or to get a tax receipt as the first priority). But we will also pay attention to the larger context of the parable, for this parable doesn't just appear out of the blue. It is shared in the midst of a fairly intense debate between Jesus and a legal professional, and it therefore needs to be considered as part of this dialogue. The discussion and the parable also feature echoes and allusions to other biblical texts, such as the famous instruction to "love your neighbor as yourself."[3] There is also a reference to a story way back in 2 Chronicles 28, where a group of soldiers are cared for *by their enemies* after defeat in battle. As the lawyer discovers, any conversation with Jesus results in a surprising challenge at the end.

On Trial

This parable of the Samaritan in Luke 10 is about an awful event that happens on the road to Jericho, and the parable occurs in the midst of a larger travel narrative.[4] In the previous chapter, Luke 9, Jesus has fatefully set out for Jerusalem where he is bound to be arrested. Traveling along this road, Jesus sends his disciples ahead of him, and they return with reports about miracles and spectacular happenings on the journey. Much of this activity takes place in Samaritan territory. Keep in mind that

2. Amy-Jill Levine, *Short Stories by Jesus: The Enigmatic Parables of a Controversial Rabbi* (San Francisco: HarperOne, 2014), 281.

3. For remarks on this parable as a narrative exegesis of Lev. 19:18, see Jeannine K. Brown and Kazuhiko Yamazaki-Ransom, "The Parable of the Good Samaritan and the Narrative Portrayal of Samaritans in Luke-Acts," *JTI* 15 (2021): 233–46.

4. For an overview, see James A. Metzger, *Consumption and Wealth in Luke's Travel Narrative*, BIS 88 (Leiden: Brill, 2007).

there is a deep-seated hostility between the Jewish community and their northern Samaritan neighbors. After northern Samaria was decimated in 2 Kings 17 and repopulated with a mixture of people groups, those in Judah and Jerusalem were bitterly opposed to them. The rivalry was even more intense because the Samaritans believed that northern Mount Gerizim was the superior place of worship, and they even had their own edition of the Torah.[5] There are some intriguing turns in Luke 9–10, and the series of unexpected scenes continues with the unannounced arrival of a new character in the story: a lawyer.

Most of us think about calling a lawyer when there is some sort of trouble. But we should clarify that in Luke 10 we are not dealing with an attorney like Atticus Finch, Ally McBeal, or a robed figure in a John Grisham novel. Rather, the lawyer in this episode is a learned scholar of the Hebrew Bible—the stories and poems, lyrics and legal material—and how it applies to every facet of life in the community of God's people: "The work of a lawyer, defending and interpreting the law of God, was honored and responsible work in the first century. Then, as now, the Scriptures were quoted and misquoted by anyone who wanted divine authority for his or her program. The lawyers, these Bible scholars, were responsible among other things for keeping their communities alert to the possibilities of religious craziness and/or deceit."[6] As mentioned earlier, unusual things are taking place around Jesus. Now, in Luke 10, this lawyer appears abruptly on the scene and poses a question:

> [25]On one occasion an expert in the law stood up to test Jesus. "Teacher," he asked, "what must I do to inherit eternal life?"

We are not immediately sure of the lawyer's motives in the opening line of this episode, but elsewhere in the Gospels, lawyers tend to bring an unfriendly line of questioning to Jesus. However, this lawyer aims to test Jesus by putting him on the spot. In other words, it is not just a point of curiosity

5. E.g., Neh. 4:1–4 and John 4, and note Klyne R. Snodgrass, *Stories with Intent: A Comprehensive Guide to the Parables of Jesus*, 2nd ed. (Grand Rapids: Eerdmans, 2018), 269. Note also V. J. Samkutty, *The Samaritan Mission in Acts*, LNTS 338 (London: T&T Clark, 2006). The nuances and historical complexities are surveyed by Gary N. Knoppers, *Jews and Samaritans: The Origins and History of Their Early Relations* (Oxford: Oxford University Press, 2013). A more forensic appraisal is undertaken by Matthew Chalmers, "Rethinking Luke 10: The Parable of the Good Samaritan Israelite," *JBL* 139 (2020): 543–66.

6. Eugene H. Peterson, *Tell It Slant: A Conversation on the Language of Jesus in His Stories and Prayers* (Grand Rapids: Eerdmans, 2008), 35–36.

for the lawyer but, rather, an opportunity to catch Jesus in a mistake. The same approach can be seen when the devil tempts Jesus (Matt. 4; Luke 4), so it hardly suggests a casual conversation.[7] Consequently, here in Luke 10 we are dealing with a courtroom drama, with the prosecutor trying to discredit the person on the stand. There is no indication of the lawyer's age, but he seems to be drawing on experience: He uses standard etiquette when he addresses Jesus as "Teacher"—a title that carries the same respect as "Your Honor"—as he poses his question, and so the trial begins.

The lawyer's question is fitting for a biblical expert, but it also raises an issue that would be of interest to all sorts of people: "What must I do to inherit eternal life?" We've talked about inheritance already in *the parable of rich barn builder*, and the concern there was property. But here the stakes sound much higher than material prosperity as such.[8] It could be that the lawyer is asking, "How do I make it to heaven?" or "How do I enjoy the fullness of all God has to offer both here *and* in the life to come?" If there a problem with the question, it lies in the verb "do," as it implies "single, limited action," as though the lawyer "is thinking of something to check off his to-do list."[9] Of course, we are not sure if this a personal matter of some importance to the lawyer or if he is acting in his professional capacity and *testing* this increasingly popular teacher. But we are quite sure that with a loaded question of this magnitude, any audience would agree that this debate is just as engrossing as an entire season of *Law & Order*.

The Fine Print

A memorable scene takes place in Matthew 22:15–22 where the Pharisees and the Herodians team up to try to trap Jesus in his words. Normally

7. Joshua Eugene Leim, "To Inherit Eternal Life: Jesus, the Lawyer, and Luke's Soteriological Grammar," *BBR* 31 (2021): 182: "ἐκπειράζω occurs only one other time in Luke, and this for Satan's temptation of Jesus (4:12; cf. 4:2; 11:16)."

8. On the question as phrased in Mark 10:17, see Mark L. Strauss, *Mark*, ZECNT (Grand Rapids: Zondervan, 2014), 439: "The man's question concerns inheriting 'eternal life' (ζωὴν αἰώνιον), which means ultimate salvation in God's presence (Dan 12:2). In context it is synonymous with being 'saved' (v. 26) and 'entering the kingdom of God' (vv. 23, 25). The idea of eternal life as an 'inheritance' fits the OT concept of Israel as God's children (Exod 4:22; Deut 14:1; Isa 43:6; Jer 3:4, 19; 31:9, 20; Hos 11:1), who are heirs of God's blessings. In the LXX 'inherit' is commonly used for possessing the Promised Land (Lev 20:24; Num 34:13; Ps 37:9) and came to be used in later Judaism for the reception of eschatological blessings (*Pss. Sol.* 14:10; *1 En.* 40:9)."

9. Levine, *Short Stories by Jesus*, 84.

these two groups are fiercely divided against each other: The Herodians tend to collaborate with the Romans, while the Pharisees resent any such compromises. Yet they are united in their opposition to Jesus, and they conspire to trip him up over the dreaded matter of taxation demanded by the Roman Empire. "Is it right to pay the imperial tax to Caesar," is their trick question, "or not?" Asking for a coin, Jesus then flips a question to them: Whose image is on the coin? When they concede that the emperor's image is on the coin, Jesus says, "Therefore render to Caesar the things that are Caesar's, and to God the things that are God's" (22:21 ESV).

Either a "yes" or a "no" answer would have given the Pharisees and the Herodians exactly what they wanted, and they would have posted on social media that Jesus is either pro-Roman or a dangerous rebel. But instead of getting burned, Jesus takes the opportunity to impart something more valuable and provides some wisdom about directing what is most important to God. In this episode Jesus is hard to beat in a debate. In fact, Matthew 22 features a number of sparring matches. Every time, the opponents lose, and the final line of the chapter informs us, "from that day on no one dared to ask him any more questions" (22:46). So then, if our lawyer in Luke 10 intends to win this case, he better be well prepared for his next round. In response to the difficult question of how to inherit eternal life, Jesus poses a legal question to the prosecutor:

> [26]"What is written in the Law?" [Jesus] replied. "How do you read it?" [27]He answered, "Love the Lord your God with all your heart and with all your soul and with all your strength and with all your mind"; and, "Love your neighbor as yourself." [28]"You have answered correctly," Jesus replied. "Do this and you will live."

With the agility of skilled litigator, the roles are quickly reversed as Jesus returns the ball to the opponent's court. In a Jewish context, it is natural that questions about inheritance and eternal life should involve Scripture and its interpretation.[10] In a matter of seconds, now the lawyer is on trial! Whether

10. G. Anthony Keddie, "'Who Is My Neighbor?' Ethnic Boundaries and the Samaritan Other in Luke 10:25–37," *BibInt* 28 (2020): 264: "The interlocutor is a lawyer (νομικός) and Jesus is identified by the lawyer as a teacher (διδάσκαλε, 10:25). The word νομικός refers to someone specifically trained in the application of Mosaic law (νόμος). It appears primarily in Luke in the New Testament and often designates those who contest Jesus's actions as they regard the Judaean law."

he was anticipating this ploy or not, the lawyer deftly refers to the heart of the Hebrew Bible, the *Shema* (from the Hebrew verb meaning "to hear") in Deuteronomy 6:4–5: "Hear O Israel, the LORD our God, the LORD is one. You shall love the LORD your God with all your heart, and with all your soul, and with all your strength." It is no accident that this becomes such a central statement, involving the whole person (emotion, passion, drive, intelligence) in a full-bodied and faithful response to the character of God.[11]

Without pause, the lawyer continues seamlessly with a follow-up reference to Leviticus 19:18, the full text of which reads: "Do not seek revenge or bear a grudge against anyone among your people, but love your neighbor as yourself. I am the LORD" (NIV). At this point we probably need to acknowledge that in our present day, not many people are reading Leviticus. It seems to be all about sacrifice, and such concerns are far from our minds in this modern era. But if we recognize for a moment that sacrifice is a way to say "thank you" or "I'm sorry" to God, that might be a helpful way to approach the book. Sacrifice is a practical means for reconnecting with God, and it points toward a life of gratitude and forgiveness. The Israelites were rescued from slavery, and thus cultivating an attitude that reflects God's goodness poured out on them was important from the outset. Leviticus 19:18 teaches us that our devotion to and love for God are expressed through how we treat our neighbor, and that's why the lawyer quotes it here. And given the affirming response of Jesus—"do this and you will live" (Luke 10:28)—we expect the case is closed.

For better or worse, in our modern age we often think of lawsuits as dragging on for extended periods of time. Indeed, in *Bleak House* by Charles Dickens, a lawsuit lasts for the *entire book*, and it is a really thick novel. But interminable lawsuits are found in the ancient world as well, and an example is found in the book of Acts. The apostle Paul is on trial for several long chapters, and he speaks in his own defense numerous times before royalty, governors, and religious leaders in Acts 21–26. One particular scene occurs in chapter 24, where a notorious solicitor named Tertullus takes the stage (the term for lawyer here is *rhetōr*, implying skill in speech).[12] Tertullus's rhetorical flourish is evident from his opening

11. Darrell L. Bock, *Luke*, 2 vols. (Grand Rapids: Baker, 1994–96), 1025–26.

12. On the term ῥήτωρ in this context, note C. K. Barrett, *A Critical and Exegetical Commentary on the Acts of the Apostles*, vol. 2, *Introduction and Commentary on Acts 15–28*, ICC (Edinburgh: T&T Clark, 1998), 1093–94.

remarks: "Since through you we enjoy much peace, and since by your foresight, most excellent Felix, reforms are being made for this nation, in every way and everywhere we accept this with all gratitude" (24:2–3 ESV). Whether or not Felix is greasy and corrupt we can leave for others to adjudicate. Rather, on the basis of Tertullus's flattery, we suspect that the trial in Acts 24 is going to be very tiring. My point here is not to pass judgment on Paul's legal proceedings in the book of Acts but instead to give a warning: Always beware that court cases have the potential to drag on much longer that you might anticipate (or can afford).

Legal Loophole

The debate could have ended in Luke 10:28 with the affirming statement, "You have answered correctly," as the lawyer's response is entirely consistent with the mission and message of Jesus.[13] If matters did end here, it would be reminiscent of Mark 12:28–34, a scene that features a dialogue with a scribe that has some similar contours.[14] On that occasion, the scribe overhears Jesus in another debate and poses a question himself about which commandment is the greatest. Jesus's response is almost identical to the lawyer's answer in Luke 10, and upon hearing this, the scribe heartily agrees (prompting Jesus to exclaim, "You are not far from the kingdom of God!"). Quite different, however, is our scene here with the lawyer, and akin to the trial in *Bleak House*, there is yet another round of questioning. If we were wondering about the lawyer's motives—whether to gain some wisdom about how to inherit eternal life or to discredit his opponent in public debate—then the next line provides some clarification:

> [29]But he wanted to justify himself, so he asked Jesus, "And who is my neighbor?"

Any interest in eternal life seems to be replaced with a more immediate goal of finding a loophole in order to *win the point* in this debate. Other translations render the lawyer's purpose as "wanting to justify himself" (NRSV)—that is, wanting to look straight and proper. Recalling that Jesus

13. Joel B. Green, *The Gospel of Luke*, NICNT (Grand Rapids: Eerdmans, 1997), 428.
14. John P. Meier, *A Marginal Jew: Rethinking the Historical Jesus*, vol. 5, *Probing the Authenticity of the Parables*, AYBRL (New Haven: Yale University Press, 2016), 201–3.

had just replied, "Do this and you will live," it certainly takes the debate to another level: Alongside belief, some action is also necessary. Did this answer trigger a shift in the lawyer's tactics? It is hard to tell if the question "Who is my neighbor?" is preplanned, but it certainly sounds like the lawyer is trying to win the debate on a technicality. It is increasingly obvious that he is intent on tripping up his opponent, but now his question gives Jesus another turn in this chess game.

Countermove

In a previous chapter we looked at an episode that takes place earlier in Luke 7, when Jesus is invited to dinner at the house of Simon the Pharisee. Outwardly polite, Simon is inwardly seething as he watches a disreputable woman lavishly showing gratitude to Jesus. This action prompts Simon to grumble in his heart, "If this man was the prophet I thought he was, he would have known what kind of woman this is who is falling all over him" (7:39 *The Message*). Not only does Jesus know all about the woman, but he also sees right into Simon's mind and gives him a parable suited to the occasion about gratitude that flows from the forgiveness of a debt.

The parable of the moneylender illustrates the kind of reaction we have to the amount of forgiveness we receive. That short parable in Luke 7:41–42, we remember, ends with a question. Now, the same strategy is about to unfold again here in Luke 10. The lawyer has just asked for clarification: "Who is my neighbor?" Presumably, he doesn't believe the answer is "everybody" or else he wouldn't be debating the criteria. As we listen to this parable, the question will be reconfigured, because Jesus isn't going to answer directly. Instead, Jesus will end up asking him—after some traveling down the road—whether *he* is a neighbor.

> 30In reply Jesus said: "A man was going down from Jerusalem to Jericho, when he was attacked by robbers. They stripped him of his clothes, beat him and went away, leaving him half dead."

The parable opens with an anonymous character making a journey, and the lack of any description means we should understand him as an average Jo(seph), a typical person walking down the street. There is no reason given for his trip, only the Google Maps coordinates of the road: *from Jerusalem to Jericho*. Scholars tell us that this eighteen-mile stretch of uneven road is dangerous, with plenty of caves and hiding places that are optimal for criminals. An ominous landmark is the Pass of "Adummim" (see Josh. 18:17), a name that echoes the word "blood" in Hebrew.[15] The scholarly theories about danger certainly seem legitimate, for the anonymous tourist at the beginning of the parable fails to reach his Jericho destination because he is viciously attacked by a gang of thugs.

While traveling, he is set upon by this band of brigands, and the term implies a random encounter rather than a specific targeting. The same word is used elsewhere in the New Testament for falling into adversity—that is, when bad circumstances or accidents happen that aren't necessarily our fault (e.g., James 1:2–3). Earlier in Luke we had the money squandering of the dishonest manager; now we have highway robbery in this parable. Indeed, the word for robbers carries the nuance of plundering and is used to describe self-seeking religious leaders who take advantage of the faithful (Luke 19:46; John 10:1), all kinds of petty criminals, and even political terrorists.[16] In the end, Jesus will be crucified between two thieves (Matt. 27:44 uses the same Greek word that is used for the robbers in the parable). The robbers in the parable don't appear to have a political agenda. They are most likely motivated by material gain, since they steal the traveler's clothes and nearly beat him to death in the process. Such violent actions appear in other texts: In Matthew 27:28 Jesus is stripped of his clothing, much as the suffering servant in the book of Isaiah is beaten and afflicted (Isa. 53:4). And so, here is our unnamed tourist, the victim of an act of violence, lying half dead in the ditch at the side of this lonely road less traveled.

Expert Witnesses

When we introduced the lawyer of Luke 10 in our discussion above, we emphasized that he is an expert in biblical literature, a theologian with a dedication to upholding community standards. Other religious authorities in the New Testament world include priests and Levites, and are mentioned

15. Bock, *Luke*, 1029.

16. Ruben Zimmermann, *Puzzling the Parables of Jesus: Methods and Interpretation* (Minneapolis: Fortress, 2015), 307.

frequently in the Gospels.[17] It is worth remembering that you don't *choose* to become a priest in ancient Israel. You are *born* into the priesthood. Priests and Levites therefore are part of a privileged line, and their genetic entitlement carries considerable weight in first-century Jewish society. Both of these experts show up in our parable, and the first one arrives *by chance*. No reason is given for his journey, and his arrival at the crime scene is not intentional, but there may be another force at work: "That a priest 'happened' to be going down the road," says one commentator, "would suggest to believing Jews the arrival of providentially arranged aid."[18] To have such a highly respected first responder would have encouraged our victim and would have been perceived as the best thing that had happened on this very bad day.

> 31A priest happened to be going down the same road, and when he saw the man, he passed by on the other side. 32So too, a Levite, when he came to the place and saw him, passed by on the other side.

It was terrible timing for this man to fall into the hands of the brigands, but it is great timing that a priestly passerby is now on site, for who better to show up than someone who is well-versed in the very book that says, "Love your neighbor as yourself"? Since there are positive (Zechariah) and negative (Caiaphas) images of priests throughout the book of Luke, probably the most important aspect of this parable is the lawyer's perception: The lawyer can relate to these figures because they are his fellow professionals. It is jarring, to say the least, when the priest walks right by. And when the Levite likewise passes by on the opposite side of the road, hearers must have wondered how this could have happened. Some interpreters might argue that the priest and Levite fear that they too will be ambushed by the robbers, so they hurry away. Others may speculate that neither wants to be contaminated by contact with a dead body. However,

17. For a short survey of scholarly positions on the characters and roles of the priest and the Levite in the parable, see Michel Gourgues, "The Priest, the Levite, and the Samaritan Revisited: A Critical Note on Luke 10:31–35," *JBL* 117 (1998): 709–13; e.g., "By having first a priest and then a Levite come on stage, Luke's narrative is taking up only the first two categories from the traditional postexilic trilogy. One would then normally expect the appearance of a lay member of Israel as the third character. Thus, the surprise effect occurs when the tale substitutes a Samaritan" (712).

18. Craig L. Blomberg, *Interpreting the Parables*, 2nd ed. (Downers Grove, IL: InterVarsity, 2012), 300.

neither of these excuses is very persuasive. For whatever reasons, these characters are not moved with the desire to help, and so they continue down the road and are never heard from again. They do not interrupt their personal schedules and are consigned to oblivion.

A New Hope

This larger section of Luke's Gospel has featured a number of episodes that take place in Samaritan territory, and we've already noted the long-standing hostility between the Samaritans and the Jewish community. An example of such tension is found in Luke 9:51–56, when Jesus had just dispatched messengers to go ahead of him. These messengers entered a Samaritan village, but the locals "did not welcome [them]" (9:53). We have to realize, then, that the animosity works both ways, and Samaritans have their own issues with the Jewish community. In response to this lack of hospitality, the brothers James and John (nicknamed "the sons of Thunder") asked permission to "call fire down from heaven to destroy them" (9:54), but Jesus does not grant their request.

In the parable in Luke 10, we know that Jesus is talking to the lawyer, but we have to assume that his own disciples are also listening to this story. Now with a Samaritan ready to arrive on stage, a more controversial scenario could hardly have been scripted for the occasion.

> [33]But a Samaritan, as he traveled, came where the man was; and when he saw him, he took pity on him. [34]He went to him and bandaged his wounds, pouring on oil and wine. Then he put the man on his own donkey, brought him to an inn and took care of him.

At the outset of the parable the certain person who falls into the hands of thieves is given very little description. As a result, we are starting to think that he is a *representative* character, and he could be a picture of *any* of us. Moreover, the situation is getting worse: Two people have already passed by, and surely this victim does not have much time left. Like the priest and the Levite, the traveling Samaritan sees the victim at the side of the road, but his reaction is the opposite of theirs: He is moved with compassion, even though this is probably an enemy member of the Jewish community. The term for "compassion" means to be "touched to the very heart" (literally, to the bowels) of one's being, and refers to the deepest identification with the plight of another person: "The suffering of others is not only noticed but rather moves one to the core; it is experienced completely; it is suffered; it is 'suffering with' in the deepest sense of the word."[19] Throughout the New Testament, this kind of compassion is most commonly associated with Jesus. At various points Jesus is filled with pity for the multitudes who are lost and wandering aimlessly (Matt. 9:36), as well as moved with compassion when two blind men cry out to have their sight restored (20:34). The term should be kept in mind because it will be seen again in *the parable of the prodigal sons*. Here in Luke 10, it is the compassion of the unnamed Samaritan that saves the life of the victim at the side of the road, who is bandaged and taken to a place of safety.

Back to the Future

We can imagine the lawyer listening to this parable, and how he might react to the patient narration of the Samaritan's actions of bandaging the victim, tending the wounds with antiseptic wine, mounting the victim on his own donkey while he walks alongside, and driving him to an inn, most likely in Jericho itself. Is this sequence of actions ringing a bell for our lawyer, the expert in the Bible? Because, as it just so happens, the Samaritan's extraordinary compassion has some precedent. The high point of the parable is very similar to an episode from Israel's history found in 2 Chronicles 28, a story about a raging civil war. It takes place during the days of the divided kingdom, and there is a civil war between Israel (the future Samaritans) in the north, and Judah (the future Jewish community of Jerusalem) in the south.

During this period, the king in southern Jerusalem is Ahaz, and his evil reign plunges the nation into an Ahab-like darkness. As a consequence, the land of Judah is invaded by northern Israel in 2 Chronicles 28, with great damage inflicted.[20] The northerners inflict wounds on their southern counterparts, plunder them, and take away two hundred thousand people as prisoners. But as the army is marching into the capital city of Samaria

19. Zimmermann, *Puzzling the Parables of Jesus*, 323.

20. Cf. Nick Spencer, *The Political Samaritan: How Power Hijacked a Parable* (New York: Bloomsbury, 2018), 93–94.

with their captives, suddenly they are confronted by a new character, the prophet Oded (whose name is associated with the term for restoration). In a passionate speech, Oded declares that they have acted cruelly and are no different from these prisoners! It was God who allowed the southerners to lose, but the northerners need to acknowledge their own waywardness and release the slaves: "Don't all of you surely have your own transgressions against the Lord your God? So now, listen to me, and hand back the captives you have captured from your brothers, for the burning anger of the Lord is upon you" (28:10–11). The prophet's speech is reinforced by other northern leaders, and in yet another plot twist, the warriors listen to this counsel:

> [14]So the soldiers gave up the prisoners and plunder in the presence of the officials and all the assembly. [15]Those who were personally assigned tended to the prisoners, and from the plunder they clothed all who were naked. They provided them with clothes and sandals, food and drink, and healing balm. All those who were weak they put on donkeys. Then they took them back to their relatives at Jericho, the City of Palm Trees, and returned to Samaria.

Is it reasonable to the think that the inquisitive lawyer in Luke 10 would have caught this reference to 2 Chronicles 28? When he hears the story of a bleeding figure who is the object of mercy from an enemy Samaritan, does he catch the deliberate echo of an earlier episode in Israel's history, replete with bandages and donkey rides to Jericho? As an expert in biblical literature, it is highly probable that he would have recognized this shift in the direction of the parable. And all of sudden, new evidence is introduced in this trial. When the lawyer asks, "Who is my neighbor?" he should already know the answer, because the Bible tells him so. The prophet Oded commands the northern Samarians not to gloat about their plunder but to release the prisoners and show them some pity. They need to do this because they are just as guilty, and it is only through God's mercy that the roles are not reversed. The story of the good Samaritan has already happened in the past, and it should now be changing the future because the kingdom of God insists on breaking down the boundaries of prejudice and transforming the definition of our neighbor.

Money Talks

As we arrive at the inn, even the most aggressive anti-Samaritan would have to admit that exemplary care has been shown to the victim so far.[21] There's still more to come. To this point in our study we have seen wealth and resources used in a number of ways: It has been lost, found, squandered, stolen, invested, and hoarded, and substantial debts have been canceled. We are about to see one more use of resources here: Money is used to care for another person with no chance of any return. When Jesus explains *the parable of the shrewd manager* to his disciples, he urges them to consider using their resources for investments in the kingdom of God. As this parable in Luke 10 moves into its final scene at the inn, we see another tangible sign of the economy of grace at work. Apparently, some innkeepers have a bad reputation; some of them are not exactly trustworthy, and the chance of extortion is a very real one.[22]

> [35]The next day he took out two denarii and gave them to the innkeeper. "Look after him," he said, "and when I return, I will reimburse you for any extra expense you may have."

We will recall from reading *the parable of the lost coin* that a drachma is a day's wage in ancient Israel, and here a denarius is the equivalent. Here at the inn, the Samaritan pulls out a pair of denarii (that is, two days' wages) to cover the expenses. Even beyond being rescued, the victim in the parable is being treated like a pearl of great price, like a treasured possession. For the first and only time in the story, we hear the actual words of the Samaritan, a comparatively long speech that details his plan: Whatever additional costs are incurred, he assures the innkeeper that he'll pay them on his way back. So in addition to meeting the immediate needs of the victim, the Samaritan also pledges to look after his longer-term

21. Gourgues, "The Priest, the Levite, and the Samaritan Revisited," 712: "In the context of the book of Leviticus, 'neighbor' (רע) included the גר as well as Israelites, that is to say, it included the stranger who shared the land with them. Scribes included this category among the proselytes and were in general agreement about admitting them to the group of those covered by the injunction to neighborly love. The case was different for pure and simple non-Israelites as well as other categories of strangers, among whom Samaritans were sometimes formally classified—as they are by Luke himself in 17:16–18: '. . . Now he was a Samaritan. Then Jesus said: Was no one found to return and give praise to God except this foreigner (ἀλλογενής)?'"

22. J. Green, *Gospel of Luke*, 432.

healing. Evidently the Samaritan is banking on the innkeeper doing the right thing. In a parable brimming with reversals, here's one more: The Samaritan trusts in the innkeeper, regardless of any reputation, and blasts the stereotype with a deposit of cold hard cash. And for his part, the innkeeper is likewise trusting and evidently chooses to believe the Samaritan's promise that he'll return in due course. The innkeeper has just seen the Samaritan's care for the injured traveler, and no doubt that elevates the Samaritan's integrity in the eyes of the innkeeper. Altogether, acts of mercy are changing things in this story, and this is an image of what can happen when the kingdom of God breaks into our lives.[23]

Cross-Examination

With the bill paid and the promise of return extended, it is now time to go back to the lawyer who has been silent for a while and might well be stunned by the climax of the parable: "By depicting a Samaritan as the hero of the story, therefore, Jesus, demolished all boundary expectations. Social position—race, religion, or region—count for nothing. The man in the ditch, from whose perspective the story is told, will not discriminate among potential helpers"[24] The lawyer has just heard not only about mercy shown to the victim at the side of the road but also about a new kind of neighborliness and reciprocal trust with the innkeeper. Now it is his turn to answer one more important question as this trial is close to a final verdict:

> [36]"Which of these three do you think was a neighbor to the man who fell into the hands of robbers?" [37]The expert in the law replied, "The one who had mercy on him." Jesus told him, "Go and do likewise."

23. Bruce W. Longenecker, "The Story of the Samaritan and the Innkeeper (Luke 10:30–35): A Study in Character Rehabilitation," *BibInt* 17 (2009): 446: "In the empires of the world, such relationships are unprecedented. In the empire of God, where grace and mercy overflow in abundance, such exceptional partnerships are (to be) the norm." Further, "Jesus' parable depicts an exceptional association of dubious characters as the means through which to get a momentary glimpse of the embodied reign of God" (447).

24. R. Alan Culpepper, "The Gospel of Luke," in *NIB* 8:229. Cf. Mark A. Proctor, "'Who Is My Neighbor?' Recontextualizing Luke's Good Samaritan (Luke 10:25–37)," *JBL* 138 (2019), 218: "Jesus's parabolic response to the lawyer's question thus plays on the reciprocity inherent in the word πλησίον in an effort to tease out of his interlocutor a response to the parable's concluding query, which effectively shatters the lawyer's world."

Perhaps the lawyer responds with gritted teeth, and despite all he's heard, it seems he can't quite bring himself to utter the loathed word "Samaritan." The trial started with the question "What must I do to inherit eternal life?," a question that "presumes eternal life is a commodity to be inherited or purchased on the basis of a particular action rather than a gift freely given."[25] But upon further reflection, the answer-by-parable turns the question upside down. The economy of grace it not about what *we do* in the first instance but, rather, about what *has been done* for us. These parables are teaching the disciples that all of us are lost sheep who can be rescued by the ultimate shepherd, or like injured victims at the side of the road who now can be restored to health.[26] In response, we have a chance to love our neighbor as we have been (and are) loved. And we don't need anything in return—whether reward or repayment—because of the lavish amount we have been given. The lawyer would know that the messiah is the one who binds up the wounds of the broken and applies the balm of healing. It could be that he will look back and realize there is more going on in this parable. Jesus tells the lawyer to "go and do likewise," and meanwhile, he is walking on the road to crucifixion as the definitive act of compassion.

25. Levine, *Short Stories by Jesus*, 84.

26. For some resistance to allegorical avoidance in scholarship from Adolf Jülicher onward, see Mikeal C. Parsons, "The Character of the Good Samaritan: A Christological Reading," in *Let the Reader Understand: Studies in Honor of Elizabeth Struthers Malbon*, ed. Edwin K. Broadhead, LNTS 583 (London: T&T Clark, 2018), 132: "Furthermore, the radical claims of the parable of the Good Samaritan are not avoided when one excludes Jesus as the referent of the parable, since Jesus calls the lawyer to 'act like a Samaritan.' Why should Jesus, a Jew, expect something of a Jewish lawyer that he himself is not prepared to expect of himself? It is in the very offense of the image of the Samaritan as a Christ figure that the parable has its evocative power in its fullest sense. Thus, we conclude that the exegetical tradition that has understood the Good Samaritan as Christ logically presents a more compelling reading in light of the text of Luke itself than the modern critical consensus."

4

A Billionaire and a Beggar

AMONG THE MOST hyped-up events on the calendar is the Super Bowl, annually blitzing viewers around the globe. Yet a recent survey indicates that some people tune in not for the game but, rather, for the *commercials*. How can that be? While there is hardly any time in a thirty- or sixty-second advertisement for any depth of storyline, it is nonetheless possible in a short space to create memorable characters who are instantly recognizable to the audience. By its very nature, the genre of the parable is immersive, quickly catches our attention, and involves our imagination in the episode at hand. We just heard *the parable of the good Samaritan*, which in two minutes or less sketches an extraordinary character who shows mercy to a hurting victim from an enemy people group, while others just pass by and forfeit an opportunity to lend a hand.

Such character contrasts are a main feature in the next installment of our study, as we now turn to *the parable of the rich man and Lazarus* in Luke 16:19–31. The two prominent figures in the story are worlds apart on the socioeconomic scale, and there is some continuity with themes found in *the parable of the good Samaritan*. There, we recall, the Samaritan deposits two days' wages with the promise to pay more down the road, whereas the rich man in this next parable has a human being at his gate but quite literally doesn't give a scrap. Indeed, the Samaritan saw the victim lying in the ditch and had compassion, but others saw the same person and just continued on their way; in this parable, that same *passing by* will evidently happen every day. But there are several surprises in store, both for the rich man and for poor Lazarus. And here is yet another parable with a jaw-dropping plot twist: *We will never even meet most of the main characters.*

Purple Haze

In *the parable of the rich barn builder* in Luke 12, it becomes clear that this character's riches gradually shift his priorities. Jesus tells that parable to an unnamed member of the crowd who is squabbling with his brother over their inheritance. Such acquisition, so the parable teaches, should have a warning label attached. Through the man's soliloquies, it is revealed that the rich barn builder has daydreams of luxury and visions of slothful self-indulgence, giving no thought to anyone but himself. Regrettably, he does not consider the real estate of his soul, and the parable ends with a call to accountability for more than just his money. While this cautionary tale lingers in the background, our attention turns to another rich man in Luke 16.

Just before sharing *the parable of the rich man and Lazarus*, Jesus is talking about various dangers associated with the pursuit of money. How many crimes, shady practices, arguments, or anxieties involve money in the ancient world, and is it so different today? "Nobody," says Jesus in Luke 16:13, "can serve two masters. You will end up hating one and loving the other, or going along with the first and despising the other." On the positive side, the disciples are encouraged to be faithful with their resources. As emerged from the discussion around *the parable of the shrewd manager*, any disciple can shrewdly use resources—however meager—to invest in noble and generous purposes. But also listening here in Luke 16 are some Pharisees who "loved money" (16:14), and they are unmoved by such teaching.[1] Jesus insists that what is highly prized by the world is worthless in God's eyes, and he then unfolds this parable while issues of basic justice and the dangers of unchecked wealth are fresh in the audience's mind:

1. E.g., Stephen I. Wright, "Parables on Poverty and Riches (Luke 12:13–21; 16:1–13; 16:19–31)," in *The Challenge of Jesus' Parables*, ed. Richard N. Longenecker (Grand Rapids: Eerdmans, 2000), 230: "The Parable of the Rich Man and Lazarus in Luke 16:19–31 is set as a warning to the Pharisees about the dangers of the love of money, which was a love they denied but secretly embraced (16:14)."

[19]"There was once a rich man," said Jesus, "who was dressed in purple and fine linen, and feasted in splendor every day."

The first mystery is: How did the rich man generate his money? In the case of the barn builder, we know that his land produced a bumper crop, and the Oil Baron is wealthy through dealings in oil and grain. It is also obvious that the shrewd manager makes money by fraudulent means. But there is no backstory provided for the rich man here, and so the focus shifts from *how* he gets his money to *what* he does with it. The camera zooms in on his clothing, on which he spends a vast amount. Purple is both really expensive and among the highest expressions of status in the ancient world.[2] In Daniel 5, for example, whoever interprets the writing on the wall will be dressed in purple and made the third highest ruler in the kingdom. In Luke 16, the purple attire of the rich man clothes him in an aura of opulence. The robes of purple also cover his fine linen undergarments, rumored to be purchased from Egypt.[3] In our day only the most popular social media influencers would be so bold as to advertise their underwear, and thus it is possible to infer that the rich man is quite proud of his wardrobe.

Spending money on his clothing, however, is exceeded by lavish fare at the rich man's table each day of the week. The term used here for "feasting" implies sumptuous parties; this kind of daily event was something that the barn builder could only dream about: "And I shall say to my soul, 'Soul, you've got many good things stored up for many years. Take it easy! Eat, drink, have a good time!'" (12:19). But the very fact that such feasting happens every single day might raise concerns for the audience here in Luke 16. After all, the calendar in ancient Israel sets apart all kinds of days for fasting and other observances. Does the rich man take seriously the high points of the year such as Passover, the commemoration of the nation's rescue from slavery? Is the rich man thoughtful and solemn on the Day of Atonement, or does his partying continue? If he enjoys a feast every day, the audience might wonder about the place of the weekly Sabbath in the schedule of this wealthy man, who is certainly not looking like a worthy

2. Reuben Bredenhof, *Failure and Prospect: Lazarus and the Rich Man (Luke 16:19–31) in the Context of Luke-Acts*, LNTS 603 (London: T&T Clark, 2019), 50: "In first-century Palestine wearing purple garments was associated with elite status."

3. David E. Garland, *Luke*, ZECNT (Grand Rapids: Zondervan, 2011), 669.

role model at this early point in the parable.[4] Given such questions, it is not surprising to find the following paraphrase in *The Message* version that captures the excessive self-indulgence of this rich and famous lifestyle: "There once was a rich man, expensively dressed in the latest fashions, wasting his days in conspicuous consumption" (16:19).

Drop Off

Amid the details about his imported outfits and continuous buffet, there is no description of the rich man's house. But we soon find out that his house is equipped with a *gate*, not a common feature for a private citizen in the world of first-century Palestine. Usually walled cities or temples had gates, suggesting here that the rich man's house is something of a fortress, although on a smaller scale. In Israelite cities the gate was the equivalent of a law court, the place of justice. The prophet Amos was disappointed about the lack of justice in ancient Israel in the eighth century BCE, and was angry with those who afflicted the righteous, who took a bribe, and who pushed away the needy at the gate.[5] Whether the rich man feels safe inside or is trying to keep certain people away is not stated, but his gate will remain shut for the duration of our story. Of immediate interest is a new character at this gate who is not sporting any purple or Egyptian finery but, rather, is clothed with painful lesions:

> [20]A poor man named Lazarus, who was covered with sores, lay outside his gate. [21]He longed to feed himself with the scraps that fell from the rich man's table. But the dogs came and licked his sores.

In a short scene in Mark 12, Jesus notices various people donating money to the temple treasury, with some of the rich tossing in large amounts. Then a poor widow comes along and gives two small coins, only worth pennies, but Jesus calls his disciples and points out that the others gave from their surplus, but she gave all she had. The poor widow's poverty

4. Douglas D. Webster, *The Parables: Jesus's Friendly Subversive Speech* (Grand Rapids: Kregel Academic, 2021), 144.

5. Amos 5:11–12; see David B. Gowler, "'At His Gate Lay a Poor Man': A Dialogic Reading of Luke 16:19–31," *PRSt* 32 (2005): 249–65, esp. 264; Joel B. Green, *The Gospel of Luke*, NICNT (Grand Rapids: Eerdmans, 1997), 609.

can be measured; her spirit of generosity cannot. Here in the parable of Luke 16 there is no reason given for the poverty of the new character at the rich man's gate, but his wasting disease and inability to walk must contribute. He may not have any money, but he does have something that nobody else in our parables has so far: a proper name. Another form of "Eliezer," the name Lazarus means "one whom God helps."[6] There is another Lazarus in John 11, a friend of Jesus who dies but days later is raised from the grave.[7]

The Lazarus in Luke 16 could use some help, and so he is dropped off (or even *thrown*) at the gate of the rich man's compound.[8] It seems that he was carried, and therefore can't walk, and we have to assume it is to beg. The shrewd manager was ashamed to beg, but it looks like Lazarus hardly has a choice since he is covered with sores. Despite his potentially favorable location outside the gate, Lazarus, we might suspect, is not given very much, since he is yearning for even the scraps from the rich man's table. The contrast could not be greater between the rich man's sumptuous fare *every day* and the absence of anything for the beggar. It would appear that the only attention that Lazarus receives is from a pack of dogs. Many people nowadays would have a sympathetic view of the dogs licking the sores of Lazarus, as though these friendly creatures are the only ones showing mercy to the beggar. But some scholars argue that for a first-century audience, the mention of dogs here would not be positive: "Although we may be tempted to think of the dogs of Jesus's story in sentimental terms, we should rather imagine pariahlike mongrels that roamed the outskirts of town in search of refuse."[9] Perhaps there is a pointed contrast at work, as these dogs in the parable have something

6. Amy-Jill Levine, *Short Stories by Jesus: The Enigmatic Parables of a Controversial Rabbi* (San Francisco: HarperOne, 2014), 262. On the background of the name and various antecedents in the Hebrew Bible, see Keith L. Yoder, "In the Bosom of Abraham: The Name and Role of Poor Lazarus in Luke 16:19–31," *NovT* 62 (2020): 2–24.

7. Richard Bauckham, "The Rich Man and Lazarus: The Parable and the Parallels," *NTS* 37 (1991): 225–46.

8. Cf. Arland J. Hultgren, *The Parables of Jesus: A Commentary* (Grand Rapids: Eerdmans, 2000), 112: "The Greek verb is ἐβέβλητο, the perfect passive of βάλλω, which is used to depict a person confined to his or her sickbed (cf. Matt 8:6, 14; 9:2; Mark 7:30). The use of the verb points to his helplessness. He has to be placed at the gate every day by friends (cf. the words of the paralytic at John 5:7)."

9. J. Green, *Gospel of Luke*, 606. Alternatively, see Justin David Strong, "Lazarus and the Dogs: The Diagnosis and Treatment," *NTS* 64 (2018): 178–93.

of a meal, whereas Lazarus in his misery does not.[10] Overall, Lazarus has a lot in common with the victim at the side of the road in *the parable of the good Samaritan*, as both are ignored by those in better health.

This Mortal Coil

Among the strangest stories in the Bible is an anecdote about a funeral in 2 Kings 13:20–21, in the dreary days of the northern kingdom: "Elisha died, and they buried him. Now raiding parties of Moab entered the land in the spring of every year. As they were burying a man, behold they saw the raiding party, and threw the man in the grave of Elisha. The man went, touched the bones of Elisha, lived, and arose to his feet." In the context of 2 Kings, part of the message of this story is hope and consolation. If the nation listens to the prophetic word, they can receive the gift of life even in the despair of their circumstances. For our purposes here, whatever this short scene is about, it dramatically illustrates that the grave is not the end of the story. It also reminds us that the Bible has something to say about the afterlife, and such ideas should be kept in mind as *the parable of the rich man and Lazarus* in Luke 16 continues.

> 22In due course the poor man died, and was carried by the angels into Abraham's bosom. The rich man also died, and was buried.

Poor Lazarus's death, we suspect, did not attract much attention or fanfare. He had been carried to the rich man's gate, and there he probably passed away. But what might be lacking in any lavish funeral is more than compensated after his death. We might think of angels with halos on Hallmark cards, but in this setting they are better imagined as heavenly warriors, escorting the honored guest to a banquet. Abraham's bosom is usually interpreted in terms of a special seat at an important occasion, with proximity to the host as a sign of privilege.[11] Other narratives in

10. John T. Carroll, *Luke: A Commentary*, NTL (Louisville: Westminster John Knox, 2012), 481–82: "While the poor beggar cannot taste scraps of food from the extravagant daily feasts at the wealthy man's home, dogs are able to make a meal by licking the poor man's sores."

11. Alexey Somov and Vitaly Voinov, "'Abraham's Bosom' (Luke 16:22–23) as a Key Metaphor in the Overall Composition of the Parable of the Rich Man and Lazarus," *CBQ* 79 (2017): 620: "In v. 23, Luke uses the spatial difference between the postmortem positions of the rich man and Lazarus to mark the difference in their afterlife status: The lower position the rich

the Bible include the theme of banquets as an image of God's presence. Exodus 24 describes an incredible scene where Moses and a group of leaders walk up to the top of the mountain and see the God of Israel. On this mountain, God is enthroned on brilliant pavement, and this group is privileged to eat and drink before God. Lazarus is carried into the bosom of Abraham, and although it wasn't reported earlier, in all likelihood he is to be understood as an example of someone who was rich toward God. From the parables of the lost sheep and the lost coin, we might wonder if Abraham's bosom can be pictured as a place of celebration.

Staying with the topic of life after death, the rich man's hourglass also runs out of sand. There is no indication in the parable, but we can probably suppose there was a splendid funeral replete with a signature feast for the impressive guest list. But there is no fanfare mentioned in the parable, which would have given the audience an uneasy feeling, and there is certainly no mention of Abraham's bosom. It is true that Abraham is wealthy in the book of Genesis, but he is also a pillar of hospitality (e.g., Gen. 18:1–8). And now, as the parable declares, Lazarus is enjoying the company of this preeminent ancestor of the faith. What about the rich man? We did get a fleeting glimpse of the afterlife in *the parable of the rich barn builder*. In Luke 12 he is called a fool, and God does not mince words: On that very night his soul will be required of him. The rich man has just shuffled off his mortal coil, and we await further insight as to the next stage of his journey.

Titanic Reversal

"We considered the ship unsinkable," an executive for the White Star Line is reputed to have said in the aftermath of the *Titanic*'s calamitous voyage, "and it never entered our minds that there had been anything like a serious loss of life."[12] In the wake of perhaps the most written about nautical event since Noah's ark, an abundance of eulogies were published from the likes

man occupies in Hades corresponds to his worse fate and humiliated condition, while the higher position of Lazarus (as well as Abraham) marks his honorable and exalted state. The orientational metaphor used for the wicked rich man—*down*—confirms that he is condemned; the orientational metaphor used for the righteous Lazarus—*up*—stands for the blessed reality reserved for him."

12. Frances Wilson, *How to Survive the Titanic: The Sinking of J. Bruce Ismay* (London: Bloomsbury, 2011), 34.

of Thomas Hardy (In the solitude of the sea / Deep from human vanity, / And the Pride of Life that planned her, stilly couches she) and the Bishop of Winchester ("The *Titanic*, name and thing, will stand as a monument and warning to human presumption").[13] These cautions from a poet and a preacher could fit quite well in Luke 16, with the concern about the potential disaster of riches and the lure of material gains that can divide our loyalties and impair our judgment. Early in Luke's story the looming potential for reversal is outlined in straightforward terms (e.g., "He has filled the hungry with good things / but has sent the rich away empty," 1:53 NIV), and the man previously clothed in purple is about to become an incendiary illustration.

> [23]As he was being tormented in Hades, he looked up and saw Abraham far away, and Lazarus in his bosom. [24]"Father Abraham!" he called out. "Have pity on me! Send Lazarus to dip the tip of his finger in water and cool my tongue! I'm in agony in this fire!"

Usually in the New Testament, "Hades" is the abode of the dead, and it has some similarities to "Sheol" in the Hebrew Bible.[14] Our key point here is that whatever Hades is exactly, evidently you can't buy your way out of it, and it is much better to be in Abraham's bosom. In the absence of any lengthy description of Hades in the parable, our attention turns to its latest occupant, the rich man. Amid his torment, his gaze falls on Abraham off in the distance, and perhaps for the first time in a long time the rich man's eyes are *not* on himself. Most notably, he is begging for pity, and so we have our first major plot reversal: The billionaire has now become the beggar in the parable.

An entirely new set of contrasts also emerges. Lazarus had earlier longed for just a scrap that dropped from the rich man's table, whereas now the rich man longs for a drop of water. It has become obvious that the rich man knows the name of Lazarus, suggesting a more intentional strategy

13. Quoted in Anna Anselmo, ed., *Twentieth-Century Poets: A Selection with Notes* (Milan: EduCatt, 2011), 7–8.

14. I. Howard Marshall, *The Gospel of Luke: A Commentary on the Greek Text* (Grand Rapids: Eerdmans, 1978), 816. Note also Outi Lehtipuu, *The Afterlife Imagery in Luke's Story of the Rich Man and Lazarus*, NovTSup 123 (Leiden: Brill, 2007); Ed Christian, "The Rich Man and Lazarus, Abraham's Bosom, and the Biblical Penalty *KARET* ('Cut Off')," *JETS* 61 (2018): 513–23.

of ignoring him while he was at the gate. Yet the rich man also has the audacity to treat Lazarus as a kind of courier or servant, asking that he deliver the required drop of water. For all the torment, the rich man doesn't exactly sound humble or contrite. And his request has some irony: He asks Abraham to send Lazarus over to him, which is interesting, because not so long ago Lazarus couldn't walk and needed to be dropped off at the unopened gate.

The Abyss

To review what we have heard in the parable so far, there were no overt reports about the faithful deeds of Lazarus or the lack of any charity from the rich man.[15] There is some circumstantial evidence, and the audience is invited to at least make a few assumptions. But nonetheless there are mysteries about each person that only God knows, and so we also consider the divine character, especially God's passion for justice, which we have already heard about. The theme of accountability for our actions is woven throughout each of these parables as well, along with an opportunity to allow God to *help* with our lives (as the very name "Lazarus" highlights). Meanwhile, we wonder what is going to happen with the rich man's request for a drop of water, as he is asking for the mercy that he never seems to have extended himself.[16]

> [25]"My child," replied Abraham, "remember that in your life you received good things, and in the same way Lazarus received evil. Now he is comforted here, and you are tormented. [26]Besides that, there is a great chasm standing between us. People who want to cross over from here to you can't do so, nor can anyone get across from the far side to us."

The formal title the rich man uses in verse 24 is "Father Abraham," which takes us back to a scene in Luke 3:7–9, where John the Baptist is fairly sharp with the growing crowd: "Produce fruit in keeping with repentance. And do not begin to say to yourselves, 'We have Abraham

15. From a literary point of view, the shift in spatial setting is telling; see Bredenhof, *Failure and Prospect*, 40: "The parable's second narrative scene, after the deaths of Lazarus and the rich man, continues the depiction of starkly differentiated settings. The setting is no longer an urban residence and street, but the afterlife with its own geographical features."

16. J. Green, *Gospel of Luke*, 608.

as our father.' For I tell you that out of these stones God can raise up children for Abraham" (3:8 NIV). The point is that one's lineage is not a network that can be leveraged for some sort of spiritual advantage, and such privilege is a gift, not an entitlement. When Abraham responds to the rich man, he seems to acknowledge the relational connection, but he immediately points out the lack of fruit, something that would have come with repentance (as John the Baptist would have put it). Again the irony is underscored, because the rich man is listening to someone who lavished hospitality on strangers in Genesis 18.

Abraham explains the measure-for-measure approach that is frequent in the Bible. David steals the poor man's lamb and loses most of his kingdom in the process. Jacob deceives his relatives and gets deceived by his own family. The rich man was not generous and should not expect generosity in return. As for the chasm that no one can cross, it becomes a potent reminder that we are accountable for our actions: "The rich man is not condemned because he is rich, but because he slipped into the coma of callousness that wealth often produces. He became consumed with his own joy, leisure, and celebration and failed to respond to the suffering and need of others around him. His callousness made his earthly riches all that he would receive from life."[17] Why can't you get across to the other side? Because the *chasm* is like a gate that remains closed, as the rich man is gradually learning.

Band of Brothers

So far in our study of parables, we have documented a few surprises along the way. The shrewd manager earns the praise of the very employer he stole from! A Samaritan on the Jericho road pulls over to help not just somebody stranded but a bitter enemy in a seven-hundred-year feud. Of course, these parables have other layers: Through the shrewd manager, Jesus encourages the disciples to invest in real enterprises that will last. Instead of procrastinating on matters that are eternally important, disciples have a chance to be "all-in" for the kingdom of God. The Samaritan's care for the victim at the side of the road, moreover, provides an insight as to how the Messiah offers to rescue all of us and bring us to a place of healing.

17. Darrell L. Bock, *Luke*, 2 vols. (Grand Rapids: Baker, 1994–96), 1372.

In this parable of the rich man and Lazarus, there have also been some plot twists. Not least, Lazarus is now at a banquet in a stunning reversal. We don't exactly know why, so we have to guess that he was rich in faith and receives God's invitation to this party: In Matthew 8:10–12 we discover that "many will come from east and west and will eat [that is, recline at the table] with Abraham and Isaac and Jacob in the kingdom of heaven."[18] We do know that the rich man is not at any banquet, and instead, he is thirsty in Hades. Even though his situation has drastically changed, his attitude apparently has not, and he still orders people around as though they exist solely for his benefit.

Unlike the Samaritan who stumbles upon a helpless victim on a lonely road, Lazarus is dropped off right at the rich man's doorstep. And we now learn that the rich man knows Lazarus by name, suggesting that on earth he knew exactly who he was, and yet did nothing. Even the dogs showered Lazarus with more attention than the rich man. Yet still he sees Lazarus and barks orders, and he almost willfully refuses to accept that Lazarus is busy, because he's the guest of honor in Abraham's bosom. And one more plot twist is going to be revealed as this dialogue continues. We are about to hear of some main characters in the story, even though they never formally enter the stage.

> 27"Please, then, father," he said, "send him to my father's house. 28I've got five brothers. Let him tell them about it, so that they don't come into this torture-chamber."
> 29"They've got Moses and the prophets," replied Abraham. "Let them listen to them."

Once in a while, when we are watching a good movie, new information is disclosed that changes our perceptions of the story. At this point in the dialogue with Abraham, we learn two new things about the rich man. First, he has *five brothers*. Second, he sounds concerned about them. While such passion might be commendable—and certainly has not been seen before—it is also possible that he continues to ignore some of the basic facts: "The rich man's paternal invocation and familial emphasis continue, but again he has not yet learned what landed him in torment in the first

18. Levine, *Short Stories by Jesus*, 267.

place. He wants to save his brothers from torment, not to ease the pain felt by the millions who lack food, shelter, or health care."[19]

How Lazarus is supposed to warn these five guys, and what exactly he is supposed to say, is not specified by the rich man: "Would he warn them that living in the lap of luxury while ignoring abject poverty at their doorstep is dangerous to their spiritual health?"[20] Apart from these practical questions, it is notable that the rich man persists in referring to Lazarus as someone to be used to further the rich man's interests, as though Lazarus is a personal employee to send on an errand. Granted, there is a sense of urgency here, but even this apparent concern gives us a further glimpse into the rich man's soul: "The wealthy man, accustomed to extra considerations, will not take No for an answer. Continuing to speak from his supposed position of privilege, the wealthy man insists that, for his family, more is needed, that a special envoy is required."[21]

In yet another twist, Abraham insists that he doesn't need to send Lazarus to the five brothers because they've *already* been warned! At their disposal, they have the words of Moses. Should they choose to listen, what would they hear? They would hear God's promise to childless Abraham: Through your descendants every family on earth will be blessed. The five brothers can hear the account of Pharaoh who enslaved the Israelites and threw their children into the water, until a later Pharaoh was thrown into the water in a stunning act of rescue. And those liberated slaves were then led on a sojourn through the wilderness, as God faithfully led them to their promised destination despite rebellion and complaints! "I've set before you life and death," says Moses in his final address on the end of the promised land. "Now choose life" (Deut. 30:15–16).

If they listened to the prophets, the five brothers would hear again the astonishing promise to David, as God announced in 2 Samuel 7, that he will always have a descendant on the throne of Israel. They can hear stories in the prophets about a wayward people and a God who is utterly committed to them, sending them messages of hope and healing, warnings of impending judgment alongside reminders of everlasting love. These five brothers could quite easily access these divine words shared by Moses: "If

19. Levine, *Short Stories by Jesus*, 275.
20. Garland, *Luke*, 673.
21. J. Green, *Gospel of Luke*, 609.

your brother becomes poor and cannot maintain himself with you, you shall support him as though he were a stranger and a sojourner, and he shall live with you" (Lev. 25:35). They can also hear the prophetic warning: "Many of those who sleep in the dusty ground will awake—some to everlasting life, and others to shame and everlasting abhorrence" (Dan. 12:2).[22] And the parable could have ended on this note. But as in the story of the lawyer who wanted to justify himself, there is still one more round in this dialogue.

All They Need Is a Miracle

We overhear a number of conversations in the Gospels about being raised from the dead.[23] Take Herod in Mark 6:14–29 for instance.[24] He gets nervous when he hears about the various deeds of Jesus's disciples, as they go around announcing that people should repent and are casting out demons and healing the sick. Herod is scared: "It's John the Baptist," he said, "risen from the dead! That's why these powers are at work in him" (Mark 6:14). Since Herod had previously ordered John's execution, no wonder he's deeply disturbed. But we need to notice something here: Herod is certainly affected by these rumors, but he does very little in response.

To return to the parable in Luke 16, we've just heard the rich man pleading with Abraham to send Lazarus to them. He is so insistent because he "knows from personal experience that his family do not take seriously

22. Levine, *Short Stories by Jesus*, 270.

23. For overviews, see Outi Lehtipuu, *Debates over the Resurrection of the Dead: Constructing Early Christian Identity*, OECS (Oxford: Oxford University Press, 2015); Markus Bockmuehl, "Resurrection," in *The Cambridge Companion to Jesus*, ed. Markus Bockmuehl (Cambridge: Cambridge University Press, 2001), 102–18.

24. Cf. Garland, *Luke*, 674: "Herod heard rumors that John or one of the prophets was raised from the dead. It piqued his curiosity but did not lead him to repentance (9:7–9; 13:31). In John's gospel, when Jesus raised a man from the dead, coincidentally named Lazarus, it did not produce repentance but precipitated a plot to kill Jesus (John 11:45–53). In Matthew, the story by the guards at the tomb about Jesus' resurrection only provoked the leaders to invent a lie and bribe the guards to squelch the truth (Matt 28:11–15). Something more than a dramatic return from the dead must soften hardened hearts."

Note also Levine, *Short Stories by Jesus*, 268: "In John 8.56, Jesus tells his Jewish interlocutors, 'Your ancestor (father) Abraham rejoiced that he would see my day; he saw it and was glad.' In Luke 13.28, Jesus speaks of the division of the righteous and the sinners: 'There will be weeping and gnashing of teeth when you see Abraham and Isaac and Jacob and all the prophets in the kingdom of God, and you yourselves thrown out.' The parable is a visual enactment of this prediction."

what the law and the prophets say."[25] We now get the sense that the rich man did not take the message of the Scriptures to heart, and neither do his five brothers, who are just like him. Yet the rich man persists and feels that all they need is a miracle. But that raises another question: Do miracles cause us to change our minds, lifestyle patterns, or thinking habits?

> 30"No, Father Abraham," he replied, "but if someone went to them from the dead, they would repent!"
> 31"If they don't listen to Moses and the prophets," came the reply, "neither would they be convinced, even if someone rose from the dead."

The five brothers never make a formal appearance in the story, but they are negatively characterized because the (formerly) rich man virtually admits they won't listen to the Bible. No doubt they know the Scriptures are around, but evidently they have little interest in taking the message to heart. This is Abraham's logic: If they don't listen to God's word now, why would they listen to Lazarus from beyond the grave when he was ignored at the gate? This parable ends with the words of Abraham, and the ending is a cliff-hanger: Will the five brothers ever really listen or learn to pay attention to another Lazarus at their own gates?[26] Can they ever be rich toward God? Will they—like their brother who has recently shuffled off his mortal coil—continue on the treadmill of self-indulgence, or will they experience the economy of grace?

Like a profitable movie franchise, this parable carries hints of a sequel. The brothers may be important, but they aren't the real focus at the end; instead, it's the listener! Parables, as we've discussed, have a more personal application than we may realize, and so every member of the audience is challenged: How would I respond to the message of Moses and the prophets? Would I listen to Lazarus? Would I be persuaded about the truth of Scripture if someone were raised from the dead? Just as the acts of the good Samaritan give us some insight into what a divine rescue might

25. Marshall, *Gospel of Luke*, 809.

26. N. T. Wright, *Jesus and the Victory of God* (Minneapolis: Fortress, 1996), 256: "The five brothers at home correspond quite closely to the older brother in the prodigal son. 'Resurrection' is happening, but they cannot see it. The story takes for granted that the poor and outcast were rightly being welcomed into the kingdom, and it turns the spotlight on to the rich, the Pharisees, the grumblers: They, too, now needed to repent if they were to inherit the new day that would shortly dawn. They were refused the extra revelation of someone going to them from the dead; the message of repentance was clear enough in Moses and the prophets."

look like, so this parable points to a resurrection that is a game-changing moment in the larger storyline.[27] In fact, that resurrection points to an outpouring of God's favor that cannot be earned no matter what our income or status might be and that gives us an opportunity to repent, or "turn around." And for another illustration of what it means to "turn around," we now turn to our next parable.

27. Cf. Josh Stigall, "'They Have Moses and the Prophets': The Enduring Demand of the Law and Prophets in the Parable of the Rich Man and Lazarus," *RevExp* 112 (2015): 554: "Abraham's further comment, 'If they do not listen to Moses and the Prophets, neither will they be persuaded if someone rises from the dead,' (v. 31) leads to the question, 'Who is this someone?' Whereas in the context the referent is certainly meant to be Lazarus, in Luke's Gospel only one character's resurrection has soteriological significance, namely, that of Jesus."

5

Bankruptcy, Bitterness, and the Banquet

IN AN AVERAGE WEEK, our news feeds have ample reports of excess and greed. Corruption seems to be found in every sector of society: from the business world to college-admissions bribes and from the political arena even as far as fraud in the health-care system. We are intrigued by *the parable of the shrewd manager* because it captures an all-too-familiar pattern of employee theft and insider trading. But Jesus then turns the story upside down with a memorable closing line about how disciples should invest their time and energy for an ultimately much more profitable cause. As we turn to our next case study, the topic of a rebellious youngster is our immediate focus. This unnamed youthful character demands his share of the family inheritance from his father but then pours it down the drain through a debauched lifestyle. When all is lost, he finally comes to his senses and decides to return, only to discover—in a major-league plot twist of the parable—that the father has long been waiting for his restoration. Some of the questions raised by this parable include how you might deal with someone who has just blown a vast portion of your income.

The parable of the prodigal sons in Luke 15 inspired some of Rembrandt's paintings and is probably the inspiration for Shakespeare's Prince

Hal in *Henry IV, Part 1*.[1] But here is another example where the traditional title of the parable ("the prodigal son") is slightly misleading, as there are *two* sons in the story, along with several other elements that would have been a bit scandalous to the original audience. It is worth reviewing *why* Jesus chooses this genre of short stories. Using the kinds of family dynamics that most people can immediately relate to—even if they haven't personally had these exact experiences—draws the audience in. Like the Trojan Horse allowed the Greeks to sneak into the city of Troy, when people listen to a parable, it provides a sly way to access matters of the heart: "Jesus spoke in parables deliberately. He was interested in something much more than mere clarity of thought and a routine answer. He didn't teach in order for someone to learn the right response. His teaching was not a mere cerebral exercise. He taught so that the soul would be surprised into experiencing a new, authentic revelation of truth, one that would pour over into life and living. For that, Jesus needed to slow down reception and infuse an element of participation—and a dose of doubt."[2]

Overall, this parable of wayward sons and a faithful father draws on several core themes in biblical literature and provides us with some remarkable insight on the character of God, what human rebellion and failure feels like, and the qualities of forgiveness and repentance. There are several layers of meaning in the story, and the reader is able to glimpse a vision of the Christian faith that is memorable and compelling. Like the other parables we have seen so far, this short story about wasted money brings out other dimensions of the economy of grace that is part of Jesus's larger message. We will also see the idea of redemption in this parable. What does it mean to be redeemed? This parable will take us beyond the dictionary definition to witness an outrageous story of recovery and restoration.

Show Me the Money

At the start of Luke 15 there are two short parables. Earlier we looked briefly at the parables of *the lost sheep* and *the lost coin*, and I suggested that they illustrate several facets of how God is actively searching for

1. See Alison M. Jack, *The Prodigal Son in English and American Literature: Five Hundred Years of Literary Homecomings* (Oxford: Oxford University Press, 2019).

2. Leonard Sweet, *The Bad Habits of Jesus: Showing Us the Way to Live Right in a World Gone Wrong* (Carol Stream, IL: Tyndale, 2016), 62–63.

those who have gone astray, that human beings are immensely valuable to God, and that there is great rejoicing when someone lost is recovered. These themes are going to be expanded on in the longest parable we will read in this book. It has an elaborate plot with two movements, exploring the profiles of two sons who are both lost in different ways. The opening movement unfolds in some detail: the initial demand, fractured relationships, the harsh reality of adverse circumstances, and steps toward a return home.[3] In the second movement attention turns to the older son, who may never have left home but who nonetheless is alienated from his father.

All three parables in Luke 15 are spoken to a diverse group of listeners. The beginning of the chapter is captured this way in *The Message* version: "By this time a lot of men and women of questionable reputation were hanging around Jesus, listening intently. The Pharisees and religion scholars were not pleased, not at all pleased. They growled, 'He takes in sinners and eats meals with them, treating them like old friends.' Their grumbling triggered this story." Recall that this longer narrative of Luke 11–19 take place in a travel context and is often referred to as the "gospel for the outcasts."[4] The centerpiece of this travel narrative, as Jesus is heading for Jerusalem, is *the parable of the lost sons*.

Our story starts with an introduction to an unnamed landowner. It is hard to determine how wealthy he is, although he certainly seems well off, and sizable property is mentioned in this parable. But he is not defined by riches as in some of our other cases, like the barn builder or the Oil Baron. Matters of inheritance and capital are big parts of this story, but they are not mentioned in the opening sentence. Instead, this character is primarily introduced as a father with two sons. The father makes the most appearances in the story as he deals with his sons who are both rebellious but in quite different ways. In the first half of the story, the younger son gets the most attention because of a very controversial demand.

> [11]Jesus continued: "There was a man who had two sons. [12]The younger one said to his father, 'Father, give me my share of the estate.' So he divided his property between them."

3. Cf. Eugene H. Peterson, *Tell It Slant: A Conversation on the Language of Jesus in His Stories and Prayers* (Grand Rapids: Eerdmans, 2008), 94.

4. Klyne R. Snodgrass, *Stories with Intent: A Comprehensive Guide to the Parables of Jesus*, 2nd ed. (Grand Rapids: Eerdmans, 2018), 85.

The Bible contains no shortage of narratives about fathers and brothers, often featuring rivalry and jockeying for position. Such accounts start early with Cain's jealousy of his brother Abel, and continue through the book of Genesis and beyond. It is soon clear that *firstborn status* is a big deal. We learn in the tales of Esau and Jacob that the firstborn can formally expect the birthright—that is, a significant share of the family property upon the father's death. The birthright is later codified in the legal section of the Hebrew Bible: "According to the Mosaic law, which may have been designed to protect the rights of the elder brother against favored younger brothers, the elder brother received a double portion of the inheritance (Deut. 21:17)."[5] Among other reasons, this principle is designed to keep property within the family network as it is handed down through the generations.

An early signal that we are dealing with a story of shocking upheaval is that the firstborn—normally the focus of all the attention—is moved off the stage for the entire first act of the parable.[6] The spotlight is instead focused on the younger son and his deeply disrespectful words. We just noted that the inheritance would usually be divided at the father's death, but this renegade younger son wants the timeline accelerated. We have seen some unusual moves in the parables so far. For example, the Samaritan asks the innkeeper to take care of the wounded victim and keep track of any further expenses. But that gesture is full of generosity. Here in Luke 15, the younger son's demand is surely an insult. In effect, he is saying, "I would prefer you were dead, because I want my share now!"[7]

Fyre Fest

Questions of inheritance have surfaced before. *The parable of the rich barn builder* back in Luke 12 arises out of a squabble, as someone from the crowd wants Jesus to intervene: "Teacher, tell my brother to divide the inheritance with me" (12:13). Hardly any details are given—so we

5. R. Alan Culpepper, "The Gospel of Luke," in *NIB* 8:301.

6. On the eschewing of favoritism, see Abraham Smith, "A Prodigal Sings the Blues: The Characterization of Harriett Williams in Langston Hughes's 'Not Without Laughter,'" in *Yet with a Steady Beat: Contemporary U.S. Afrocentric Biblical Interpretation*, ed. Randall C. Bailey (Atlanta: SBL, 2002), 154–55.

7. N. T. Wright, *Jesus and the Victory of God* (Minneapolis: Fortress, 1996), 129.

have to make an educated guess—but it sounds like a younger brother is angry about money that is apparently withheld by an older brother. Why would an older brother do this? Is he concerned that his (rather confident) younger brother won't manage the inheritance properly? Given that Jesus then goes to talk about the dangers of riches, there is reason to suspect that the guy who wants his share of the family inheritance needs to hear the warning of the rich fool who builds bigger barns. Here in Luke 15 it seems that the younger son is acting in a way that dishonors his father, the community, and the larger tradition of Israel's law embodied in the Scriptures, and his request certainly sounds immature and self-centered.

During their sojourn in the wilderness, the people of Israel could be quite demanding. Despite being rescued from slavery in Egypt, the lack of resources in the desert caused lots of complaining. In Numbers 11:4–5 some members of the community get carried away: "The rabble among them had a strong craving; and the Israelites also wept again, and said, 'If only we had meat to eat! We remember the fish we used to eat in Egypt for nothing, the cucumbers, the melons, the leeks, the onions, and the garlic'" (NRSV). It is all too common for the people to treat God like a slot machine or a candy dispenser, and now in Luke 15 the younger son is following in those rebellious footsteps by treating his father in a similar way. So why would the father give in? Why would he divide up his property and allow the younger son to have his way? Most fathers in this situation, one might argue, would *not* be willing to grant the son's disrespectful demand. Whether it is heartbreaking or not, the father divides the inheritance, and the younger son now has the assets that he eagerly desired.

> [13]Not long after that, the younger son got together all he had, set off for a distant country and there squandered his wealth in wild living.

In the very short and one-sided conversation about the inheritance, there was no mention of the older brother and what he might do with his share. The parable will return to him down the road, but right now the focus is squarely on the younger brother who opts for liquidity. Since there are no transaction records, we are not quite sure how he pulls it off, but somehow he gathers together all of his possessions. In *the parable of the hidden treasure*, the finder sells everything in order to buy the field of dreams. Here, the younger son has rather different desires. He buys a ticket for a distant place; we assume it is nowhere near the promised land and far away from any kind of faithfulness to the Torah.[8] The exact country may be unknown, but we do know exactly what happens there: The inheritance recently received from the father and presumably converted to some form of liquidity is squandered.

It's one thing to lose your money, say, after being deceived in a Ponzi scheme. It's quite another to completely waste it, squandering the wealth. The Greek word for "squander" is also used in *the parable of the shrewd manager*, who is accused of squandering his master's property and promptly loses his job. In a country far away, the younger son uses the converted cash to fuel a freewheeling ride on the wild side. Without much effort, anyone reading this parable today can probably imagine the posts he would have made to his social media accounts were this phase of the story taking place in our postmodern era.

And yet, we hardly need a psychologist to explain *why* the younger son wanted to live this way, since the same examples can be seen all around us. Besides, in the end more energy is expended in the parable's description of the banquet than the reasons the younger son goes bankrupt. To be sure, the elder brother will give more details of the wild things the younger son did later. In the same vein, lots of preachers graphically describe the ancient equivalents of casinos, brothels, nightclubs, ecstasy, and related toxins that must have entered the younger brother's bloodstream. That is the easy part; the more difficult question for interpreters is not why the rebel wants to live in such a self-destructive way but, rather, why the father granted the disrespectful demand in the first place.

Theoretically, it is quite possible that many listeners in the audience would object to the father's conduct and question his premature release of the inheritance, especially if he had any suspicion of what the younger son was liable do with the money. On this score the parable might be called *the parable of the prodigal father*, owing to his reckless generosity. But in the end, we are going to ask if the image of the father in this parable gives us further insight into the economy of grace. Will the father demand repayment of this considerable debt, or will another approach be taken?

8. For a different interpretation of the younger son's journey (and several other provocative points), see Peter Baker, "The Prodigal Returns? Karl Barth's Christological Interpretation of Luke 15:11–32," *JTI* 16 (2022): 57–73.

Global Recession

Some misery has occurred in the parables so far. The traveler on the Jericho road falls into the hands of robbers and is beaten and left half dead in the ditch. Poor Lazarus is covered with sores and reduced to begging at the gate of an indifferent rich man who is busy feasting. The shrewd manager is dismissed from his post by the Oil Baron, but it is difficult to feel bad for a con artist who then proceeds to swindle his master *again*. Similarly, the younger son is about to fall on hard times, but since this is almost entirely a self-inflicted problem, the audience may not be overwhelmed with sympathy for him. The timing is unfortunate, however, for the younger son's bankruptcy in Luke 15 coincides with some serious climate change:

> [14]After he had spent everything, there was a severe famine in that whole country, and he began to be in need.

People have burned through money throughout human history, and the younger son does not appear to have invested any of his inheritance or made any real friends who will welcome him into their homes now that his trust fund is empty. After all of his careless spending, the faraway country is hit with a famine. On the basis of other stories in Scripture, such as in 2 Kings 6, we know that times of famine can be awful. That episode takes place in the days of Elisha, when the Aramean army from the north has laid siege to the capital city of Samaria. Inflation skyrockets to the point where the head of donkey costs eighty shekels, and people are increasingly desperate. In our parable in Luke 15, the younger son is far from home, he has no cash, and is "in need." The same Greek word occurs in John 2:3 where it describes the wine running out at the wedding in Cana, causing the host to panic. The younger son has nothing in his wallet, and now that the market has collapsed, he is quickly running out of options.

Minimum Wage

Famines and other natural disasters are a common occurrence in the biblical world. Sometimes these events are divinely sent, as in the catastrophic flood in the days of Noah. But other times famines occur and no divine cause is mentioned, as in the era of Abram in Genesis 12, when a famine prompts his idea to seek safety in Egypt. The central question in these instances is not just "Did God send this famine?" We may also ask, "How do the various characters respond to a crisis situation? Do the characters in a given story use the opportunity to consider major life changes, or just continue in their previous way?"

For our younger son, who has just squandered his inheritance, the arrival of the famine compounds his problem because he is in a foreign land. While some might say "he's in Vegas," the term "exile" is a better description here. For example, the man and the woman are banished from the garden of Eden in Genesis 3, and they go into exile. David is guilty of some monstrous sins, and his son Absalom enters Jerusalem and attempts to take over the nation. Fleeing from this threat, David goes into exile on the other side of the Jordan River, and he is able to return only after a brutal civil war. When you are dislocated from the place you really belong, you are in exile.

The younger son has departed to a far-off place, and he has become a stranger in a strange land. Moreover, his situation of exile is worsened because he is now destitute in a time of famine, and we suspect that he is gradually having everything stripped away. The victim in *the parable of the good Samaritan* gets stripped of his clothes by the band of thieves. Loss of clothing represents humiliation and also the loss of identity.[9] We find out later in Luke 15 that this younger son needs sandals and presumably is in rags. And now, as he has little choice but to labor in hard conditions, the younger son is gradually losing the shirt off his back, so to speak, as a mark of his growing humiliation in this distant land:

> [15]So he went and hired himself out to a citizen of that country, who sent him to his fields to feed pigs. [16]He longed to fill his stomach with the pods that the pigs were eating, but no one gave him anything.

Pigs are the most obvious sign that the younger son is deep in Gentile territory. The legal sections of the Hebrew Bible designate pigs as unclean creatures, and therefore pigs don't feature on the menu in Israelites homes. Notable references are Leviticus 11:7 (where swine are listed as unclean) and Isaiah 65:1–5 (which describes a scene where eating pig's meat is a

9. See Michael P. Knowles, "What Was the Victim Wearing? Literary, Economic, and Social Contexts for the Parable of the Good Samaritan," *BibInt* 12, no. 2 (2004): 145–74.

shameful act). Pigs also play a notorious role in an episode in Mark 5:11–13: A legion of demons are cast into a herd of swine and then rush down the slope and are drowned in the sea. These texts variously underscore that pigs are uniformly viewed with disdain, and help us to understand why pigs don't get much positive press in the Bible. So when the younger son has little choice but to take a job with a local *who then sends him out to the pigs*, it signals how far he has fallen since he left home. Not only is his menial job the lowest of the low, but feeding the pigs would have been religiously offensive to the Jewish community.

Having squandered his inheritance, the destitute younger son is reduced to feeding the swine during this time of famine in a distant land. Even worse, he is craving their food, and he must be desperate if pig slop looks appealing. The term for "pods" or "husks" that the pigs are enjoying only occurs here in Scripture, and it could be describing the kind of food that is only given to animals or the poorest folk.[10] We can deduce that the younger son's belly is as empty as his bank account, and he trudges to work with a gnawing hunger. In this scene, the point of view is the younger son's: He is watching the pigs eat and is *longing* for the husks. Such hunger is also seen in *the parable of the rich man and Lazarus*, as the beggar is lying at the gate and *longing* (same Greek verb: ἐπιθυμέω) for any crumb that falls from the rich man's table. But only dogs lick Lazarus, while the rich man and everyone else pass by. The younger son is likewise passed by, and nobody gives him anything. Because of the famine, perhaps no one is in the mood for sharing; regardless, the younger son receives no mercy.

The Comeback

If you are out in the field longing for the husks that feed the pigs, could you not just help yourself to a few of the pods? We have to wonder, therefore, if the younger son is being monitored, and if there are severe penalties for stealing. It is quite possible that in the eyes of the owner, the pigs are a more valuable asset than his (foreign) worker. Indirectly, we are meeting a new character, a citizen of that country who might be a horrible boss, like Ahab. This owner of the field, in other words, doesn't look like the

10. I. Howard Marshall, *The Gospel of Luke: A Commentary on the Greek Text* (Grand Rapids: Eerdmans, 1978), 781.

kind of guy who would divide his property because of a selfish demand from one of his sons. There is a bit of a reversal here, as now the younger son is reduced to working for a property owner who is totally unlike his own father. Is there a moment of illumination on the horizon? It appears that the younger son's experience of tough labor in miserable conditions opens his eyes to the reality of his situation. He hasn't just squandered wealth, but he has also turned his back on an uncommon father.

> [17]When he came to his senses, he said, "How many of my father's hired servants have food to spare, and here I am starving to death!"

Fellowship with the swine marks a pivotal moment in the parable. There is no indication of how long it takes, but the adversity wakes him up and "he came to himself" (a more literal rendering of the Greek at the beginning of verse 17).[11] The younger son's awakening prompts further discussion about the idea of repentance that we have raised earlier. In terms of definition, we are understanding "repentance" as a change of mindset and a change of direction. This is not quite the same as "regret." An example of a character who regrets his actions is Pharaoh in Exodus 10:16. After enduring numerous plagues and ecological disasters because of his refusal to release the Israelites from slavery, Pharaoh is desperate for a ceasefire: "Pharaoh hurriedly called Moses and Aaron and said, 'I have sinned against the Lord your God and against you.'"[12] A very short time later, however, Pharaoh flip-flops and resumes his hostility. The question we might have about the younger son in Luke 15 is whether he is genuinely sorrowful for all of his actions, including embarrassing his father and squandering his inheritance in distant land, or merely disgusted with his present circumstances in the pigpen.

However, the motives of the younger son are less important than the eventual outcome. It is difficult to discern the heart of this impoverished character, especially at this stage in the parable. And this might be a crucial element: As it stands, the situation is hopeless for the younger son, and any plan depends on whether the father is willing to extend mercy to his rebellious child. No doubt the younger son, wallowing in filth, regrets some

11. François Bovon, *Luke 2: A Commentary on the Gospel of Luke 9:51–19:27*, Hermeneia (Minneapolis: Fortress, 2013), 426.

12. David E. Garland, *Luke*, ZECNT (Grand Rapids: Zondervan, 2011), 627.

of his past behavior. But if he is to repent, it will result in some movement and a commitment to change.

The first signs of a shift are heard through a soliloquy, presumably while the younger son is working at his miserable job. Soliloquys are a frequent occurrence in our parables, and they provide a window into the character's thought process. For example, in a soliloquy the shrewd manager formulated a strategy for surviving after getting caught pilfering from his master. The shrewd manager's internal monologue began with an appraisal of his own predicament: He claims that he doesn't have enough muscle for manual labor and has too much pride to start begging at the gate of some rich guy with linen underwear (Luke 16:3).

For the younger son in Luke 15, thoughts of day laborers start his soliloquy. He is longing for the pig husks, and he then compares his current fate in this distant land with memories of his father's hired servants back home. The lowest wage-earner on the scale, a hired hand, depends on daily work that may or may not be continued.[13] At the beginning of Job chapter 7, there is a similar reference to a hired worker, and it sounds like a difficult grind without much security or any benefits. Here the younger son realizes that his father's hired hands are treated much better than he is. Even those workers who are lowest on the food chain in his father's service have a preferable situation in comparison, as they have plenty to eat.

Hunger Games

As the lengthy soliloquy continues, it is worth reviewing the plot so far: The younger son demands his inheritance from the father, converts it to cash, journeys to a distant land where he squanders his money, and now that he has nothing in a place of exile, he is starting to contemplate a return journey. These kinds of movements are seen elsewhere in the Bible, and the idea of exile and return is a significant theme. The life of Jacob, for instance, follows a similar pattern: He leaves the promised land after cheating his older brother but eventually comes back.[14] As discussed previously, the famous King David made some horrendous decisions that include adultery and murder, and he is forced to evacuate the palace when

13. Darrell L. Bock, *Luke*, 2 vols. (Grand Rapids: Baker, 1994–96): 1312.

14. See Kenneth E. Bailey, *Jacob and the Prodigal: How Jesus Retold Israel's Story* (Downers Grove, IL: InterVarsity, 2003).

Absalom, his son, tries to seize the throne. Walking out of the city in 2 Samuel 15:25, David himself admits that if God grants him favor, only then will he have a chance to return to Jerusalem. Is it possible that the journey of the younger son in this parable is configured on the life of Jacob and the trials of David, or even on the people of Israel as a whole with their journey of exile and return? We will return to this question in a little while. For now, the younger son is still a long way from home, but he has a plan:

> [18]I will set out and go back to my father and say to him: Father, I have sinned against heaven and against you. [19]I am no longer worthy to be called your son; make me like one of your hired servants.

Recognizing that even his father's hired hands have a way better deal, the younger son outlines the journey home. As his soliloquy continues, he opts to start with a confession. To reiterate, it must be said that some interpreters raise an eyebrow here and wonder if the younger son is simply acting like a "classic manipulator."[15] Does his soliloquy reflect a heart of genuine repentance? Or is he only playing a game because of his hunger? The example of Pharaoh cited above is instructive, because the language used by the king of Egypt is almost identical: Pharaoh acknowledges, "I have sinned against the Lord your God and against you" (Exod. 10:16 NIV). The emergency situation in Exodus prompts these words from Pharaoh, and it is clear that there is no real change of direction because he soon marches out and tries to recapture the Israelites he's just released. With this backdrop in mind, how should we hear the younger son's confession?

It could be that the younger son's confession begins with a *synecdoche*. By way of definition, a synecdoche is a figure of speech where a part of something stands for the whole.[16] So if a student drives up in a sparkling new Lexus and a professor says, "Nice wheels," this is a figure of speech whereby "wheels" is one component that stands for the entire vehicle (purchased with a squandered inheritance). The younger son plans to say, "I have sinned against heaven and against you" (15:18), which could

15. Note the discussions of Bailey, *Jacob and the Prodigal*, 115; and Amy-Jill Levine, *Short Stories by Jesus: The Enigmatic Parables of a Controversial Rabbi* (San Francisco: HarperOne, 2014), 59.

16. J. A. Cuddon, *The Penguin Dictionary of Literary Terms and Literary Theory*, rev. C. E. Preston (London: Penguin Books, 1999), 890.

be interpreted as a synecdoche for all his violations, ranging from flouting the traditions of inheritance and the values of the Torah to parental disrespect and a self-centered attitude.

We can compare the younger son's soliloquy to that of the shrewd manager here: That scamming manager gets caught squandering but displays no remorse for his conduct.[17] As he deliberates, he only comes up with a scheme that involves more cheating. In contrast, the younger son plans to ask his father to make him a day laborer, one of the lowest-ranking workers (minimal wage and hired on a short-term basis without the longer-term commitment of a household servant). While we cannot be 100 percent certain of his motives—and we should acknowledge the possibility that he is merely trying to sound sorrowful in order to deceive his father—at this point he sounds more honest than the shrewd manager. He certainly seems to know that his only chance is to cast himself on the mercy of his father, whom he has not seen since his disgraceful request for the inheritance, which he proceeded to burn through. There is no hint of what kind of reception he can expect from his father, but some listeners may well expect that the father has a right to be furious with his younger son.

The Embrace

After the younger son makes the decision to arise and return to his father, the parable's point of view shifts, and the younger son is no longer the central focus. In his worst moment of hunger, when "no one gave him anything" (15:16), his thoughts turned toward his father. Yet as we will see, the father's thoughts were already turned toward his lost son, and so now the focus of the parable shifts to the father's perspective. At best, the younger son is hoping for the status of a hired hand working for his father, a much better situation than he enjoyed with the pigs in the distant land. But after blowing the money, he might well be blown away by the reception that he receives after making the long trip back:

> [20]So he got up and went to his father. But while he was still a long way off, his father saw him and was filled with compassion for him; he ran to his son, threw his arms around him and kissed him. [21]The son said to him, "Father,

17. See Philip Sellew, "Interior Monologue as a Narrative Device in the Parables of Luke," *JBL* 111 (1992): 239–53.

> I have sinned against heaven and against you. I am no longer worthy to be called your son."

While we have previously wondered about the younger son's sincerity, the father's reaction when he glimpses his lost child far away on the horizon is on a completely different level. Perhaps the message of the parable is that even partial repentance—prompted in the first place by lousy choices and dire predicaments—nonetheless is enough to open the floodgates of grace. And "floodgates" is not overstating the matter, as the father is deeply moved by this sudden turn of events. More specifically, he is filled with "compassion," the exact same word as we see in *the parable of the good Samaritan*.

The quality of compassion in both parables can quite literally give life to the dead: In Luke 7:11–17, Jesus sees a widow who has just lost her only son, and Jesus is deeply moved with compassion.[18] He interrupts the funeral march, touches the coffin, commands the dead son to rise, and in due course the mother receives her child back. When the Samaritan sees the victim at the side of the road, he has compassion on someone who might well be a bitter enemy, since Samaritans and the Jewish community had long been estranged. While others pass by, the Samaritan shows mercy and tends to the wounded man. The father's compassion on his lost son can be compared with the Samaritan, as both are lifesaving, albeit in slightly different ways.

Since the father sees his younger son "while he was still a long way off" (15:20), the audience might wonder "if he had not been regularly looking for him down the road by which he had left."[19] The woman in *the parable of the lost coin* was actively searching for the missing item of value. But here we see a picture of intense waiting over a long period of time. If the father has been waiting for a long time, it might help explain why he starts running to meet his returning son. Several interpreters make a big deal about this action, arguing that running is undignified conduct for a highly respected father, as he would have to lift his robes and would kick up dust with his feet.[20]

18. Joel B. Green, *The Gospel of Luke*, NICNT (Grand Rapids: Eerdmans, 1997), 582.

19. Craig L. Blomberg, *Interpreting the Parables*, 2nd ed. (Downers Grove, IL: InterVarsity, 2012), 208.

20. E.g., Bailey, *Jacob and the Prodigal*, 120–21.

I suppose it is possible that a cultural code is violated when the father runs, but there are other ways to view this scene. Perhaps there is an echo and a poetic reversal of the soaring lyrics in Isaiah 40:31: "Those who wait on the Lord will renew their strength. They will rise up with wings like eagles; they will run and not grow weary." Isaiah 40 envisions a return from captivity in a foreign land, not unlike the recent experience of the wayward son. The father's running is an expression of joyful energy as he catches sight of the rebel's return. Followed up with a lavish embrace, the long-waiting father's actions overflow with the adrenaline of surprise at the son's arrival.

Who Says You Can't Go Home?

Having carefully rehearsed his speech earlier in the pigpen, the younger son arrives back home and duly apologizes after receiving his father's embrace and a kiss of reconciliation. But it is notable that the kiss from the father *precedes* the younger son's speech. The kiss is therefore an expression of forgiveness that is extended before any apology or the acknowledgment that the son has sinned against heaven and against the father himself.[21] Despite the obvious facts that the son is disgraced, insolvent, and a source of embarrassment, the father hugs him. Instead of discussing repayment plans or some sort of financial rehabilitation program, the father embraces this lost sheep who has returned to the flock.

As the fractured relationship begins to be restored through the father's response, this scene provides an altogether compelling illustration of the economy of grace. Maybe the son should have expressed more sorrow over his terrible behavior and offered to somehow pay back his considerable debts.[22] But the point of this scene is more direct: A handful of steps in the right direction results in the father's embrace, even if the words of repentance are not quite complete. Similar to the victim at the side of the road, the younger son and his wasteful ways are the object of compassion.

21. Bock, *Luke*, 1314.

22. Cf. Bailey, *Jacob and the Prodigal*, 118: "He considers neither the agony of rejected love his father has endured nor the financial loss the entire family has sustained." For another perspective, see Alex Damm, "Gandhi and the Parable of the Prodigal Son," *BibInt* 29 (2021): 90–105.

To what extent, interpreters ask, is a portrait of God available in this scene of the running father who welcomes the returning son?[23] Earlier we have seen God pictured as a shepherd who adventurously seeks the wandering sheep. Now, in this parable, Jesus is teaching that God's embrace of grace is not earned. Rather, it is a gift, and most often a gift that is scarcely deserved. Does the younger son grasp this massive concept? Presumably he was ready to launch into the rest of his speech about being a mere hired hand, even lower in status than a household slave who enjoyed more privileges. He is not given the chance to become a day laborer, because there is an interruption.

> [22]But the father said to his servants, "Quick! Bring the best robe and put it on him. Put a ring on his finger and sandals on his feet. [23]Bring the fattened calf and kill it. Let's have a feast and celebrate. [24]For this son of mine was dead and is alive again; he was lost and is found." So they began to celebrate.

As we know, the younger son was prepared and planning to ask for a menial position. But having confessed, "I am no longer worthy to be called your son" (15:21), he doesn't get a chance to finish his speech. Maybe the son breaks down because of the undeserved embrace his father offers, or maybe the father interrupts the speech by ordering clothes and preparations for a party. Either way, in this scene the younger son's confession takes a back seat to the father's joyful reaction. The father's speech starts with "Quick!" (ταχὺ), implying that the father has been waiting a long time for this moment, perhaps scarcely hoping for such a return. There is also a bit of irony: The father quickly gives a series of instructions to the household staff, having interrupted the speech where the younger son is about to ask for a lower status than the household slaves who are now preparing a party to celebrate *his* homecoming.

No mention has been made about the younger son's outward appearance at this point. But it is not hard to imagine that he is in rough shape from the combination of having worked with swine and traveled a long distance. However, the father's call for the "best robe" is not just a practical

23. See Jack, *Prodigal Son*, 8: "God may be presented as suffering the loss of the son very deeply, and loving the son beyond human comprehension. Even when he is presented as the judge, the purpose of the trope is to motivate an individual's response, rather than to condemn. God here is the instrument of relief for the believer, rather than a transcendent figure from whom humanity is separated by their own sin."

matter, nor is it about looking good in the story. More precisely, he calls for the "first robe," which brings to mind other biblical accounts where (re)clothing occurs. When Joseph is brought out of prison to interpret the dreams of Pharaoh in Genesis 41, his appointment over the entire royal house of Egypt is sealed with a ring on his finger and garments of the finest linen. The man and his wife are banished from the garden of Eden in Genesis 3, yet God replaces their fig-leaf clothing with robes of dignity. Despite their offenses, they are nonetheless human beings created in the divine image, and these durable leather robes indicate that the divine image cannot easily be erased. The poet of Isaiah 61 rejoices in anticipation of a day when former captives are clothed in robes of righteousness. These various texts combine to provide a background for the younger son's clothing as an image of restoration, and the outfit is complete with sandals for his (bare) feet.

Only on the most special occasions will a fattened calf enter the storyline. Not every household can afford such a luxury, since the time and the cost of raising the calf were considerable. Eating meat, therefore, was comparatively rare. This is why the rich man clothed in purple would have been viewed as an indulgent outlier with his *daily* feasting. As mentioned earlier, there are a number of important spiritual holidays on the Israelite calendar, such as Passover, which commemorates the rescue of the Israelites from slavery. Some scholars wonder if the fattened calf in this parable is understood to be reserved for a commemoration like the Feast of Weeks or the celebration of Purim.[24] Bringing the fattened calf signals a major occasion, and it is not an exaggeration to state that a feast such as this could probably feed a village.

If the entire village is invited to the party, then it would stand to reason that the newly returned younger son is the guest of honor.[25] He is certainly dressed for the occasion, and it might bring to mind images of Lazarus at Abraham's bosom and the banquet scene in that parable. Here, the banquet is the spatial setting for a number of contrasts. In that distant land where the wayward son squandered his liquidated inheritance with wild living, he longed for the unclean pig slop in his desperate circumstances. Now, he can partake of the most expensive kind of meat in ancient Israel. Furthermore, during the famine in Gentile territory, nobody could be

24. Cf. Bock, *Luke*, 1315.
25. Blomberg, *Interpreting the Parables*, 207.

bothered to give anything to this hungry younger son. But having arrived back home, he is given an extravagant banquet sponsored by *the very person* whom he insulted and treated in the most shameful manner.[26] He wasted his father's money, and now that father welcomes him back with an expensive public celebration.

Does the younger son deserve a banquet of this magnitude in light of his rebellious past? The father's explanation—"This son of mine was dead and is alive again; he was lost and is found"—sounds like more than just instructions to the household staff about party arrangements. Surely he would not have to explain or justify himself to his own employees. So who is the father addressing with these weighty words that touch on a number of important themes in Luke's larger story? The heightened language that the father uses points to a connection with the character of God. Even after the son's long history of bad choices, the father responds with an embrace. Similarly, God is interested in extending grace to anyone who is spiritually impoverished, and a move toward repentance is met with joyful reception. Recall that in *the parable of the lost sheep*, there is a celebration at the end. But in this parable there are elaborate details of the party, virtually immersing the audience in an experience of forgiveness. Just as the father rejoices when his rebellious child returns, so God is full of joy when any lost human being is found and returns home.

Exile and Restoration

If we step back for a moment, we can see that the younger son's journey of exile and return evokes a larger pattern in the Bible. A moment ago we discussed Jacob and David, two prominent characters who are both devious (in their own unique ways) and need to flee from their homes. Yet both are able to come back, and like the younger son in the parable, both experience a restoration. But as Jesus is telling this parable, even more echoes of the biblical story come to mind, because the younger son's journey can also be compared to the people of Israel as a nation.

Much earlier in the book of Genesis, God makes a promise to Abraham that through his descendants every family on earth will be blessed. Given that Abraham is seventy-five years of age in Genesis 12, has no children,

26. Garland, *Luke*, 629.

and his wife Sarah is barren, it is a remarkable promise to say the least. But Abraham sets out from Ur of the Chaldeans (ancient Babylonian territory) and walks to the land of Canaan, the land that God gives him and his promised descendants. The odds are against it, but by the end of Genesis, Abraham has twelve grandsons who eventually become the twelve tribes of Israel. God rescues the Israelites from Egyptian slavery, and they eventually return to Canaan where they have the privilege of living for God in covenant relationship.

In other words, the people of Israel are given an inheritance, and yet the books of Joshua through 2 Kings illustrate how this inheritance is squandered. Through the period of the Judges and into the era of the monarchy, persistent unfaithfulness is the people's default position. The various leaders fall short, and despite the encouragement and warnings of the prophetic voices, the wrong pathway is chosen far more often than the right one. Consequently, in 2 Kings 25 the Babylonian military is allowed to invade the city of Jerusalem and bulldoze the temple, and a significant percentage of the citizens are marched into captivity. Years earlier Abraham ventured from Babylonian territory because of God's promise to his descendants, but now those descendants are forced to reverse that journey and begin a long walk of shame into exile.

We should note, however, that in 1 Kings 8, near the midpoint of the story, an intriguing prayer is uttered by a Davidic heir.[27] Solomon's official prayer, given before a large crowd at the temple dedication ceremony, covers a range of subjects (including the inability of a temple to contain God, a theology of battle, and a theology of natural disasters such as famines). Toward the climax of the prayer and looking to the future, the king asks that God forgive those who will act disobediently and get carried off to a foreign land:

> [47]If they come to their senses in the land to which they have been taken captive, and repent, and plead with you in the land of their captors, saying, "We have sinned, and have done wrong; we have acted wickedly"; [48]if they repent with all their heart and soul in the land of their enemies . . . [50][then] forgive your people who have sinned against you, and all their transgressions that they have committed against you; and grant them compassion in the sight of their captors, so that they may have compassion on them [51](for they are

27. Noted in Garland, *Luke*, 627.

your people and heritage, which you brought out of Egypt, from the midst of the iron-smelter). (NRSV)

Besides this long prayer of Solomon, dozens of lyrics in the great prophets, such as Isaiah and Jeremiah, likewise forecast a return to the land after a season of banishment. Psalm 23 also provides a snapshot of Israel's national experience. In this famous psalm, the poet speaks on behalf of the entire community.[28] Despite wandering through the dark valley of death's shadow—a picture of the bleakness of exile—God is faithful to the people and brings them back to the land and allows them to return to the house of the Lord that they previously rejected. The image of a banquet table completes the story of restoration in Psalm 23, a poem that begins with a picture of God as the divine shepherd who cares for the flock.

To summarize, it is entirely possible that the parable of the younger son's sojourn in a distant land evokes the story of Israel's own national journey of exile and restoration, an interpretive dimension that has been trending in recent decades.[29] In this case, the audience is invited to think about how God, who is represented by the father figure in this parable, is willing to restore members of the community who have gone astray. Lest we forget, Jesus is talking to *all the tax collectors and sinners who had gathered* to listen to the parables of Luke 15. By means of this story about a rebellious child, Jesus is preparing the way for anybody to experience restoration and a reconnection with God. And because Jesus is on his way to Jerusalem, his death and resurrection will open the door for people of all nations to be reconciled.

Meanwhile, the audience listening to this parable might also wonder if every human life is somehow represented by the younger son. It might be suggested that each person has been given gifts by God, but in various ways they have squandered these gifts through ingratitude or indifference.

28. See the discussion of Richard S. Briggs, *The Lord Is My Shepherd: Psalm 23 for the Life of the Church*, Touchstone Texts (Grand Rapids: Baker Academic, 2021), 50–53.

29. E.g., N. T. Wright, *Jesus and the Victory of God*, 126; Kevin J. Vanhoozer, *The Drama of Doctrine: A Canonical-Linguistic Approach to Theology* (Louisville: Westminster John Knox, 2005), 52. For several points of critique, see Richard B. Hays, "Knowing Jesus: Story, History and the Question of Truth," in *Jesus, Paul, and the People of God: A Theological Dialogue with N. T. Wright*, ed. Nicholas Perrin and Richard B. Hays (Downers Grove, IL: InterVarsity, 2011), 41–61.

The message of the parable, however, is that anyone who returns to the father will be welcomed with an embrace and a celebration. As we read all of Luke's Gospel, this is the good news in a nutshell. In the context of Luke's story, Jesus is announcing that all who are lost have a chance to repent and receive forgiveness. All who have wasted their gifts can be given a second chance in the economy of grace. Even more shocking, this news is not just for a select few: For people all over the world, the floodgates of divine welcome are now being opened. Who could object to such an expansive notion? We do recall, however, that beside the tax collectors and sinners in Luke 15 sits another group: "But the Pharisees and the teachers of the law muttered, 'This guy welcomes sinners and eats with them!'"[30] Although the Pharisees arguably have been unfairly maligned in the history of interpretation, perhaps they are part of the group who are now addressed more directly as the parable continues.

The Sound of Music

Despite depicting a sumptuous party to celebrate the return of the younger son, this parable is far from over. Of course, it could have ended here and been considered a classic story of redemption. If the portrait of the father in this parable has any correspondence to the character of God, then it is notable that when the younger son returns, we don't hear any "I told you so" or harsh word of condemnation. Neither is there any indication of a debt-repayment scheme, so we have to assume that God somehow makes sure that any debts are covered.

At the outset of the parable, we were told that once upon a time there was a man with *two* sons. A fairly long time has passed in the story, we can assume, and lots has happened since we heard about the older brother. He is an easy character to forget, and with the whirlwind of the younger son's riotous ride, many sermons do seem to forget about the older brother who stayed close to home. But the next installment of the parable is just as important as the first part, and we should keep in mind once more that the parable is spoken to a combination of outcasts *and* privileged insiders who are sneering and grumbling. The older brother has been in

30. Cf. Eckhard J. Schnabel, *New Testament Theology* (Grand Rapids: Baker Academic, 2023), 167–70.

the background and out of the picture since the opening sentence of the parable, but he is now poised to burst on to the stage:

> [25]Meanwhile, the older son was in the field. When he came near the house, he heard music and dancing. [26]So he called one of the servants and asked him what was going on. [27]"Your brother has come," he replied, "and your father has killed the fattened calf because he has him back safe and sound."

Further details about the party are disclosed in this next scene. We know about the new clothing and the fattened calf, but the music and dancing are new pieces of information that suggest the celebration is in full swing. Nonetheless, with the instruments tuned and the band amped up, somebody else is still hard at work in the fields. The elder brother is pictured as a responsible son, diligently cultivating the agricultural land. To be sure, he looks like the guy who has been growing the grain that would have fed the fattened calf that is now being enjoyed by a multitude. His steady work supplies the food for the feast in honor of the recently returned rebel.

Still, we have to wonder why the older brother was not immediately informed of this big news about his brother and invited to join the party. "It is strange," one commentator remarks, "that nobody went to tell him what had happened, and that he must find out for himself: is there some suggestion that he was not on the best of terms with his father? Or is the point simply that he labors away all day in the fields until his duty is complete?"[31] Presumably, the older brother has been working the non-squandered acres of the property *the entire time* that the younger son was burning through his liquidated share. Does he hold a grudge? We've seen a seven-hundred-year grudge against the Samaritans, so it is certainly possible here.

Back when the father divided the inheritance between the two sons, there was no word about how the older brother responded. We did not learn how he felt about either his younger brother's request for the money or his father's indulgence. But now, in the second half of the parable, the point of view shifts to his perspective, and the audience learns a great deal about how he feels.[32] Arriving home after a long day of responsible hard

31. Marshall, *Gospel of Luke*, 784.
32. Culpepper, "Gospel of Luke," 8:303.

work, the eldest son hears the sound of music from the house. A new minor character is introduced when the brother calls to a household servant to inquire about what's going on. Another spin on the earlier irony appears again: The younger son was going to ask his father to become a worker on a lower level than household servants, and now a servant informs the eldest son that his brother has been restored to his former status.

Excitement from this servant is a natural enough reaction under the circumstances. It is a happy occasion with a splendid banquet and live music, so who wouldn't be in a good mood? However, the servant's enthusiastic response might unintentionally come across as quite grating to the older brother. To begin with, the servant reports that the party has started, and it obviously has started without the eldest son in attendance. Furthermore, the servant's language is slightly different from the father's speech.

In his joyful outpouring, the father emphasized the younger son's spiritual restoration from the zone of the *lost* and his virtual resurrection from the dead. But through the servant's filter, the eldest son hears a slightly different nuance. Not only has "your brother" returned, the servant exclaims, but "your father" has also sacrificed the special calf, highlighting the uniqueness of the occasion and inviting a large crowd to share in the expensive meal. The servant also informs him that his brother is "safe and sound"; in other words, he focuses on the physical well-being of the younger son after his rowdy and reckless behavior in a distant land. No doubt the servant is thinking that the older brother will be glad to hear this, and the servant is reflecting the joy of the celebration. But as we'll see in the next scene, the servant's words cause a rather different reaction than intended.

Raging Bull

Sibling conflicts can be seen throughout the Bible. When Goliath the giant is threatening the troops of Israel, young David delivers some supplies to the battlefield. But as his older brother Eliab hears him asking questions about rewards, his wrath is kindled: "Why is this you've come down? With whom have you left that little flock in the wilderness? I know your insolence and the evil in your heart. Indeed, you've come down in order to see the battle!" (1 Sam. 17:28). Eliab sounds jealous here, but when David is later guilty of adultery and murder, the older brother's words also ring true. Miriam is critical of her brother Moses because of his Cushite wife, and while the context is obscure, it could be that she (along with Aaron) is commenting on his wife's skin color. A short time later divine anger is directed against Miriam, and she is struck with leprosy. This change in skin coloration could well be interpreted as poetic justice for Miriam's conduct.[33] In the New Testament, there is a conflict between two sisters, Martha and Mary.[34] When Jesus visits their village in Luke 10, Martha opens her home to him and his disciples. Mary sits at Jesus's feet and listens to him, while Martha is frantic with all the meal preparation, and she complains to Jesus, "Don't you care that my sister has left me to do the work by myself? Tell her to help me!" (10:40).

Our parable in Luke 15 is similar. Now that the older brother in this parable has heard the music and discovered that the younger son has returned, he is about to join this fraternity of quarreling siblings.

> [28]The older brother became angry and refused to go in. So his father went out and pleaded with him. [29]But he answered his father, "Look! All these years I've been slaving for you and never disobeyed your orders. Yet you never gave me even a young goat so I could celebrate with my friends. [30]But when this son of yours who has squandered your property with prostitutes comes home, you kill the fattened calf for him!"

Maybe the older brother doesn't like the style of music coming from the house, but it sounds like there is something in the servant's report that strikes a different chord and ignites the older brother's anger. At this point, the story doesn't specify why he turns into a rage monster: Is it because of the substantial expense of the party or that yet again the father is way too lenient with the irresponsible younger brother? Whatever the exact reason, the eldest son stays outside and declines to take a step further. Now he's the one who is far from home, as it were.

It should be acknowledged that readers have often been dismissive of the older brother, and his reputation throughout interpretive history has rarely been positive. But he did remain at the family property and has

33. See Robert Alter, *The Five Books of Moses: A Translation with Commentary* (New York: Norton, 2008), 743; note also Adriane Leveen, "Becoming Israel in the Wilderness of Numbers," in *The Oxford Handbook of Biblical Narrative*, ed. Danna Nolan Fewell (New York: Oxford University Press, 2015), 150–51.

34. Levine, *Short Stories by Jesus*, 68.

apparently been diligent while the younger son was a reprobate. His anger, however, seems out of proportion with this festive occasion. He stayed with the father but does not appear to be very concerned about the father's feelings. The younger son earlier acted with selfishness and was indifferent to the father, but now we have to wonder how different the brothers really are. Is the eldest son disappointed with his brother, or is he angry with his father?

Somebody must have told the father that his older son was outside in a paroxysm of rage, refusing to join the celebration in the house. A short time earlier the father saw his younger son a long way off and was willing to start running before the welcoming embrace. Now, he is willing to leave the party in order to venture forth in search of the older brother, who is starting to look like a lost son himself. Coming outside, the father "pleads" with his eldest son, a verb that carries the sense of urging and also comforting.[35] Such efforts by the father, though, are rejected: "It turns out that the father is as powerless with the older son as he was with the youngest."[36] Because the father's speech is not included, the reader is prompted to fill in the blanks. Is he telling his oldest son that the younger brother is repentant? Sure, it wasn't until he was broke and destitute that he came to his senses, but he's alive again and has returned from exile. Whatever the exact words the father uses, it certainly looks like he is trying to get his older son to repent as well and to change his mind toward his younger brother.

At the outset of the parable, the younger son showed some bad manners when he asked his father for the inheritance. Now, the older son is acting quite rudely as well and doesn't even use the word "father" when addressing him. Instead of using a term of respect, he seems to avoid any relational language, uttering a sharp "Look!" (ἰδοὺ) before launching into his very long list of complaints.[37] Without stating the matter directly, the root of his anger seems to be a comparison with his younger brother. Thus, he starts by saying that "all these years I've been slaving for you" and working diligently in (what's left of) the fields. And while I've been hard at work, your younger son has done nothing but squander the inheritance. He has been treacherous, whereas I have "never disobeyed your orders," and I demand better.

35. Levine, *Short Stories by Jesus*, 69.
36. Garland, *Luke*, 631.
37. J. Green, *Gospel of Luke*, 585.

The crowning insult, so it would appear, is this over-the-top celebration for the younger son, who is finally mentioned outright. Indeed, this marks a transition in the catalog of grievances. It started with the older son outlining his many accomplishments but now turns to the father's irrational (and preferential) approach to the younger son's homecoming. The older brother seems to have a particular beef with the fattened calf and protests that he's never even been given a (much cheaper) goat. Matters take a very personal turn as well, with the older brother emphasizing that the younger son wasted the inheritance with prostitutes. There could be an allusion here to the book of Proverbs:

> The person who loves wisdom brings joy to his father,
> but a companion of prostitutes squanders his wealth. (Prov. 29:3)[38]

Earlier in the parable, we are told about the brother's high life, but how does the older brother know these *National Enquirer*–level details? Have rumors been circulating? Is he assuming such activities took place and trying to make his case stronger?[39] In the end, he might as well have said, "Because of what he's done, your younger son deserves to be wallowing in rags outside your gate, whereas I deserve to host a private feast with my invited friends." Of course, he's saying this to his father, who has left the party to come outside and plead with his angry older son, who is steaming about the graceful reception given to a shameful slacker.

An Offer

What's wrong with this picture? As the festivities are rocking, two out of the three characters that are part of the family in this parable are not inside. Instead, they are outside having an argument based on different reactions to the prodigal's return. Back when the father was peering into the distance, he saw his younger son from afar and was moved with compassion. But when the older brother hears the music and the report

38. Noted by Bock, *Luke*, 1318–19, and Levine, *Short Stories by Jesus*, 70.

39. On the question of how the older brother becomes aware of such sordid information, a number of scholarly views are compared by Callie Callon, "*Adulescentes* and *Meretrices*: The Correlation Between Squandered Patrimony and Prostitutes in the Parable of the Prodigal Son," *CBQ* 75 (2013): 259–78.

about the celebratory feast, his wrath is kindled. The older son has been boasting about his obedience and slave labor, but increasingly he's looking self-centered and immature, insulting the father as he recites his long list of good works. If we had only the words of the older son, the father would not appear in a favorable light: He could be accused of acting in an arbitrary manner, giving the prostitute-indulging younger son a free pass without having to pay anything back or work to restore the loss.

Some interpreters view the Pharisees as the real target in the second half of this parable. As we have already noted, at the beginning of Luke 15, the Pharisees are hovering among the crowd. Others are listening intently, but the Pharisees are complaining that Jesus is welcoming the sinners and having a meal with them. But restricting the application of this parable only to the Pharisees is too easy: Anyone who grumbles might well be addressed here—anyone who has issues with the father because the father doesn't do what is expected or act according to what is deserved. Near the beginning of this book, we made the point that parables can have a lot more personal application than we think. So I would suggest that a much bigger audience than *just* the Pharisees is included. Notably, the last words of the parable are directly from the father to the older son. In the previous section he was pleading with his son, but we had to guess what he was saying and try to fill in the blanks. Yet in the final moments of this parable, the father's actual words are included. It is the father's voice that the reader is left to consider:

> [31]"My son," the father said, "you are always with me, and everything I have is yours. [32]But we had to celebrate and be glad, because this brother of yours was dead and is alive again; he was lost and is found."

Our parable starts with a father who has *two* sons. The *younger* leaves home with a wallet full of money, but after some terrible choices he returns to the house he once left. Not only does the father receive the mutinous son, but he makes the effort to sponsor a homecoming celebration. The same effort is now expended in his final words to his *older* son, explaining the reasons for his actions and offering a chance for him to be part of the reception. The language should be carefully analyzed: The older brother refused to address him as "father," but the father immediately calls him "my son" (literally, "child," τέκνον). Stressing the relational connections is a key theme of the father's words: The father states that the younger son is "your brother" and worthy of the older son's embrace as well. It is clear that the younger son doesn't have to earn his way back to the father, and neither does the older son, who is raging outside of the house. "Everything I have is yours," the father pleads, and this is not conditional, based on attitude or behavior.

All of these words sound like they are conveyed in a peaceful tone. The father doesn't lose his temper or get angry because his older son is out of control and acting as disgracefully as the younger son once did. Without bringing up the prostitutes or any other undignified actions the younger son may have taken, the father explains that this is not an intervention or a public shaming. Rather, the party is a celebration of the younger brother's return to the house.

To what extent, the audience of the parable may well be wondering at this point, do the father's words and actions reflect something of the divine character?[40] Some most likely view God as a moral accountant who keeps track of sins on a spreadsheet. To be sure, the younger brother painfully illustrates the consequences of selfish living. But what happens when a lost child wants to come home? The older brother insists that sinners should be treated just as they deserve, and no doubt some who are listening to the parable believe that God should also act this way. Yet a different set of images emerge from this story: The father's love doesn't keep a record of wrongs but, rather, wants to find and restore what is lost.

By concluding with the language of "lost and found" coupled with "dead and alive," the father's climactic words are more than just a description of the younger son's journey. What we also hear is the father making an offer to the angry older son to surrender his prideful defiance and come inside. As a result, the parable ends with a mystery: Will he reconcile with the lost brother? We don't know if the same grace embodied by the father will eventually assuage the older son's anger, resentment, and self-centeredness or if the older son will experience a change of heart. A similar open-ended conclusion is also found in *the parable of the rich man and Lazarus*. In that story, the audience is left wondering if the five brothers of the rich man will respond to the law and prophets and thus have a chance to enjoy the banquet of Abraham. There are also some similarities to *the*

40. Note the longer study of C. Kavin Rowe, *Early Narrative Christology: The Lord in the Gospel of Luke*, BZNW 139 (Berlin: de Gruyter, 2006).

parable of the good Samaritan, as the older brother is encouraged to let go of a bitter grudge and *be a neighbor* to his own brother.

A parable that starts with a lot of wasted money ends with an invitation from the father to rejoice that a lost brother has come to his senses. If the younger son scarcely deserves such a shower of mercy, that could be true for lots of other people as well. Some interpreters have detected in this parable the tension of welcoming the Gentiles into the church, a topic that is certainly a controversy elsewhere in the New Testament.[41] Other scholars have inquired as to what extent there is a message for the more established church, as the members have occasionally been accused of looking down on those sinners who come to visit, thinking of themselves as morally superior. In this case, the older brother represents those believers who are persuaded they can impress God with their virtuous conduct. If we compare this parable to *the parable of the lost sheep*, these would be the "over ninety-nine righteous persons who do not need to repent" (Luke 15:7).

Such debates can be expected to continue, but what cannot be denied are the images in this parable of the father who patiently waits for the return of his younger rebel and who pleads with his older son to extend mercy.[42] It is worth noting that we don't hear from the younger son again after his interrupted confession. Once the father embraces him and outfits the lost son with the robe, ring, and sandals, he is absorbed into the celebration and fades from view. So it is the father's actions that eclipse any response of the son to the unmerited favor that he receives. The older brother illustrates that you can be in proximity to the father but far from home. There is a concluding offer from the father, and you don't need to be in a foreign pigpen to come to your senses. Both sons squander the wealth of relational capital at their disposal, and both sons also show the audience different sides of the economy of grace. One child is granted forgiveness for a perilous series of choices, while another child is given a chance to move away from what he thinks he is owed and toward gratitude for what he has already been given.

41. E.g., Levine, *Short Stories by Jesus*, 71, cites Barbara E. Reid, *Parables for Preachers, Year C* (Collegeville, MN: Liturgical Press, 2000), 116.

42. On the larger issue of the father's characterization, see Trevor L. Burke, "The Parable of the Prodigal Father: An Interpretative Key to the Third Gospel (Luke 15:11–32)," *TynBul* 64 (2013): 217–38, who suggests that "his behavior is highly unusual and appears to be every bit as rash and unconventional as the younger and older sons" (219).

6

A Widow and the Workers

IN THE OPENING PAGES of this book, we briefly mentioned some of the elements of a classic movie or novel: great characters, an interesting plot, and some cool special effects. All three elements can be observed in *the parable of the prodigal brothers* that we just studied. First, the story has a memorable cast of characters. The rebellious younger son wastes his money with wild living in a distant land, and after coming to his senses and returning home, he is shunned by his harsh older brother who complains about his treatment to their way-too-gracious father. Second, among the various plot twists, the older son learns about his brother's return from a household servant, an irony because the younger son was planning on begging his father to make him a hired hand, someone of even lower rank than a servant. Third, the special effects of this parable include the use of shared language ("squandering" is the action of the shrewd manager, while "compassion" is a hallmark of the good Samaritan), spatial settings (the murky locales of the distant land and the pigpen), and the soundtrack of music and dancing at the celebration of the rebel's return. The combination of all these elements in the parable provides the audience with an immersive experience in the economy of grace.

Continuing to weave our way through these parables, we now consider two more examples that have new kinds of characters and variations on the plots that we have encountered so far. Starting first with Luke 18:1–8, we will look at a story with a courtroom drama at its core. In an earlier chapter we mentioned *Bleak House* by Charles Dickens, which features a really long court case that stretches out over hundreds of pages of Victorian prose. This short parable in Luke 18 has far fewer words and features a feisty underdog as its main character: a widow who is pleading her case, but the legal odds are against her because she's dealing with a corrupt judge.[1] Not so long ago we had a dishonest manager, and now we are faced with an unjust judge. Second, after hearing about the persistent widow who demands justice, we then turn to *the parable of the vineyard workers* in Matthew 20. A group of workers make an agreement with a landowner about wages for a day's employment, but when the actual payout occurs, they suddenly become disgruntled employees who complain about unfairness. Among the various questions that arise in these parables, we will ask: How does justice work when grace is in business?

Bleak Widow

As a basic principle, the surrounding context and any preamble to a parable should be taken into consideration.[2] For example, *the parable of the rich barn builder* occurs when someone in the crowd asks Jesus to intervene in a dispute about inheritance. Here in Luke 18, the chapter begins with an address to the disciples: "Jesus told his disciples a parable to show them that they should always pray and not give up" (Luke 18:1). Lots of reasons might be suggested as to why the disciples would be tempted to give up, ranging from geopolitical upheavals and natural disasters all the way to domestic challenges and personal circumstances (such as physical health and mental well-being, as well as addictive habits and related struggles). But rather than just commanding the disciples to pray and not lose heart, Jesus takes it a step further by telling a story of someone who has every reason to "give up" but does not. The verb can also be translated "become weary," and so the parable speaks about prayer

1. Borrowing the term from Wendy J. Cotter, "The Parable of the Feisty Widow and the Threatened Judge (Luke 18:1–8)," *NTS* 51 (2005): 328–43.

2. In the previous chapter, Luke 17, Jesus is responding to the question of *when* the kingdom of God was coming; to what degree Luke 18 and *the parable of the persistent widow* continues that conversation is a matter of debate and need not detain us here. For those interested, see I. Howard Marshall, *The Gospel of Luke: A Commentary on the Greek Text* (Grand Rapids: Eerdmans, 1978), 860–61.

that seems to go unanswered for a long time, tempting the disciples to despair.[3] The protagonist in this parable is a widow who could have lost heart in the face of corruption and grown weary because of injustice but instead becomes an example of bold perseverance.

> [2]In a certain town there was a judge who neither feared God nor cared what people thought. [3]And there was a widow in that town who kept coming to him with the plea, "Grant me justice against my adversary."

Scrolling back in the Hebrew Bible, there is a story about a widow in the days of Elisha at the beginning of 2 Kings 4 that has some intriguing parallels. She has a serious legal problem, and with few options she pleads with the prophet for help: "Your servant my husband is dead; and you know that your servant feared the Lord, but a creditor has come to take my two children as slaves!" (4:1). In all likelihood the widow has incurred some kind of debt because of the death of her husband, and now reports the threat that her children will be sold into slavery as collateral. The reader is unsure of the identity of the creditor, but the widow implores the prophet Elisha to intervene, and in due course there is a miraculous flow of oil that allows her to pay the debt and live on the remainder. But apart from the prophet's phenomenal assistance, this account of a widow in crisis illustrates the vulnerability of those on the margins and helps to explain why dozens of biblical texts direct the Israelites to care for widows and orphans. As we consider the parable here in Luke 18, we are probably inclined to side with the widow in this dispute, given the precedent and the long history of predatory abuse.

Prior to the widow's introduction, the first character mentioned in the parable is a "judge" in a "certain town." Earlier in Deuteronomy 16:18 the Israelites are told to appoint judges throughout the land, "and they will judge the people with righteous judgment." In the unnamed city of this parable, however, the judge has scant interest in fairness or equity, despite the biblical imperative and the weight of his office. So when a widow from that town arrives to plead her case before this judge, the audience suspects that she will not have an easy time. Although there is no precise indication as to what the widow needs exactly, most scholars assume that she

3. Joseph A. Fitzmyer, *The Gospel According to Luke*, 2 vols. (Garden City, NY: Doubleday, 1981–85), 2:1178.

is petitioning the judge to award her property or money that she is owed (probably stemming from the death of her spouse or close relative).[4] What has her "adversary" done? Note that she is pleading with the judge to secure her rights, not necessarily to punish her legal opponent.[5] Because the audience doesn't know the details of her case, the focus is on her treatment by the judge rather than the relative merits of her case.[6]

Faced with the kind of judge described in this parable, the widow has every reason to give up. Recall that Jesus is addressing this parable to a group of disciples, encouraging them to pray and not grow weary when things don't work out as they might prefer. The widow is a comparatively powerless figure who is up against an uncaring system. In fact, she has two opponents in this legal battle, as she is forced to deal with her adversary *and* an indifferent judge. We are not sure of the adversary's identity, and this shadowy character never makes a formal appearance on stage. Enough details are given for us to suppose that the widow could quickly become demoralized, and who could fault her? But the key aspect in verse 3 is her tenacity, emphasized through the phrase "kept coming to him." Instead of losing hope because the odds are not in her favor, she opts for persistence. Her unwillingness to yield to the bullies, so to speak, leads directly to the plot twist in this parable.

Judge Dread

At various points in the history of Israel, judicial corruption has been a problem. For example, in 1 Samuel 8 the prophet Samuel appointed his sons—Joel and Abijah—as judges in the land. However, these characters accepted bribes and perverted justice, and their base conduct was clearly known to the elders of the nation (see 1 Sam. 8:5). At the outset of this parable in Luke 18, we are told that this judge in a certain city does not fear God. Usually in the Hebrew Bible the expression "fearing God" refers to a healthy respect for authority and an acknowledgment that we are ultimately accountable for our actions. During the judicial reforms of Jehoshaphat in 2 Chronicles 19, the king was careful to instruct those holding the office: "Consider what you do, for you don't judge for humanity but for the Lord. He is with you in

4. E.g., Joel B. Green, *The Gospel of Luke*, NICNT (Grand Rapids: Eerdmans, 1997), 640.
5. Fitzmyer, *Gospel According to Luke*, 2:1179.
6. See Dorothy Jean Weaver, "Luke 18:1–8," *Int* 56 (2002): 317–19.

giving judgment. Now then, let the fear of the Lord be upon you. Be careful what you do, for there is no injustice with the Lord our God, or partiality or taking bribes" (19:6–7).[7] The name Jehoshaphat means "the Lord is judge," so this matter may have some personal urgency for the king.

But this certain judge in our parable has no fear of God, and therefore does not conduct his duties according to the parameters set out by Jehoshaphat or Moses before him.[8] Furthermore, this judge cares little what people think and doesn't take seriously the court of public opinion. More precisely, the language used here "suggests someone incapable of shame" and thus a figure to whom the rules of honor likewise do not apply.[9] Assuming that this posture also includes any inner deliberation of conscience, then the widow's slim odds just got slimmer. On the basis of the Elisha analogy in 2 Kings 4, the widow is now even more hard-pressed. Not only is her adversary unyielding, but she is unlikely to receive any sympathy from this judge in her financial dispute. The audience is hardly prepared, then, for the next scene in Luke 18, which features a soliloquy and a plot twist:

> [4]For some time he refused. But finally he said to himself, "Even though I don't fear God or care what people think, [5]yet because this widow keeps bothering me, I will see that she gets justice, so that she won't eventually come and attack me!" [6]And the Lord said, "Listen to what the unjust judge says. [7]And will not God bring about justice for his chosen ones, who cry out to him day and night? Will he keep putting them off? [8]I tell you, he will see that they get justice, and quickly. However, when the Son of Man comes, will he find faith on the earth?"

Brushing the widow aside for quite some time, the judge does nothing on her behalf. Some interpreters wonder if the judge ignores the widow

7. David E. Garland, *Luke*, ZECNT (Grand Rapids: Zondervan, 2011), 708.

8. Cf. R. Alan Culpepper, "The Gospel of Luke," in *NIB* 8:336: "Judges were charged with the responsibility of hearing complaints fairly and impartially, a duty that was all the more important because they adjudicated cases without the benefit of a jury. Deuteronomy reports Moses's charge to judges: 'Give the members of your community a fair hearing, and judge rightly between one person and another, whether citizen or resident alien. You must not be partial in judging: hear out the small and the great alike; you shall not be intimidated by anyone, for the judgment is God's' (Deut 1:16–17 NRSV)."

9. Luke Timothy Johnson, *The Gospel of Luke* (Collegeville, MN: Liturgical Press, 1991), 269. Cf. Mary W. Matthews, Carter Shelley, and Barbara Scheele, "Proclaiming the Parable of the Persistent Widow (Lk. 18.2–5)," in *The Lost Coin: Parables of Women, Work and Wisdom*, ed. Mary Ann Beavis, The Biblical Seminar 86 (London: Sheffield Academic Press, 2002), 48.

because of her adversary, implying that the opponent has the kind of social standing that intimidates the judge.[10] But given his disregard for anyone else's opinion, it seems unlikely that any formidable adversary of the widow would sway the judge in this case. Others suggest that the judge shrugs off the widow because he's waiting for a bribe—assuming that there is a "system of kickbacks" from which the judge has a long history of profit—but there is no clear indication in the parable that the judge exploits his position for his own monetary advantage.[11] The easiest explanation is that the judge snubs the widow through sheer indifference, perhaps prompting us to look back to the rich man and Lazarus: Although the poor man was just outside his gate, the rich man's daily feast was never interrupted to help a fellow Israelite in a desperate predicament.

Under siege by the widow's continual pleas, the judge is unmoved for an unspecified length of time. But the standoff is broken when the audience hears an unanticipated soliloquy from the judge. He confirms his characterization as someone who neither fears God nor is moved by pricks of conscience, but he also admits that this widow is majorly annoying. While the verbal form in verse 3 indicates that she "kept coming to him," the quality of her resolve is filtered through the judge's perspective as it breaks down his wall of detachment.[12] A stark reversal is now apparent: Despite the chasm between the widow's vulnerability and judge's authority, it is the widow who is suddenly emerging as the more powerful figure, and the judge is drained of energy.[13] The shift is underscored through an image taken from the boxing ring.[14] Most translations capture the judge's concern as "so that she may not wear me out" (NRSV). A more literal rendering of the verb is "to strike under the eye," hence the option of "give me a black eye" that some commentators discuss.[15] The effect of this imagery communicates that the widow might get knocked down, as

10. Marshall, *Gospel of Luke*, 863: "Although the judge was legally required to give precedence to a widow's case, he was either unwilling to do so (perhaps through laziness) or he would not dare (θέλω, 18:13; Mk. 6:26; Jn. 7:1) to withstand her powerful opponent."

11. Noted by Barbara E. Reid, "A Godly Widow Persistently Pursuing Justice: Luke 18:1–8," *BR* 45 (2000): 25–33.

12. Michael Wolter, *The Gospel According to Luke*, vol. 2, *Luke 9:51–24*, trans. Wayne Coppins and Christoph Heilig (Waco: Baylor University Press, 2017), 314.

13. Cf. Weaver, "Luke 18:1–8," 319.

14. J. Green, *Gospel of Luke*, 641.

15. Nicholas Perrin, *Luke: An Introduction and Commentary*, TNTC 3 (Downers Grove, IL: InterVarsity, 2022), 387; Wolter, *Gospel According to Luke*, 2:317–18.

it were, but she keeps getting up. Her aggressive pursuit of justice now has the judge on the ropes.

Against all odds the parable ends with the judge planning to render a verdict in favor of the persistent widow. Some might be reminded here of the Joker's line to Batman about an unstoppable force meeting an immovable object at the end of *The Dark Knight*. Regardless, Jesus circles back in verse 6 to the matter of active prayer that never gives up. The widow lives in a hostile world, and she certainly could have succumbed to the temptation to despair because of her circumstances and a deeply flawed judicial process. But the message of this parable is that we can completely shift our perspective: If a dishonest judge responds to a widow's tenacity, how much more will God respond to his treasured children with whom he walks every step of every day? Here is another example, therefore, of a *how much more* parable, along the same lines as the story of the dishonest manager. If the widow's efforts cause a change in the unrighteous judge, how much more will the disciple's fervent prayer for justice be honored by a righteous God?[16] The widow becomes a heroic figure in our parables and gives us further insight into the economy of grace that is a hallmark of God's kingdom.

From the Widow's Distress to Workers Who Feel Ripped Off

The plot twist in the unjust judge parable revolves around justice. Our widow wanted a fair shake, and, against the odds, she prevailed without the kind of power that the judge would normally arbitrate. Such themes are extended in the next parable we'll look at, and it too features a contract dispute as a main issue. But instead of a solitary underdog battling against the forces of a hostile world, the parable in Matthew 20:1–16 has a collective character at the center. As we will see, this group rages like the older brother when he learns about the welcome home party sponsored by his way-too-generous father. Moreover, the story of the widow and the unjust judge takes place over a length of time, and in fact it is the widow's long-term perseverance that motivates the action. By contrast, the parable

16. On translating καὶ μακροθυμει, see John Mark Hicks, "The Parable of the Persistent Widow (Luke 18:1–8)," *ResQ* 33 (1991): 219–20.

in Matthew 20:1–16 has a much more limited time span, as the action takes place in the course of a single day. Altogether, if the widow's story draws attention to God's interest in basic social justice and is an encouragement to never give up hope, then *the parable of the vineyard workers* illuminates matters of status and compensation within an economy of grace.

In *the parable of the vineyard workers* there is a disruption of the workday's usual pattern, and the audience hardly realizes what is happening until the day is over: "Many of Jesus' parables do not simply follow common experience but actually reverse common experience and present a story that actually shocks the reader. This is because the kingdom reality is the reverse of this world."[17] It turns out that the reversal in Matthew 20:1–16 is disclosed through an argument about compensation, as certain employees in the parable apparently get a better deal than others, understandably creating some serious tension in the workplace. As a result, one writer has thought of a few alternate titles for the story, such as *the parable of the complaining day laborers* or *the tale of the surprising salaries*.[18] There are two main plot movements, starting with part 1: The owner of a vineyard hires several groups of workers over the course of a long day. But part 2 is where things get interesting, as the groups line up to get paid for their labor. The audience would think that those who labored longer are paid more, as do the laborers themselves. At the end of the day, however, everybody gets the same amount, causing those workers who labored longer to grumble loudly. It is quite clear that a different kind of CEO is at work in this parable, and probably not the kind who would take a massive bonus in the midst of a financial collapse.

The Owner

Three preceding scenes in Matthew 19 set the stage for this parable. First, a wealthy young man asks Jesus what good thing he is required to do in order to earn eternal life. After a conversation where the youngster claims to have kept all the commands, Jesus challenges him to sell his possessions

17. Grant R. Osborne, *Matthew*, ZECNT (Grand Rapids: Zondervan, 2010), 505.

18. Amy-Jill Levine, *Short Stories by Jesus: The Enigmatic Parables of a Controversial Rabbi* (San Francisco: HarperOne, 2014), 205. Perhaps there is an analogy to the titles of paintings; if so, see Julian Barnes, "What Are *You* Looking At?," *New York Review of Books*, May 12, 2022, 16–18.

and give to the poor, and then he will have treasure in heaven. But "when the young man heard this, he went away sad, because he had great wealth" (19:22). Second, Jesus turns to his disciples and remarks that "it is easier for a camel to go through the eye of a needle than for someone who is rich to enter the kingdom of God" (19:24). Upon hearing this, the disciples are alarmed, but then Jesus reminds them that with God, all things are possible (19:26). Third, Peter reminds Jesus that he and the other disciples have left everything to follow him and asks what their reward will be. In response, Jesus assures Peter (and the others) that whatever they've left behind when deciding to follow him, they will receive one hundred times in return and will indeed inherit eternal life. Yet he also reminds them that "many who are first will be last, and many who are last will be first" (19:30). This cryptic saying is later repeated at the end of the parable in 20:16, but in reverse order.

The occasion for the parable in Matthew 20:1–16, as we just noted above, is a conversation between Jesus and his disciples. A rich young man has just left their presence, disappointed because he can't seem to relinquish his grip on many possessions in order to take hold of something with infinitely higher value. Likewise, they have just heard about a camel going through the eye of a needle, which sounds decidedly uncomfortable and a maneuver that at some point must involve downsizing. The reader also overhears the topic of *rewards* raised by Peter, and presumably the utterance about "the last being first" will be explained by this parable that begins with an image of vineyard:

> [1]For the kingdom of heaven is like a landowner who went out early in the morning to hire workers for his vineyard. [2]He agreed to pay them a denarius for the day and sent them into his vineyard.

The vineyard is frequent metaphor for Israel, as illustrated in various texts such as Isaiah 5:1 ("Let me sing for my beloved my love-song concerning his vineyard") and Jeremiah 12:10 ("Many shepherds have ruined my vineyard").[19] Similarly, in John 15 Jesus uses the imagery of the vine to talk about the nature of discipleship, reinforcing the idea that this parable has a pertinent message for the disciples.[20]

19. Ben Witherington III, *Matthew* (Macon, GA: Smyth & Helwys, 2006), 373.
20. R. Dennis Cole, "Vine, Vineyard," in *EDB*, 1356–57.

Most commentators suggest that the vineyard's landowner represents several aspects of the character of God, and it soon becomes apparent that we are not dealing with a conventional owner by any means.[21] This parable doesn't aim to impart advice for operating or interpreting the agricultural industry in ancient Palestine, nor is it a tutorial in money matters or human resource management.[22] On the contrary, the audience is invited to hear this parable and discover ways that it gives insight into further differences between the kingdom of God and the typical ways of the world. Like *the parable of the dishonest steward*, the message here will be more indirect and will require some wisdom to extract.

At the start of the business day, the owner goes out to look for laborers. In verse 8 we will learn that the owner has a household overseer or supervisor, a different term from that used to refer to the dishonest manager, but evidently the two roles had a similar set of responsibilities. As we will see later, the owner summons his overseer and gives detailed instruction about payment of the workers at the end of the day. But rather than delegating this initial task of hiring workers to the overseer, the owner personally goes out "early in the morning" to recruit his workers at the beginning of the parable. Maybe this is micromanaging, or maybe it is the first of a number of oddities in the parable.[23] But other quirks will emerge before the day is over. For example, the owner is someone who asks a lot of questions, more so than any other character we have yet to meet in these parables. For now, though, there is nothing especially unusual about the owner's hiring practices.

Quid Game

Having secured the workers first thing in the morning, the owner consents to pay a denarius (rendered as "the usual daily wage" in the NRSV). Indeed, I noted earlier that a denarius is roughly equivalent to a day's wage, and on that basis we can calculate some approximate values.[24] In Luke 10:35 we recall that the Samaritan left two denarii with the innkeeper to

21. E.g., Ulrich Luz, *Matthew: A Commentary*, 3 vols., trans. James E. Crouch, Hermeneia (Minneapolis: Fortress, 2001–7), 2:531.

22. Cf. Thomas G. Long, *Matthew* (Louisville: Westminster John Knox, 1997), 224.

23. O. Wesley Allen Jr., *Matthew* (Minneapolis: Fortress, 2013), 270.

24. David L. Turner, *Matthew*, BECNT (Grand Rapids: Baker, 2008), 478.

care for the victim, with the assurance to pay whatever other expenses were incurred upon his return. Here in this parable, the vineyard owner and the workers agree on the day's wage. This agreement needs to be kept in mind, because it will cause a quarrel about twelve hours from now.

When the owner went out at sunrise, he was searching for *workers*. Back in *the parable of the prodigal sons*, the younger brother is more than willing to return to his father's house as a mere hired hand, a tough gig without any lasting stability or much of a benefits package. Although the term for hired hand is different than the term used here in Matthew 20, a similar notion of day labor is at work.[25] In James 5 there is a sharply worded warning to the wealthy about exploitative practices and heaping up riches for themselves at the expense of their hired workers: "Listen! The wages of the laborers who mowed your fields, which you kept back by fraud, cry out, and the cries of the harvesters have reached the ears of the Lord of hosts" (5:4 NRSV). In contrast, the contract in the opening line of the parable shines a more favorable light on this vineyard owner who agrees to pay a fair wage to his workers.[26]

We might have assumed that having recruited his workers early in the morning, the owner is good to go for the day. But the next scene causes the reader to pause, then, as the owner ventures out again a few hours later. More specifically, it is the third hour, roughly 9 a.m. or "midmorning" as it is often translated. Not only is it now slightly later in the day, but as will be evident in a moment, the gathering site is the marketplace. Usually visualized as the public square in a town or a village, the marketplace is presumably the same location where the first workers assembled and were hired at sunrise. An easily overlooked point as we move into this next scene is that all of these day laborers seem to share the same status, and this should be kept in mind since Jesus is telling this parable to the inner circle within the context of a larger discussion about the cost of discipleship.

> [3]About nine in the morning he went out and saw others standing in the marketplace doing nothing. [4]He told them, "You also go and work in my

25. For some further background discussion on day laborers, see Erin K. Vearncombe, "Redistribution and Reciprocity: A Socio-Economic Interpretation of the Parable of the Labourers in the Vineyard (Matthew 20.1–15)," *JSHJ* 8 (2010): 199–236.

26. Cf. Levine, *Short Stories by Jesus*, 213: "The agreement is precisely that; the Greek is *symphoneo*, whence 'symphony' (cf. Matt. 18.19, 'If two of you agree on earth about anything you ask, it will be done for you by my Father in heaven')."

> vineyard, and I will pay you whatever is right." [5]So they went. He went out again about noon and about three in the afternoon and did the same thing.

Without any explanation, the owner goes out again a few hours later. It might be assumed that he previously went to the marketplace and found his workers early in the morning, but this spatial setting is only now mentioned in the parable. Verse 3 indicates that when he is in the marketplace, the owner sees another group of (potential) workers. This scene is filtered through the owner's point of view. Not only does he notice them, but he also concludes that they are standing there with nothing going on. From standard English translations, the reader might gain the impression that this is group of slackers who would prefer to play video games than to find a more typical vocation. The NIV, as can be seen above, has this group standing in the marketplace "doing nothing," while in the NRSV they are "standing idle." Such translations are possible, but they perhaps attribute the lack of work to laziness or an absence of ambition.[27] But this interpretation is unlikely when considering the next sequence in the parable: The owner offers them a chance to go to the vineyard, and off they go.

It might be further argued that those standing in the marketplace are not loafers because they proceed to the vineyard without any kind of negotiation and in the absence of any definite payment plan. In hindsight, the absence of the term "denarius"—the day's wage agreed upon by the first group—will be an important omission, but for now it does not seem particularly serious. The owner assures the midmorning crew, "I will pay you whatever is right," and there is no obvious reason for distrust: "He promises them a fair recompense, which the reader naturally assumes will be a percentage of the amount paid those hired earlier."[28] Only in retrospect will the audience realize that the parable redefines "whatever is right" from the owner's perspective, and it is the hinge for the forthcoming plot twist. The new group of workers, however, register no complaint as they secure employment for the remainder of the day.

On two more occasions the owner returns to the marketplace—at noon and then again in the midafternoon—recruiting more workers on each

27. Richard T. France, *The Gospel of Matthew*, TNTC (Grand Rapids: Eerdmans, 2007), 672.

28. Osborne, *Matthew*, 729.

occasion. There is still no rationale for the owner's trips to the marketplace and no statement about any urgent situation at the vineyard that would explain why (or if) these workers are needed. The owner's hiring strategy has led some interpreters to speculate that it must be harvest time: "When the grapes get ripe, there is a need to pick them as quickly as one can to get the maximum yield."[29] It would certainly help to make sense of the owner's actions *if* we were told that it was harvest time or given some other reason for the hiring. But we are not told anything like this, so the audience has to view the matter differently: What if it is the plight of the workers rather than the owner's profit that motivates the hiring? When the owner goes into the marketplace, he sees the workers with nothing to do. The parable does not say he is moved with compassion like the Samaritan was when he saw the victim lying half dead at the side of the road. However, the owner does respond to their need for viable employment and meaningful work, and he offers them an opportunity to work for the wage.[30]

Daylight Savings

Periodically when watching the news or some other program, you might hear a report that includes the phrase "the eleventh hour," and it refers to some event that takes places or occurs at the last possible moment.[31] Examples might be "the two sides reached an agreement at the eleventh hour" or "the student procrastinated on a term paper, but finally slid the half-baked paper under the professor's door at the eleventh hour (and earned a failing grade)." As the day has unfolded in this parable, we have seen the vineyard owner make some unexpected moves. But the most unexpected action is about to occur, quite literally, at the eleventh hour (τὴν ἐνδεκάτην). Many translations opt for "around five o'clock in the

29. Witherington, *Matthew*, 373; cf. Luz, *Matthew*, 2:531, who remarks that the parable "has no intention of making the farmer's strange behavior plausible; instead, it wants its hearers to wonder about this farmer who does such a bad job of planning."

30. France, *Gospel of Matthew*, 671: "It is unlikely that he needed the extra workers, and his excessive payment of them speaks for itself. Commercially, the man is a fool. And God is as uncalculating as that."

31. Ian Boxall, *Matthew Through the Centuries*, WBBC (Oxford: Wiley-Blackwell, 2019), 304. He further notes, "This explains the title of the 2007 documentary *The 11th Hour*, narrated by Leonardo DiCaprio, warning of the dire consequences of global warning. Perhaps even more famous is the timing of the Armistice, which brought to an end the First World War: 11 a.m. on 11 November 1918, or 'the eleventh hour of the eleventh day of the eleventh month.'"

afternoon" to give us the sense that it is very late in the day when the vineyard owner goes out once more:

> [6]About five in the afternoon he went out and found still others standing around. He asked them, "Why have you been standing here all day long doing nothing?"
> [7]"Because no one has hired us," they answered.
> He said to them, "You also go and work in my vineyard."

When the owner hired workers during the past two rounds—at noon and then in the middle of the afternoon—the audience may suspect that the hiring is less about the owner's needs and more about the workers' need for employment. Now, as the day is almost over, such suspicions appear to be confirmed by means of a dialogue that takes place at the eleventh hour. I mentioned previously that this vineyard owner poses more questions than any other character so far in these parables, and in verse 6 he asks those who are standing around why they have been there all day without any work. This does not seem to be a rebuke in the form of a rhetorical question but, rather, a genuine request for information.

Speaking of questions, the audience might well wonder why this group hasn't been hired and why they are still standing in the marketplace this late in the day. Perhaps, as some interpreters assert, this excuse is merely a "cover for laziness."[32] Alternatively, the very fact that these workers are still lingering in the marketplace—long after they could have left—implies that they are willing to work, so maybe there is something about them that does not impress any employers.[33] We get the sense that this might be a hapless group who "no longer [has] any good hope of being employed," so they are probably astonished to hear the owner's positive response in verse 7: "You also go and work in my vineyard."[34] Despite being marginalized and overlooked, this crew has stumbled into some hidden treasure with darkness looming at the eleventh hour. It could be that a larger point

32. Craig S. Keener, *A Commentary on the Gospel of Matthew* (Grand Rapids: Eerdmans, 1999), 369, quoting Joachim Jeremias, *The Parables of Jesus*, 2nd rev. ed. (New York: Scribner's, 1972), 37: "Jeremias thinks that, 'Because no one has hired us' is a cover for laziness."

33. Osborne, *Matthew*, 730; cf. Donald A. Hagner, *Matthew*, 2 vols., WBC (Dallas: Word, 1993–95), 2:571.

34. Frederick Dale Bruner, *Matthew: A Commentary*, rev. ed., 2 vols. (Grand Rapids: Eerdmans, 2004), 2:319.

is emerging here: Maybe the kingdom of God is a place where anyone can be given a chance, even at the most unlikely time.

A Hard Day's Night

The most peculiar aspect of the parable so far has been the owner's repeated visits to the marketplace, and the audience is not entirely sure why. Especially so was the 5 p.m. visit, when surely he didn't need more workers, but he nonetheless hired the last desperate crew in what looks like an act of mercy. While this is strange to be sure, it is still not the climax of the story. But now, sixty minutes later, we are almost there, because it is time to pay the workers at the end of the day. Several biblical texts exhort employers to settle accounts prior to nightfall.[35] Leviticus 19:13 requires that the wages of a hired worker not be held back overnight, while a longer discussion is found in Deuteronomy 24:14–15: "You shall not withhold the wages of poor and needy laborers, whether other Israelites or aliens who reside in your land in one of your towns. You shall pay them their wages daily before sunset, because they are poor and their livelihood depends on them; otherwise they might cry to the LORD against you, and you would incur guilt" (NRSV). A payday in this parable, therefore, is not unusual, but the plot twist will come in the amount that the last group receive:

> [8]When evening came, the owner of the vineyard said to his foreman, "Call the workers and pay them their wages, beginning with the last ones hired and going on to the first." [9]The workers who were hired about five in the afternoon came and each received a denarius. [10]So when those came who were hired first, they expected to receive more. But each one of them also received a denarius.

A slightly different title is used for the main character in this scene. Initially the owner is formally referred to as "the householder," whereas now in verse 8 he is called "the owner of the vineyard." According to one scholar, this new title is "another element that makes it easy for the readers to think of God."[36] It was earlier noted that the lord of the vineyard has a "servant," or in more functional terms, a household manager. As

35. Witherington, *Matthew*, 374.
36. Luz, *Matthew*, 2:531.

we recall, the owner does not send this manager to the marketplace to recruit the workers but goes out himself and proceeds to venture forth on multiple occasions. At the end of the day, however, the household manager makes an appearance in the parable. It stands to reason that he is a loyal and faithful employee, and unlike the dishonest steward in our earlier parable, there is no report that this one steals from his boss or squanders his property. In verse 8 the household manager is directed to pay the workers, and there doesn't seem to be anything strange when he is told to start with that final crew brought in at the eleventh hour so they can receive their (modest) compensation for sixty minutes of work.

During the first round of hiring early in the morning, the initial group agreed to a denarius for their day's wage. It is not irrational, therefore, to expect that the last group will receive an appropriate percentage of a denarius based on the amount of time they've worked.[37] Indeed, the mid-morning group was told they would receive "whatever is right," so the audience expects that they too will be paid fairly under the circumstances, and substantially less than the amount received by those in the first group, who have worked the most hours. At the eleventh hour—when the vineyard owner inquires as to why the last group is still standing around—there is no negotiation over the wage. They are simply sent into the vineyard, and we guess that they will be happy with anything at the end of the day. Imagine their shock, therefore, when the manager gives them a full denarius, despite their minimal contribution. Through this example of generosity, it is now confirmed that the owner had no pressing need for the workers but, rather, showed kindness because of their situation.

If we can picture the astonishment of the last group when they receive a full day's wage for one hour's work, then we can likewise sense the frown of disappointment when the first group receives the same amount despite working eleven hours longer. Of course, everyone knows the agreement they came to early in the morning. Both parties signed the contract for a denarius, so when the manager—acting on the owner's instructions—gives the first group the correct amount, there should be no hard feelings.

37. Cf. Nathan Eubank, "What Does Matthew Say About Divine Recompense? On the Misuse of the Parable of the Workers in the Vineyard (20.1–16)," *JSNT* 35 (2013): 244: "The scandal, in other words, is in the master's decision to be generous to those who had not worked the whole day; there is little to suggest that the workers are to forget the very concept of payment in favor of duty which is its own reward."

But along with the audience, when those in the first group notice the last group getting a generous wage, they must have built up their expectations and calculated that they would receive more.[38] The question now becomes: How will they react to the owner's treatment of the last group? The owner really did not need the last group of workers, and he certainly did not need to pay them so lavishly. So will they register any complaint with this owner, even though they've been treated fairly themselves?

Money for Nothing

Let's return for a moment to the older brother in *the parable of the lost sons* to draw some comparisons. The older son officially enters the stage as he trudges to the house after a day's work in the family fields (at least, what remains of the property after his younger brother liquidates his share). Based on the sound of music and a servant's report, he flies into a rage when he finds out that the rebellious younger son has crawled back and received a resplendent celebration sponsored by the forbearing father. When that same father leaves the party and pleads with his eldest son to come inside, his efforts are met with only an angry tirade. The older son outlines his hard work and list of achievements and expresses anger that the younger brother has been given something that he has not earned. Owing to what he has accomplished, the older son deserves to be compensated better, and he begrudges the father's generosity because he has wasted money on a cause that is unworthy. It remains to be seen, now, how the first group will respond to the vineyard owner who is acting in ways that are remarkably similar to the father of the prodigal sons.

> [11]When they received it, they began to grumble against the landowner. [12]"These who were hired last worked only one hour," they said, "and you have made them equal to us who have borne the burden of the work and the heat of the day."

By their own admission, those in the first group—who were hired early and, having agreed to a denarius for their wage, had put in a long day's work—noticed all that was happening throughout their shift. They

38. Michael J. Wilkins, *Matthew* (Grand Rapids: Zondervan, 2004), 665.

observed the owner bringing in new groups at various points. Yet while they were performing their own labor, they were also computing the number of hours worked by the others. But now that the manager has paid everyone the same, the first group is deflated because they expected a bigger check on account of their longer service and efforts in the heat of the day. This unforeseen equality prompts them to "grumble," an action we have encountered previously in our study.

As we recall, at the beginning of Luke 15 a host of outcasts like tax collectors and sinners are gathering around and listening to the words of Jesus. But others—including higher-ranking members of the establishment such as the Pharisees—are "grumbling" as they watch Jesus enjoying a meal with a tableful of undesirables. This kind of grumbling has a long history, and it is frequently heard in the wilderness when the Israelites register discontent with their circumstances. The grumbling is prompted by lack of water, leadership issues, and the same menu of food over and over. Despite the exodus from Egypt and deliverance from terrible oppression, the people feel they don't deserve such adversity. They grumble against Moses, but more often they grumble against God for not acting as they would prefer.[39] Rather than limiting the capacity for grumbling to the Pharisees, though, this parable might challenge those disciples who are tempted to complain about their lot and question the ways of the owner.

Despite their opportunity to work at the outset of the day, the first group of vineyard workers take issue with the owner. On a practical level, it might be ill-advised to make their anger public. After all, they are hired hands, and presumably they need to be hired again by this employer.[40] In the heat of the moment, they could theoretically be jeopardizing their future by complaining to an otherwise openhanded boss. On another level, there is no legal basis for their grumbling. They are angry not because of any breach of contract but, rather, because other workers are treated in such a generous way: "The complaint of the leaders, if we look closely at the text, is not that the Lord broke his word or cheated them; it is that

39. Osborne, *Matthew*, 731: "This first group complains 'against' the master. This may well mean that their unhappiness is expressed first to others (probably anyone who was around) and then (v. 12) taken to the owner himself. In Num. 14:27 LXX this verb is used of Israel complaining against God in the wilderness (in 14:2, 36 it is also grumbling against Moses and Aaron)."

40. Keener, *Commentary on the Gospel of Matthew*, 369: "Jesus' hearers may have been shocked that workers would openly react so negatively to a benevolent landowner from whom they might require future favors."

the Lord was far more generous with the undeserving."[41] Much like the older brother, those in the first group believe that they deserve to be given more and that the other workers hired later in the day have not earned the same amount as them.

Cheap Grace

The German theologian and pastor Dietrich Bonhoeffer posed a searching question about some of the most important decisions that a follower of Jesus needs to make: "If we answer the call of discipleship, where will it lead us? What decisions and partings will it demand?"[42] Take the brothers James and John, for example. We will return to their story below, but in Matthew 4 they are first seen in their fishing boat, repairing their nets alongside their father. But when Jesus called to them, "immediately they left the boat and their father and followed him" (Matt. 4:22). By any measure, this is an impressive start to the brothers' journey. Nevertheless, leaving everything sometimes takes a bit longer than we think. Bonhoeffer also remarks that "costly grace is the treasure hidden in the field," and for the sake of this treasure we are willing to sell everything that we have.[43] By contrast, cheap grace doesn't require selling anything. To reiterate an earlier point, selling everything includes more than just material possessions. It also involves divesting ourselves of various ideas about merit, achievement, and calculations about what we deserve. The economy of grace is about reversal, and this includes reversing some of our own misplaced values and allowing our worldview to be recalibrated by the values of the kingdom of God.

Immediately before this parable about the dissatisfied vineyard workers comes a story in Matthew 19 about a wealthy young aristocrat who came to Jesus asking questions about eternal life. As the conversation unfolds, the youngster is soon outlining his long and impressive list of good deeds. But with the prospect of treasure in heaven within reach, he walks away from the conversation because he is unwilling to let go of what he believes is more valuable. He starts by asking about eternal life but leaves

41. Bruner, *Matthew*, 2:351.

42. Dietrich Bonhoeffer, *The Cost of Discipleship*, trans. R. H. Fuller (1937; repr., New York: Macmillan, 1979), 41.

43. Bonhoeffer, *Cost of Discipleship*, 47.

in sadness. Stumbling upon treasure in the field, he can't bring himself to sell everything. He seems utterly sincere when asking his question and just as sincere when he walks away sad.

Peter and the other disciples overhear this interaction with the rich youngster, resulting in Peter's reminder (perhaps on behalf of the entire group) that "we left everything and followed you. What do we get out of it?" (Matt. 19:27).[44] In response to Peter's question, Jesus certainly could have offered a set of abstract principles. But instead of taking a heavy-handed approach, Jesus tells *the parable of the vineyard workers*, a story that offers the disciples a chance to review their motives and expectations. When the first group of workers starts grumbling in Matthew 20:11–12, as they compare their hard labor under the searing heat with the last group's single hour of work, we have reached the heart of the story: "The first hired do not want to be treated equally to the last; they want to be treated better."[45] As we mentioned above, there are some similarities between the owner of the vineyard and the father of the prodigal son, as both are bountiful toward the undeserving. It is the extension of grace that angers both the older brother and the first group of vineyard workers, as they perceive that grace comes at their expense. The challenge for the disciples is to remember the privilege of discipleship even in hard times and to remember that costly grace has already been lavished upon them.

> 13But he answered one of them, "I am not being unfair to you, friend. Didn't
> you agree to work for a denarius? 14Take your pay and go. I want to give
> the one who was hired last the same as I gave you. 15Don't I have the right
> to do what I want with my own money? Or are you envious because I am
> generous?" 16So the last will be first, and the first will be last.

In the owner's reply to the malcontents, one particular member of the grumbling crowd is singled out. There is no obvious reason why this specific (unnamed) person is isolated, nor is he identified as the ringleader or even the loudest complainer. So we might guess that he is simply a representative of the group, and the owner's words to him apply to everyone else. In the owner's address of the representative as "friend" (ἑταῖρε), some

44. This translation is from *The Message*.
45. Levine, *Short Stories by Jesus*, 220.

interpreters sense a cold formality or a distant tone.[46] However, there is an interesting nuance from the Hebrew Bible that might be relevant here. In the story of King David, the term "friend" is an office and a title belonging to certain associates of the royal circle.[47] Perhaps the connotation here is privileged proximity. In other words, the owner starts by implying the advantages of the first group, something they may have overlooked in their anger about compensation.

As discussed earlier, the agreement was for a denarius in return for the day's work. The owner now stresses that this deal was not broken, nor has he acted dishonorably or cheated his employees. Indeed, he frames his reply as a question, and we noted that questions are a hallmark of this owner's verbal style. By asking so many questions in this closing speech, what exactly is the owner hoping to accomplish? It would seem that the owner is trying to get the grumblers to pivot—that is, to shift their perspective and view this matter from a slightly different angle. Instead of just standing in the same place and stewing in their anger, these questions from the owner challenge them to reinvent their thinking. The two rhetorical questions in verse 15 in particular are directed to this end. First, the owner asks them about his right to extend mercy to the undeserving ("Don't I have the right to do what I want with my own money?"). Again assuming that the primary audience for this story is the disciples, we can see that God's compassionate nature is illuminated here. The disciples are invited to turn away from narrow self-interest and embrace a more expansive and dynamic understanding of divine generosity.[48]

Another sharp question from the owner also focuses on the inner attitude of the heart, and several scholars note that Matthew 20:15b can also be rendered "Or do you have an evil eye because I'm good?"[49] Most modern translations (e.g., NIV and NRSV) try to avoid the translation

46. Turner, *Matthew*, 479.

47. Levine, *Short Stories by Jesus*, 221.

48. Cf. Jeannine K. Brown, *Matthew*, Teach the Text Commentary Series (Grand Rapids: Baker Books, 2015), 409: "Biblical theology rightly emphasizes God's generous nature. God's self-revelation in the covenant with Israel is marked by grace from the start: 'The Lord, the Lord, the compassionate and gracious God' (Exod. 34:6). This parable emphasizes that same quality and indicates that God's deep generosity toward others can actually trip us up if we think of the kingdom in terms of limited amounts of grace being distributed based on 'deservedness.'"

49. Charles Nathan Ridlehoover, *The Lord's Prayer and Sermon on the Mount in Matthew's Gospel*, LNTS 616 (London: T&T Clark, 2020), 119; Klyne R. Snodgrass, *Stories with Intent: A Comprehensive Guide to the Parables of Jesus*, 2nd ed. (Grand Rapids: Eerdmans, 2018), 283–84.

"evil eye," but this is exactly the point in my view. Of course, the idea of envy is being raised here, and the parable challenges the disciples to see things differently. The evil eye is also mentioned in Mark 7:22, which draws on an earlier text in the Hebrew Bible. The disciples hopefully recognize that the owner in this parable is quoting Scripture and referring to Deuteronomy 15:9:

> Be very careful that there isn't a wicked thought in your heart, saying, "The seventh year is soon approaching, the year of remission!" If you have an evil eye against your impoverished brother and give him nothing, then he will cry out to the LORD, and it will be a sin to you.

By way of background, ancient Israel had a debt-release system designed to take place every seven years. As that seventh year was approaching, some landowners might be tempted to game the system. This parable actually widens the net of application for the principle behind Deuteronomy 15:9 and asks the disciples if they could be guilty of the same kind of acquisitive mentality.[50] An immediate implication is that an evil eye is nurtured by an attitude of scarcity—that is, thinking that there is not enough of God's grace to go around. Through these rhetorical questions in Matthew 20:15, the disciples are confronted with a radical understanding of grace. This kind of grace has the potential to shift their values away from competition and scarcity toward an entirely new understanding of what values look like in the kingdom of God.

The concluding challenge is a reiteration of the "first will be last" remark at the end of Matthew 19, here reworded for creative emphasis: "So the last will be first, and the first will be last" (20:16). If the disciples refuse to let go of a worldly mentality and instead continue with an entitled attitude of rivalry, they will quickly find themselves at the back of the line. Considering the larger context, this parable about the grumbling workers cultivates a fresh view of God's capacity to act in a graceful manner.

50. Wilkins (*Matthew*, 665) notes that the evil eye refers to covetousness: "If a disciple's eyes are fixed on earthly, material treasure as his or her value, personal significance, and earthly security, then the darkness of that evil value is the state of that person's heart. When we focus on something evil, the eye becomes the conduit by which the evil fills the inner person." Wilkins also refers to a previous text in Matthew 6:22–23, where Jesus says: "The eye is the lamp of the body. So, if your eye is healthy, your whole body will be full of light; but if your eye is unhealthy, your whole body will be full of darkness. If then the light in you is darkness, how great is the darkness!" (NRSV).

Thus, the disciples are tacitly encouraged to focus on their own gratitude, not nurture grudges against other recipients of *costly grace*. God often does not act according to the strictures of the law but instead is open to dispensing mercy where it has not been earned.

Status Anxiety

Down the road on their journey of discipleship, it is entirely possible that on occasion the followers of Jesus will face discouragement and setbacks of various kinds. One of the purposes of this parable of the vineyard workers is to help anyone in the struggle with disappointment when we feel that God has not treated us fairly or not rewarded us according to our worth: "We, too, can feel like these grumblers who have worked all day in the Lord's vineyard. We compare ourselves to others and complain that God has not met our expectations."[51] If, like the rich young ruler, the disciples cling to what they possessed prior to stumbling upon great treasure, then they are sure to be disappointed.

The very next scenes in verses 17–28 after this parable are therefore an important follow-up. As he was making his way up to Jerusalem, Jesus takes his disciples aside to make a shocking prediction about his suffering, arrest, crucifixion, and resurrection on the third day. Right afterward, the mother of James and John—the sons of Zebedee mentioned earlier in our discussion (and called "the sons of Thunder")—moves into the foreground. She makes a bold and ambitious request, asking Jesus if her sons can sit at his right and left hand when he is enthroned as king. Jesus then asks if they can "drink the cup" that he's about to drink, at the very least a symbolic reference to his forthcoming ordeal on the cross. After their eager affirmative and Jesus's reply, the scene concludes with a group meeting and a word about finding distinction in an economy of grace:

> [24]When the ten heard about this, they were indignant with the two brothers. [25]Jesus called them together and said, "You know that the rulers of the Gentiles lord it over them, and their high officials exercise authority over them. [26]Not so with you. Instead, whoever wants to become great among you must be your servant, [27]and whoever wants to be first must be your

51. Douglas D. Webster, *The Parables: Jesus's Friendly Subversive Speech* (Grand Rapids: Kregel Academic, 2021), 182.

slave—[28]just as the Son of Man did not come to be served, but to serve, and to give his life as a ransom for many."

The parable of the vineyard workers—with the sour grapes of some employees at its core—is a response to questions about rewards for following Jesus. Evidently it takes a while for the new values of the kingdom of God to take root in a disciple's mindset, as indicated by Peter's questions ("What's in it for me/us?") and by the ambitions of the mother of James and John. It is notable that a parent shows up at this point in the story, indirectly suggesting that parents also might need to make some adjustments when it comes to understanding the economy of grace. This mother is serious—indicated by the fact that she bows low—and as we remarked above, she is keen that her sons are seated on the most important and prestigious thrones in the kingdom. As reported in verse 24, the other members of the group are angry with these two sons of Thunder (and their mother, by extension). But it is unclear if they are angry because the brothers are out of line (as they are so obviously trying to rise to a higher position) or because the brothers thought of it first and have the idea to enlist their mother as part of the scheme.[52]

Both the mother's request and the reaction of the other disciples reveals that they have lots in common with the first shift of vineyard workers who are complaining about their wage, as all parties are operating according to a reward system based on what we think we deserve. In fairness, several centuries afterward, theologians were still working out these matters. For example, British philosopher Alain de Botton remarks that Saint Augustine's fifth-century work *The City of God* explained that most human actions can be interpreted from the perspective of either Roman thought or Christian thought, and "that the very things esteemed so highly by the Romans—amassing money, building villas, winning wars—counted for nothing in the Christian schema, while a new set of concerns—loving one's neighbors, practicing humility and charity, and recognizing one's dependence on God—offered the keys to elevated Christian status."[53]

52. For Osborne (*Matthew*, 741), "it is a jealous anger on the part of those who are upset that James and John thought of it first and got to Jesus before they could. They are upset that the two are 'acing them out' and getting ahead of them in the race for greatness."

53. Alain de Botton, *Status Anxiety* (New York: Penguin Books, 2004), 226.

Some similarities can be spotted between Augustine's reflections and the reply of Jesus to his disciples about servant leadership and humility. First place in the kingdom of God, Jesus explains, is not attained with the same approach as in the empire. Perhaps the disciples have started to calculate how following Jesus will gain them a series of rewards or degrees of prosperity and status, but the parable and its surrounding context invites the view that discipleship is its own reward, and learning to live this truth involves learning to live by the economy of grace.[54] Within the larger world of the New Testament, it might be suggested that the two brothers James and John *did* learn this lesson, so it would seem. James is martyred for his faith by Herod in Acts 12, while John—if he is the seer of the Apocalypse, as early tradition maintains—suffers exile for his beliefs on the island prison of Patmos.[55] In all likelihood, then, they took seriously the closing words of Jesus about giving "his life as a ransom for many." A ransom is commonly defined as the price that is paid so that a slave can go free. Because Jesus is willing to pay the highest possible ransom price with his own life, paradoxically the disciples are given a status that is higher than anything they could ever achieve on their own.

54. Allen, *Matthew*, 276.

55. See the arguments for and against in R. Alan Culpepper, *John, the Son of Zebedee: The Life of a Legend* (Columbia: University of South Carolina Press, 1994), 95–98.

7

Taxes, Towers, and Bags of Gold

AS WE START TO APPROACH the finish line in this short book, we now turn to three more parables of Jesus that further illuminate how to live in an economy of grace. So far we have noticed that in some cases grace is a freely given benefit, and there may not even be a previously existing relationship between the one who gives and the other who receives.[1] On other occasions, acts of grace can involve someone in a stronger position arriving to assist another in a weakened position because of circumstances or choices. Such assistance can be a large-scale rescue, like the exodus from Egypt, or a smaller gesture of mercy to those in need,[2] like the embrace of a son who has wasted the family inheritance or paying the medical bills for an enemy who has been attacked by thieves. Responses to grace can look like pouring out expensive perfume in gratitude or like sponsoring a celebration and inviting the whole neighborhood. Living in an economy of grace starts with an awareness of divine mercy that has been lavishly extended, as the recipient now understands that typical schemes of human merit are displaced by the values of the kingdom of God.

1. John S. Kselman, "Grace," in *ABD* 2:1085–86.

2. Hans-Helmut Esser, "Grace, Spiritual Gifts," in *The New International Dictionary of New Testament Theology*, 3 vols., ed. Colin Brown (Grand Rapids: Zondervan, 1975–78), 2:116–17.

Moreover, we have been suggesting that the parable genre is an effective medium for conveying pictures of grace. Perhaps we can further define a parable as an extended metaphor that unfolds a series of images "with a certain shock to the imagination which directly conveys a vision of what is signified"; the audience not only participates in this drama but is actually "invaded" by the story-world.[3] In the sequence of parables explored in this chapter, we will notice how mercy is extended to someone with a posture of humility, the importance of counting the cost when embarking on the adventure of discipleship, and how to wisely steward the gifts we are given. Various qualities of grace are available in these three parables that feature a tax collector, the building of a tower, and investments of gold. After hearing these stories, we are further encouraged to view the world through a different lens and to see ourselves as the recipients of grace, which can reboot our imaginations with the potential to transform every relationship we have and every transaction we experience in a typical week.

In God We Trust?

To begin, the first example is a parable found in Luke 18:9–14 featuring two quite different characters who both venture to the temple for prayer. Immediately preceding, in Luke 18:1–8, is *the parable of the persistent widow* that we've already studied, a story that encourages the disciples to pray and not grow weary or lose heart. The widow has lots of reasons to give up in the face of a corrupt judge, but her perseverance is eventually repaid after a surprising twist. Other dramatic reversals have been seen in most of the parables that we have sampled. After a luxurious life of feasting in the finest clothes, a rich man is thirsty in Hades while the poor beggar dropped outside of his gate is elevated as a guest of honor at Abraham's banquet. The widow's tireless commitment, despite a glaring imbalance of power, forces the corrupt judge to grant her justice *in spite of* his gruff indifference.

3. Amos Wilder, *The Language of the Gospel: Early Christian Rhetoric*, rev. ed. (New York: Harper & Row, 1971), 92, quoted in David B. Gowler, *What Are They Saying About the Parables?* (New York: Paulist Press, 2000), 17. Cf. Charles W. Hedrick, "Parables," in *EDB*, 1006–8: "A recent approach argues that the parables are freely invented narrative fictions that are to be read in the context of the ways that first-century Palestinian Jews understood themselves. They are not referential, but are designed to bring the reader into the story where discoveries about self and the world may be made."

In this next parable of two characters who pray at the temple, there will be another unexpected reversal. If we assume that *the parable of the persistent widow* illustrates how God responds to faithful prayers over a lengthy period of time, then we need to appreciate that it is followed by another parable that shows how God responds to desperate prayers in a very short period of time. Together the parables form a compelling storyline: Pray and don't grow weary, Jesus teaches, and also pray with an awareness of God's character and capacity for graceful reception.

> 9To some who were confident of their own righteousness and looked down on everyone else, Jesus told this parable.

In some instances, we are told about the specific audience to whom a particular parable is directed. At the beginning of Luke 18, *the parable of the persistent widow* is spoken to the disciples, and there is no indication that the audience has changed. It stands to reason that this parable is therefore directed toward the disciples from the outset. Of course, there may be other listeners in view, but we should understand that the disciples are the primary target. Some scholars seem to assume that the Pharisees are the focus of the parable, but the reality is much more complicated.[4] Since the parable is oriented toward any who are confident that their behavior is pleasing to God and therefore view others with derision, the uncomfortable truth is that even disciples can drift off course by slowly starting to trust in their own righteous deeds that give them a feeling of superiority. Disciples can be tempted to become self-absorbed, and this sense of entitlement shifts the focus to their own accomplishments and pious words and away from the Lord's mercy toward them. Jesus begins the parable this way:

> 10Two men went up to the temple to pray, one a Pharisee and the other a tax collector.

Since the main characters in the parable are unnamed, they are likely intended to be representative figures who can stand for various types of people, regardless of age, gender, or ethnicity. It is notable that both of them "went up" to the Jerusalem temple. The upward direction is a

4. R. Alan Culpepper, "The Gospel of Luke," in *NIB* 8:341.

reference to the temple being the highest point of the city and Jerusalem itself standing at a relatively high elevation.[5] But perhaps more is being communicated with these words, and it could be that going up suggests a sense of transcendence or rising above worldly obsessions. The book of Psalms often celebrates "ascending" to the house of the Lord, perhaps envisioning that the temple itself has a series of steps.[6] Consequently, the audience might expect a degree of reverence on the part of these two characters as they make an appearance before God at the central place of worship.

It is entirely possible that those who have been in church circles for a while have heard the Pharisees used as a negative foil. When the term "Pharisee" comes up, many instantly recoil and give thanks that they themselves are *not* like the Pharisees! But such a caricature proves unhelpful when approaching this parable, and there is more to the Pharisees than what we typically hear: "The proliferation of hypotheses about the Pharisees," as one scholar remarks, "shows how poorly they are understood."[7] Although historians continue to puzzle over the background details and origins of the Pharisees, in general the movement, which spanned several centuries, was rooted in rigorous observation of the Torah and opposed to Roman occupation.[8]

If we survey the New Testament, we will not find a uniform presentation of the Pharisees. Collectively, they rarely get good press, but when individual Pharisees are mentioned, we find a bit more diversity in how they are depicted. The ambivalence of Simon in Luke 7 has already been noted, but Nicodemus in the Gospel of John comes across as even more complex, with his nocturnal conversations with Jesus and his presence in the aftermath of the crucifixion (John 3; 19:39). During an important

5. I. Howard Marshall, *The Gospel of Luke: A Commentary on the Greek Text* (Grand Rapids: Eerdmans, 1978), 871.

6. Psalms 120–35 are referred to as the "Songs of Ascents."

7. Anthony J. Saldarini, "Pharisees," in *ABD* 5:289.

8. Steve Mason, "Pharisees," in *EDB*, 1043–44. Cf. N. T. Wright and Michael F. Bird, *The New Testament in Its World: An Introduction to the History, Literature, and Theology of the First Christians* (Grand Rapids: Zondervan, 2019), 124: "In the Christian tradition, 'Pharisee' has become the most strident and vitriolic term to describe religious hypocrisy and self-righteousness. The result is a caricature of the original Pharisees in which they become nothing more than guardians of an external, ritualistic religion and legalistic merit-seeking. Yet the reality is that Jesus' debates with the Pharisees would be better seen as torrid insider debates between different visions of the same goal: the coming of God's kingdom on earth as in heaven. Jesus was thus in some ways closer to the Pharisaic movement than to any other sect."

meeting of the Sanhedrin in Acts, the highly respected Pharisee Gamaliel makes an influential speech when the apostles Peter and John are on trial. The speech is wise and persuasive, and it results in the apostles being released (albeit after a flogging). Indeed, Gamaliel's most famous student is none other than Saul of Tarsus, whose various writings eventually form a significant portion of the New Testament itself.

Though individual Pharisees ought to be considered on a case-by-case basis, it is nevertheless probable that in this parable the Pharisee would be perceived as the more positive of the two characters. This is because the second actor in our story is a tax collector, and historians are quite clear that such characters are contractors who gather taxes from their Jewish citizens on behalf of the loathed imperial colonizers.[9] Already in Luke's Gospel we have seen that even though tax collectors might be despised by the general population, a number of them seem to be attracted to Jesus, who treats them with certain dignity and seems quite comfortable to invite them for dinner. Nowadays we might be inclined to automatically be sympathetic because of these portrayals of their close interactions with Jesus, but in that time they were collaborators with the imperial powers.[10] It is most unlikely that Jesus's audience would have viewed the tax collector in heroic terms, and the first lines of the story convey a more negative impression of the tax collector than of the Pharisee.

Signal Virtue

As one commentator summarizes, in this parable we are dealing with two characters who can be perceived as complete opposites in the world of first-century religious culture. Not only does the Pharisee represent the most prominent movement that takes the Torah seriously for every part of life, but the tax collector is part of a most despised line of work and would hardly be met with open arms at the temple.[11] Furthermore, these characters create certain expectations in the mind of the audience, who probably assume that the Pharisee is quite comfortable in the temple setting,

9. John R. Donahue, "Tax Collector," in *ABD* 6:337–38.

10. Fred B. Craddock, *Luke*, Interpretation (Louisville: John Knox, 1990), 293: "Working for a foreign government collecting taxes from his own people, a participant in a cruel and corrupt system, politically a traitor, religiously unclean . . . a publican was a reprehensible character."

11. Darrell L. Bock, *Luke*, 2 vols. (Grand Rapids: Baker, 1994–96), 1461–62.

whereas the tax collector would not be a frequent visitor. But here both of them have ascended to this special place in order to pray, a unique kind of communication that intimately connects God and humanity, based on the belief that God is available and open to relationship and restoration.[12] To reiterate, the account of the persistent widow teaches the disciples to pray without giving up, while this very next parable emphasizes the inner disposition we should have when we pray. Now the audience has the opportunity to hear both of these characters in prayer, starting with the more religiously respectable of our two main figures:

> [11]The Pharisee stood by himself and prayed: "God, I thank you that I am not like other people—robbers, evildoers, adulterers—or even like this tax collector. [12]I fast twice a week and give a tenth of all I get."

In the chatter of contemporary society, one occasionally hears the term "virtue signaling," which is usually defined as sharing opinions or morality in a public way in order to impress others with one's character and correctness, also including well-timed expressions of disgust at certain modes of conduct or political positions.[13] Regardless of whether or not we agree with this particular definition, a similar dynamic is addressed in Matthew 6 where Jesus talks about matters such as practicing piety when conscious of onlookers, sounding a trumpet when giving to the poor in order to gain applause, or praying in such a way as to gain notice and forge a reputation for elevated spirituality. Jesus is quite clear that God has little interest in such grandstanding, and it is worth noting that he speaks these words in the famous Sermon on the Mount (Matt. 5–7). At the beginning of Matthew 5, we note the proximity of the disciples: "Now when Jesus saw the crowds, he went up on a mountainside and sat down. His disciples came to him, and he began to teach them." Because of their ringside seats, we have to infer that when Jesus starts talking about trumpeting our good deeds in Matthew 6, it is inevitable that at some point down the road the disciples will be tempted to indulge in virtue signaling or shameless self-promotion.

12. Samuel E. Balentine, "Prayer," in *EDB*, 1077–79.

13. E.g., Jillian Jordan and David Rand, "Are You 'Virtue Signaling'?," *New York Times*, March 30, 2019; Justin Tosi and Brandon Warmke, *Grandstanding: The Use and Abuse of Moral Talk* (New York: Oxford University Press, 2020).

Just before his prayer, the Pharisee is described as moving into position, but there are several different ways to translate this phrase. The NRSV has the Pharisee "standing by himself," whereas *The Message* says that the Pharisee "posed." Does this character maneuver himself so that he is in a prominent place—that is, in a strategic location? Or is he standing with a certain assurance, confident about his status before God? The NASB translates the beginning of verse 11 this way: "The Pharisee stood and began praying this in regard to himself, 'God, I thank You that I am not like other people . . ,'" implying that his prayer is about himself as much as it is directed to God. Presumably, God knows all about our good deeds, so why does this character feel a pressing need to recite them? When the Pharisee catalogs his achievements, is it for the benefit of the temple crowd rather than the divine ear? And is it possible that some showboating is taking place here in the parable?

Since there are many ways to translate verse 11, it is difficult to be 100 percent certain of the Pharisee's posture here, and perhaps the story is deliberately ambiguous. But we should have little doubt that the parable is exposing the danger in finding our security by comparing ourselves to others or by smugly publicizing our spiritual lives. If the disciples start showcasing their various religious successes, it would indicate that they have lost their focus regarding the graceful favor that has embraced their lives. The problem this parable highlights may be not so much that the Pharisee recounts a lengthy list of achievements but, rather, that he draws attention to his feeling of superiority over the tax collector. Perhaps even worse is his tacit insinuation that because of *who* this person is, and because of *what* they do, they are surely not worthy of receiving God's favor. The Pharisee's prayer is twenty-nine words long, a significant contrast to the much shorter prayer of the tax collector to which we now turn as we finish this parable.[14]

> 13But the tax collector stood at a distance. He would not even look up to heaven, but beat his breast and said, "God, have mercy on me, a sinner."
> 14I tell you that this man, rather than the other, went home justified before God. For all those who exalt themselves will be humbled, and those who humble themselves will be exalted.

14. David E. Garland, *Luke*, ZECNT (Grand Rapids: Zondervan, 2011), 717.

Whether the Pharisee is posing or not, the tax collector "stood at a distance." The same language is used in an earlier parable to underscore the chasm between the rich man in Hades and Lazarus in the bosom of Abraham.[15] When the tax collector stands away in the background maybe he's social distancing, or his location might indicate that he feels unworthy to be there with other worshipers; regardless, his distance seems to emphasize his feeling of alienation from God. That sense is further stressed as he is not even willing to raise his eyes to heaven because of his shame.[16] Beating the chest (or striking the heart) is a gesture of sorrow. In this case the heart would be understood as the seat of sin, so the tax collector's action is one of remorse.[17] The Pharisee might be drawing attention to his admirable conduct as a basis for heavenly reward, but the tax collector can only cry out for divine pity.

If God is everywhere, why does the tax collector feel compelled to pray at the temple, where he is certainly going to be seen and probably won't be very popular? His movement *toward* and prayer *at* the temple might be interpreted as steps of repentance. As we recall, after the prodigal son wallows in regret and longs to go home, he makes a decision to admit his sins to his father and declare that he's no longer worthy to be called his son. He then takes a step toward home, and before long he discovers a world of forgiveness. A parallel between the prodigal son and the tax collector is plausible when we consider Jesus's concluding words in the parable, as he commends the more "miserable" character and affirms that he is the one who goes home justified. Whoever is listening to this parable is invited to turn away from self-righteousness and contempt and instead turn toward the same divine mercy that the tax collector badly needs.

Decoding a parable usually involves identifying a disruption. The audience has a series of attitudes or viewpoints that are gradually upended in order to provide a fresh perspective on important issues. The intention of Luke 18:9–14 is not to bash Pharisees or elevate tax collectors but, rather, to make the more serious point that everyone starts at the beginning on the road to humility. Still, we might consider why Jesus features a tax collector for a starring role in this parable. One obvious reason is because

15. Amy-Jill Levine, *Short Stories by Jesus: The Enigmatic Parables of a Controversial Rabbi* (San Francisco: HarperOne, 2014), 196.

16. Joel B. Green, *The Gospel of Luke*, NICNT (Grand Rapids: Eerdmans, 1997), 649.

17. Marshall, *Gospel of Luke*, 873.

of the economic choices faced by a repentant tax collector: Should such a figure decide to start following Jesus, an immediate shift in priorities would need to take place. Perhaps we're all spiritually bankrupt, and, like the tax collector, we've sold out to the empire in various ways. At the end of the parable, the unlikely figure goes home justified but nonetheless has more work to do. In fact, the conclusion is more open-ended: Will the tax collector continue to humble himself? Within the larger context of Luke's story, becoming a shareholder in the kingdom of God (or using the imagery in Luke 9:23, a *cross carrier*) is part of the continual challenge of staying on the pathway of humility.

Cost-Benefit Analysis

Shockingly, *the parable of the Pharisee and the tax collector* might be implying that a disciple could be either of these characters at different times. Falling prey to the temptation to boast about achievements but then realizing how desperately the grace of the Lord is needed may well be part of a disciple's ongoing journey toward *humbling oneself*.[18] It may not be an accident that a tax collector is a prominent character in the parable, since such a figure needs to count the cost of discipleship and begin to invest in a completely different portfolio. These themes continue in our next parable, told earlier in Luke 14:28–30 and nestled in a stretch of text that features some sharp-edged remarks about what it means to be a true follower (rather than just an admirer) of the Lord. Arguably the sharpest is found in Luke 14:27, where Jesus insists that "whoever does not carry their cross and follow me cannot be my disciple." Right after this declaration, Jesus tells a short parable about tower construction:

> [28]Suppose one of you wants to build a tower. Won't you first sit down and estimate the cost to see if you have enough money to complete it? [29]For if you lay the foundation and are not able to finish it, everyone who sees it will ridicule you, [30]saying, "This person began to build and wasn't able to finish."

18. John P. Meier, *A Marginal Jew: Rethinking the Historical Jesus*, vol. 5, *Probing the Authenticity of the Parables*, AYBRL (New Haven: Yale University Press, 2016), 144: "The whole problem with the Pharisee's prayer (18:11–12) is that, while it is ostensibly addressed to God in thanksgiving, it is actually a self-congratulatory message addressed to the Pharisee himself."

Towers appear in a number of biblical texts, serve several different purposes, and are found in various locations. Military towers were constructed as defense fortifications and could be used as a strategic vantage point to send signals or provide refuge for citizens in times of siege (e.g., Judg. 9:51; 2 Kings 9:17). Agricultural towers were built as observation decks to track livestock (e.g., Migdal Eder, "tower of the flock," in Gen. 35:21) or as storages facilities (e.g., the vineyard watchtower of Isa. 5:2). In this parable, it sounds like an agricultural tower is in mind, which probably functioned as a security system "to provide a lookout for farmers protecting their crops from thieves or animals."[19] The advantage of such a tower standing on a property is that it increases the value and helps to safeguard the revenue stream. Any audience listening to the parable could quite easily imagine the effort that it takes to build such a tower, and that such a project involves a considerable outlay of resources.

Just a few verses earlier in Luke 14:25 we are told that "large crowds were traveling with Jesus" as he was journeying to Jerusalem, and it is this crowd that is addressed at this point in chapter 14. The tower parable begins with the hypothetical question ("Suppose one of you . . .") directed to anyone in the crowd who needs to consider the commitment and the cost of discipleship. One scholar notes that the Greek term for disciple (*mathētēs*) is a learner—that is, a student who is mentored by a teacher such as Plato or Socrates or by a great rabbi in Judaism. But "the difference between Jesus and these other models of discipleship is that Jesus' call requires more, even everything, in terms of priority from the disciple."[20]

In another parable, the kingdom of God is compared to a pearl of the highest price; here, the call to discipleship is compared to building a tower, and before starting construction the costs ought to be computed carefully. Otherwise, the project will grind to a halt, with only a half-finished memorial to a failed initiative that invites "ridicule" from passersby.[21] There is a slight possibility that such babble from onlookers evokes a memory of the most infamous unfinished tower in biblical history, the Tower of Babel, a monument to human overreach and misplaced ambition (Gen. 11:1–9).

19. Edward B. Banning, "Towers," in *ABD* 6:622–24.

20. Bock, *Luke*, 1286.

21. Note the same Greek word translated here as "ridicule" is used ironically for the mocking of Jesus in the scenes leading up to and including the crucifixion in Luke 18:32; 22:63; 23:11, 36.

Projecting the costs of a construction project in advance is always difficult. Most of us know how easy it is to go over budget, and unanticipated expenses happen all the time. So is Jesus asking disciples to guarantee, from the outset of the journey of discipleship, that they will be faithful? If that were the case, few people would qualify.[22] But through this parable, we get the sense that Jesus is challenging the crowd to think about what they really want, and if they are willing to pay the price.

Once again, the tax collector from our previous parable is a helpful comparison. When this character takes a step toward the temple, there is a cost involved. Given the negative press surrounding the tax-collecting industry, this character has to endure scorn and ridicule when he decides to start *humbling himself*. Following Jesus probably will have financial repercussions (as is the case for the tax collector), and it will undoubtedly carry social implications as well. If potential disciples estimate such costs in advance, perhaps they will be less likely to abandon the project of discipleship when periods of stress and pressure arrive.

As noted, most of the towers mentioned in the Bible serve a military or agricultural purpose. But occasionally, as in the Babel experiment mentioned above, a metaphorical dimension can be glimpsed. The tower in this parable is clearly functional, but it might have another purpose as well. Let's consider two poetic texts in this regard, starting with Psalm 61:2–3:

> From the ends of the earth I call to you,
> I call as my heart grows faint;
> lead me to the rock that is higher than I.
> For you have been my refuge,
> a strong tower against the foe. (NIV)

The poet in this psalm is under assault in a faraway place and yet declares that God has been an unshakable skyscraper of safety. In other words, when opponents have attacked with words or with weapons in the past, God has been a mighty fortress of protection, and the poet is asking for a similar intervention in this psalm.

Second, Proverbs 18:10 is similar: "The Lord's name is a strong tower: / the righteous run to it and are protected in a high place" (my translation). It celebrates the divine character as a reliable stronghold that

22. Culpepper, "Gospel of Luke," 8:293.

offers elevated protection in any time of emergency. It is surely intentional that the very next proverb in 18:11 then emphasizes the illusory security of wealth: "The wealth of the rich is their strong city: / in their imagination it is like a high wall."[23] These texts undermine our idea that wealth can protect us in every storm of life, and all such confidence is profoundly misplaced.[24] This teaching might seem counterintuitive, because material wealth appears to be a more obvious source of security than spiritual wealth. But when the city wall is knocked down, the elevated position of the tower suddenly looks way more inviting. In light of these examples from Psalms and Proverbs, it might be argued that the parable in Luke indirectly points to the flip side of failure. If someone can count the cost of discipleship and not give up in times of difficulty, then a *tower* of strength becomes a sturdy image of completing the journey of discipleship.

We now have a towering view of the *plot twist* at the end of the parable in Luke 14. On the surface it looks like a story about an unfinished project, but the audience is invited to imagine things differently. Clearly, if construction is not finished, all that remains is an incomplete pile of rocks that serves no useful purpose. But the reverse is also true: If someone is willing to count the cost and understand in advance the incredible advantages of making an "all-in" commitment, then such a disciple will be in much better shape to finish well. In the Christian life we will experience storms, adversities, setbacks, and suffering, but we will also experience the fulfillment of world-changing promises. And it is wise to keep in mind that Jesus is sharing this parable on the road to Jerusalem, where he will soon be crucified but also raised from the grave.

Capital Gains

From the illustration of tower building in Luke 14:28–30, we further discover that a commitment to long-term discipleship involves some careful planning. Moving on from the images of counting the cost of following Jesus, we now transition to another parable about energetic investing and entrepreneurship as facets of discipleship as well. While Matthew 25:14–30

23. Translation from Bruce K. Waltke, *The Book of Proverbs, Chapters 15–31*, NICOT (Grand Rapids: Eerdmans, 2005), 76–77.

24. Tremper Longman III, *Proverbs* (Grand Rapids: Baker Academic, 2006), 296–97.

is usually called *the parable of the talents*, here we will understand that a "talent" should be imagined as a bag of gold in the first instance.[25] Nowadays we think of "talents" as various gifts or abilities that a person has been given. While the parable might ultimately allow for that kind of expansiveness, the audience would have heard the term "talent" and envisioned a substantial amount of money. Commentators often point out that a talent is a measurement—a sum of cash that equivalent to twenty years' worth of wages for an average worker.[26]

The larger context of this parable in Matthew 25 revolves around the theme of alert *readiness*. Immediately preceding in verses 1–13 is *the parable of the ten bridesmaids*. Unlike those who are prepared in advance, five of the bridesmaids fail to properly invest in oil stocks, and they end up missing the wedding party.[27] Right afterward, we hear *the parable of the talents* in verses 14–30, where active planning is likewise central. The plot is straightforward enough: A property owner goes away on a long trip and entrusts three stewards with extraordinary sums of money in his absence. The parable revolves around the decisions each steward makes about what to do with the gold and the response of the owner upon his return some time later. At the heart of this parable is a challenging question about how we use the gifts we have been given and an encouragement to use such resources with fearlessness and flair.

> [14]Again, it will be like a man going on a journey, who called his servants and
> entrusted his wealth to them. [15]To one he gave five bags of gold, to another
> two bags, and to another one bag, each according to his ability. Then he
> went on his journey. [16]The man who had received five bags of gold went at
> once and put his money to work and gained five bags more. [17]So also, the

25. The focus here is on Matthew 25:14–30, but for discussion on the several variations in Luke 19:12–27, see R. Alan Culpepper, *Matthew*, NTL (Louisville: Westminster John Knox, 2021), 490–91.

26. Jeannine K. Brown, *Matthew*, Teach the Text Commentary Series (Grand Rapids: Baker Books, 2015), 383; cf. Ben Witherington III, *Matthew* (Macon, GA: Smyth & Helwys, 2006), 462: "Though in modern English the word 'talent' refers to some native ability of a human being, here the word is used in its original sense of a large sum of money. But as we shall see, a talent is a two-sided coin—on one side it says ability and on the other side responsibility."

27. See Richard T. France, "On Being Ready (Matthew 25:1–46)," in R. Longenecker, *Challenge of Jesus' Parables*, 184, who notes that these parables together speak "of a period of waiting before the master's return, and it calls on those who hear to be ready when he comes"; cf. Dale C. Allison Jr., "Matthew," in *The Oxford Bible Commentary*, ed. John Barton and John Muddiman (Oxford: Oxford University Press 2001), 878.

> one with two bags of gold gained two more. [18]But the man who had received one bag went off, dug a hole in the ground and hid his master's money.

A stubborn silence initially surrounds the identity of the property owner, and the parable gives no indication on the destination or the purpose of his journey. Despite the vagueness, the next lines provide enough clues for the audience to quickly learn quite a bit about this wealthy character. We learn that he isn't a workaholic who refuses to take time off and actually go on a trip somewhere, because that is the initial action in the parable. Moreover, he seems content to delegate and entrust what he owns to others, rather than keep a white-knuckled grip on his possessions. Not only does he bestow responsibility on his employees, but he does so willingly with no trace of miserliness. It might be too much to say that the property owner is excited to see what will happen in his absence, but there is no question that he knows his employees well, to the point that he is able to give to "each according to his ability."

To emphasize, the distribution of the bags of gold is not arbitrary but strategically based on the property owner's knowledge of the aptitudes and strengths of each servant. By depositing such phenomenal wealth with his slaves, is this owner acting counter to the audience's expectations? He is certainly the polar opposite of the Egyptian pharaohs in the world of Exodus. These despots ruthlessly exploit their Israelite slaves, piling on unreasonable demands and ordering them to make bricks without straw. If there is a contrast in this parable between the tyrants of Egypt and this property owner, then the reaction of the first slave to the five talents entrusted to him is telling: Without hesitation he goes out and starts putting the bags of gold to work. Just as his master knows him, this servant certainly appears to know his master. Hence, he acts immediately, and plunges headfirst into this opportunity that he's been given.

No explanation or further definition is provided for how the gold is put to work, so the audience is not made aware of precisely how this servant manages to double the five talents. Scholars usually speculate that some sort of buying and selling commodities is involved, usually on the basis of Luke 19:15 where the term "trading" is used, and it certainly sounds like smart investments are made.[28] Still, the focus is not on how

28. Walter T. Wilson, *The Gospel of Matthew*, vol. 2, *Matthew 14–28*, ECC (Grand Rapids: Eerdmans, 2022), 410: "Whereas Luke 19:15 indicates that the successful slaves earned their

the money is doubled but, rather, on the immediate energy invested and the servant's commitment to taking necessary risks in order to use the talents effectively. We can assume that these actions are based on his beliefs about the character of the property owner. Moreover, the second servant must have the same views, because he also goes out and doubles the two talents he received, and he must be confident that the owner will approve of and applaud his efforts.

Lots of people dream of winning the lottery and fantasize about spending the winnings on every conceivable impulse purchase. Quite wisely, the first two slaves chose *not* to waste their talents. Of course, we earlier saw the shrewd manager squander his master's money and the younger son go off to a distant land and drain his inheritance with wild living. But without any instructions from their master, these two slaves act in an entirely different manner: "In other words, everything in this story leads us to see the master as an extraordinary man," says one commentator, "trusting, welcoming, generous, and benevolent. That is the way the narrator of the parable presents him; that is the way the first two slaves view him—otherwise they would not have been so free to risk and act—and that is the way the master conducts himself."[29]

Altogether puzzling, therefore, is why the third slave has the direct opposite investment strategy. Instead of going forth and putting the money to work, or doing anything productive, this slave digs a hole and buries the master's gift. At this point the audience is unsure as to the reason(s) he acts this way. Is he bitter about being given only one talent, or is there some sort of fear of failure that paralyzes this character? Equally unclear is why he buries the money. There are other instances of *hiding* in biblical stories, but often there is guilt involved: Achan buries some gold, silver, and a cloak from Babylon in Joshua 7, while Gehazi buries the loot that he received under false pretenses from Naaman the Syrian in 2 Kings 5. At the same time, we should acknowledge that the servant does not squander the money like the shrewd manager does, but burying a bag of gold in a field may not be advisable (What if someone stumbles upon it and then buys that field?). There are more questions than answers here, but digging a hole for his talent must be based on his particular view and understanding

profits through trading [διαπραγματεύομαι], Matt 25:16 states simply that they 'worked' with the money (cf. Mark 13:34)."

29. Thomas G. Long, *Matthew* (Louisville: Westminster John Knox, 1997), 282.

of the property owner's character, and in this regard his beliefs are diametrically opposed to the first two more proactive servants.

Return of the King

Let's consider once more the placement of this parable in Matthew 25. The reader should keep in mind that we are in the midst of a longer conversation dealing with the theme of how followers of Jesus can stay alert and prepared when the master is absent from the scene. Recall *the parable of the ten bridesmaids*, in which the idea of active duty is illustrated through the image of keeping oil in a lamp. Moments before, in Matthew 24:43, Jesus also tells an anecdote about a nocturnal robbery: "But understand this: If the owner of the house had known at what time of night the thief was coming, he would have kept watch and would not have let his house be broken into." Rather than slackness, vigilance and energy should mark the journey of discipleship.

At this point, it appears that *the parable of the talents* continues along this trajectory. If the property owner represents the Lord and the slaves are disciples, then perhaps the thrust of this parable inclines toward stewardship and responsibility when handling the most valuable gift in human history: the message of the gospel. By this measurement, the first two servants emerge as quite impressive indeed. As they go forth into the world and put their talents to work, they multiply their master's capital and "illustrate the zest of discipleship" in the process.[30] Similar to the merchant who quickly sells everything else in order to buy the pearl of great price, these slaves take some risks to work with the talents they've been given. The third slave, however, hides the money and does not take advantage of the investment opportunity and the potential for profit in the master's absence. Given the emerging point in this parable in Matthew 25 about being active and prepared, we now reach the moment when the property owner returns from his trip:

> [19]After a long time the master of those servants returned and settled accounts with them. [20]The man who had received five bags of gold brought

30. Frederick Dale Bruner, *Matthew: A Commentary*, rev. ed., 2 vols. (Grand Rapids: Eerdmans, 2004), 2:579.

> the other five. "Master," he said, "you entrusted me with five bags of gold. See, I have gained five more."
> [21]His master replied, "Well done, good and faithful servant! You have been faithful with a few things; I will put you in charge of many things. Come and share your master's happiness!"
> [22]The man with two bags of gold also came. "Master," he said, "you entrusted me with two bags of gold; see, I have gained two more."
> [23]His master replied, "Well done, good and faithful servant! You have been faithful with a few things; I will put you in charge of many things. Come and share your master's happiness!"

In popular culture, "judgment day" is a phrase that most people are familiar with through various forms of art or the media. Often the phrase implies a reckoning at the end of one's life or the end of the world, but—whether at work, school, or home—other days of judgment can be faced along the way. Back in *the parable of the rich barn builder* (Luke 12:13–21), the main character faces a night of reckoning for which he is ill-prepared. The land produces a great yield for the barn builder in the parable, but how does he use this bountiful gift? As we recall, the main character is not your typical villain: Instead of being guilty of stealing or rapacious behavior, he is "careful and conservative" rather than squandering his bounty like the prodigal son.[31] What he does is refuse to share with others or acknowledge God as the ultimate source of his increase, and for most of the parable, the barn builder's only conversation partner is himself. But everything changes that very night when another voice appears in the parable, and the barn builder hears the words, "You fool!"

Here, in *the parable of the talents*, the property owner returns from his trip, and it is time for those who received bags of gold to be held accountable for how they handled their talents. By analogy, their day of judgment has arrived. The barn builder did not adequately prepare for such a day, but two characters in *the parable of the talents* enjoy a quite different fate. Based on the response of the first slave, settling accounts does not seem entirely unexpected, and it actually appears as though he was anticipating this moment. Hence, he comes forward with a sense of purpose, announcing to the master how he "made good and effective use of what

31. Craddock, *Luke*, 228.

had initially been given him."[32] The eagerness of this report stems from the slave's knowledge of his master's character, and as he steps forward he must believe that a warm reception is on the way. This interpretation is backed up by the action of the second slave, who likewise reports how he too creatively went to work with the talents he was given. Both slaves were entirely committed to the master's interests, and both made impressive returns on their investments.

Despite entrusting different amounts of money to his servants, the master gives the same compliment to both investors when hearing about their efforts: Both are commended for their loyalty and trustworthiness, both are promoted to bigger things, and both are invited to share in their master's happiness. The fact that these compliments are identical prompts us to think that the master is less interested in the money and more concerned with matters of the heart. In other words, because "the praise and the reward for both is the same, we may assume that what the master was really concerned about is what they did with what they had, not who made the most money."[33] Furthermore, the reader might be inclined to suspect that the master really doesn't need more money; rather, the master is interested in developing his servants, and he delights to see them flourish and maximize their potential.

On television screens nowadays, the viewer can occasionally glimpse a show that features an alternative history, whether that means Germany winning World War II or the Americans losing the race to land on the moon. Such storylines that present an unrecognizable political or social landscape appeal to some viewers and require them to consider other kinds of plot twists and possible outcomes. One scholar suggests an alternative history for *the parable of the talents* that is worth our attention: "It is too bad that the parable does not tell of an additional slave who invested his capital, failed, and then declared bankruptcy. Would the master have invited him to 'enter his joy'? One hopes so!"[34] There is a challenging question here about how the property owner would have dealt with failure. Or what if the money was distributed to the poor by building a homeless shelter for widows and orphans? Because the master is willing to entrust

32. Donald A. Hagner, *Matthew*, 2 vols., WBC (Dallas: Word, 1993–95), 2:735.

33. Witherington, *Matthew*, 463.

34. Ulrich Luz, *Matthew: A Commentary*, 3 vols., trans. James E. Crouch, Hermeneia (Minneapolis: Fortress, 2001–7), 3:255.

a considerable fortune to his servants, it does not seem that money is the endgame here. If it was, we may have expected the master to micromanage the servants' investment strategies. Overall, the parable presents him as more interested in human resources than in his financial balance sheet and as keen to empower his employees rather than merely hoard his wealth.

Fear and Failure

In our analysis of the master's commendation to the two slaves who multiply their investments, we will notice that a key phrase is repeated: "You have been faithful" (Matt. 25:21, 23). Other translations render the Greek term (πιστός) as "trustworthy," underscoring that the two servants must be full of faith and trust as they go about their master's business. Along with their promotion to now being in charge of "many things," these servants are also invited to "come and share your master's happiness." Details are not provided about the "many things," but those who are reliable can count on getting more responsibility in the other enterprises of the master.[35] Similarly, details about the master's happiness are not elaborated on, but the language of intimacy and rejoicing evokes memories of Abraham's banquet that we noted earlier in our study of Lazarus (Luke 16:22–23).[36] It is gradually starting to look like the talents in this parable represent more than just money. When the master commends the two servants for their trustworthiness with small things, he implies that money is not as valuable as other qualities. Consequently, the idea that disciples of the Lord have a remarkable opportunity to serve their master with all of their gifts and resources appears to be a good reading of this parable. But it remains to be seen how the third slave—who buried the bag of gold—will report on how he used his talent (or not).

The audience has been uncertain about the third slave's motives for burying the talent. Perhaps he is bitter about receiving only a single talent, but, of course, then there is less pressure to perform, even though he was

35. Grant R. Osborne, *Matthew*, ZECNT (Grand Rapids: Zondervan, 2010), 925: "The slave has shown he can be trusted with a great amount of money and deserves to be raised higher and given more responsibility in the business (equivalent to being made a vice president and given a corner office today)."

36. For comments on imagery here that echoes other parables about wedding celebrations, joy-filled worship in the presence of God, and deliverance from captivity and return to the promised land after exile, see Culpepper, *Matthew*, 492–93.

still given a vast sum of money. Is he upset than any profit won't belong to him, or does he doubt his own ability to invest the gold? When he buries his talent, it is the direct opposite of what the first two slaves do, and at this point we wonder if he hid the money from a desire to act safely, or if it was a kind of squandering of an unprecedented opportunity. The first two slaves vibrantly put their talents to work, and like others before them (Joseph comes to mind, as do Moses and David) went on to greater positions of responsibility.[37] However, when the third slave takes the stage and gives his report, the parable takes a much darker turn.

> [24]Then the man who had received one bag of gold came. "Master," he said, "I knew that you are a hard man, harvesting where you have not sown and gathering where you have not scattered seed. [25]So I was afraid and went out and hid your gold in the ground. See, here is what belongs to you."

Over the course of our analysis so far, we have noticed that a central purpose of the parables is to unfold various aspects of God's character through metaphor and analogy. Each of the parables, we might suggest, captures a particular angle or profile of how human beings relate to God and to one another. In general, authority figures in the parables represent some contour of the divine, but there also is a diverse cast of other characters who variously stand for disciples or other seekers.[38] Through the lens of these parables, the reader gets snapshots of life in and around the kingdom of God. In *the parable of the prodigal sons*, the images of the father who longs for the return of the wasteful younger child *and* who tries to reason with the angry older brother both provide some insight in the character of God. Similarly, with *the parable of the talents*, we notice how God entrusts his disciples with immense possibilities and seems excited to discover how

37. On Moses and David taking care of herds and flocks prior to their positions of leadership, see Luz, *Matthew*, 3:252. Joseph was a slave in Potiphar's house (Gen. 39), and although he was imprisoned on false charges, he rose to prominence in the Egyptian government after interpreting Pharaoh's dreams.

38. See the longer discussion of Garwood P. Anderson, "Parables," in Green, Brown, and Perrin, *Dictionary of Jesus and the Gospels*, 2nd ed., 661: "While each parable ought [to] be judged on its own merits, readers can expect authority figures (kings, fathers, judges, etc.) to depict God (if even sometimes problematically) . . . and subordinates (servants, laborers, stewards, children, widows, etc.) to stand for persons or groups and types of persons, not infrequently bifurcated as the good or wise over against the evil or foolish. This is not to allegorize the parable, but rather merely to follow its own conventions with sensitivity to genre and milieu."

they use such gifts. The warm reception of the first two "investors" indicates that the property owner is keen to promote and empower anyone who makes an effort and that he delights in their resourcefulness. But the third investor has a quite different interview with the newly returned master.

Not much has prepared us for the third slave's harsh description of the master. He begins by referring to the master as "hard," a term that is at odds with the openhanded distribution of the bags of gold and the congratulations given to the first two investors. In other contexts this same term is translated as "difficult," "fierce," or "harsh," and so here it is used to graphically depict a kind of person who is rough on the outside with an unmerciful heart on the inside (compare other uses in John 6:60 and James 3:4). Not only is the master cold and unyielding, but the third servant also claims that he takes profits that don't belong to him and exploits the weak ("harvesting where you have not sown and gathering where you have not scattered seed"). These are the reasons, so this character asserts, he hid the talent: He feared the master's negative personality traits. Because the master was such a ruthless dictator, he was left with little choice but to bury his bag of gold.

At this point the reader needs to ask if the third servant's characterization of the master is accurate or instead based on some sort of hypothesis. One scholar argues that such conclusions are not based in reality but rather come from the third servant's harsh imagination: "He fell victim to his own pessimistic conservatism and projected his paranoia onto the master. He responded to the opportunity as he would act if he were the master. He refused to acknowledge the investment as a gracious trust. He saw it only as a dangerous liability."[39] Rather than viewing the bag of gold as a gift to be invested with joyful creativity, the third servant interprets it as an albatross hanging around his neck. Whether he is trying to persuade the master to deal leniently with him is unclear. But his speech reveals that a tyrannical view of the master is used as an excuse for not investing the talent that he was given.

Double or Nothing

The third slave's use of agricultural metaphors—sowing and harvesting—prompts us to return for a moment to *the parable of the sower*, which

39. Douglas D. Webster, *The Parables: Jesus's Friendly Subversive Speech* (Grand Rapids: Kregel Academic, 2021), 223.

might be helpful. As we recall, that parable in Mark 4 is about the message of the good news as it scattered into various kinds of soil, and the soil represents various aspects of the human heart. At a key moment in the parable, some of the seed falls among thorns, and this suffocates the seed. When Jesus later explains the parable, we discover that the seed sown among thorns represents those who hear the word "but the cares of the world, and the lure of wealth, and the desire for other things come in and choke the word, and it yields nothing" (Mark 4:19 NRSV). An obvious implication is that sometimes our anxieties, misplaced desires, or fears can inhibit growth in the kingdom. This seems to be the case with the third slave. Whatever the cause, his incorrect beliefs about the master prompt his irresponsible use of the talent entrusted to him. How should the third slave's remarks be interpreted? The plot twist in this parable is that his words are about to be turned back against him, and he will be condemned on the basis of his own testimony as his hypocrisy is exposed.

> [26]His master replied, "You wicked, lazy servant! So you knew that I harvest where I have not sown and gather where I have not scattered seed? [27]Well then, you should have put my money on deposit with the bankers, so that when I returned I would have received it back with interest."

Statistically, almost 50 percent of this parable revolves around the single-talent slave: his act of hiding, the long justification of his conduct that is based on his view of the master, the master's response, and the conclusion of the story.[40] The third slave projected his own deficient view of the master, but now the master responds by describing exactly who this third slave is. The use of the terms "wicked" and "lazy" mutually indicate that his projection of the master's character is dangerous, so he refuses to carry out his obligation with the bag of gold. Moreover, his own testimony is inconsistently hypocritical because if he thinks the master so harsh, why does he not even do the bare minimum of putting the money in a savings account? Even low interest rates are better than nothing. In stunning contrast are the efforts of the first two slaves, who gladly take risks because they believe that bags of gold are for investing, not hiding. Those two get spectacular promotions, but this third slave gets a demotion. With echoes

40. Culpepper, *Matthew*, 493.

of King David and the ewe lamb, the third slave has effectively pronounced his own sentence, as the master declares:

> [28]So take the bag of gold from him and give it to the one who has ten bags. [29]For whoever has will be given more, and they will have an abundance. Whoever does not have, even what they have will be taken from them. [30]And throw that worthless servant outside, into the darkness, where there will be weeping and gnashing of teeth.

Periodically there are popular movies that provide a warning about reckless conduct, whether in the realm of risky relationships, substance abuse, illegal dealings, or unwise stewardship. These kinds of stories are often referred to as "cautionary tales," and they serve to warn an audience about dangerous pitfalls that should be avoided. The disturbing ending of this parable indicates that it can be understood as a cautionary tale for disciples but that it ultimately offers a better way to respond to the Lord's grace. The warning revolves around wasted opportunity. The third slave not only squanders a chance to multiply his talent and look after his master's interests but also justifies his inaction with a twisted account of the master's character. Disciples evidently can be tempted to rationalize their actions with false descriptions of God. The consequence for the third slave is that he has to remain outside—that is, he has forfeited his opportunity to enter the "house" of the master. "Weeping" and "gnashing of teeth" are pictures of regret and disappointment: The third slave cared little about the master's interests, and therefore he is ineligible to join the celebration.[41]

The intense ending of this parable indicates the earnestness that ought to mark how disciples respond to the Lord's gifts. This parable overall commends an approach of freedom, instead of paralysis or fear of God's punishment, and encourages the followers of Jesus to go forth with joy-filled enterprise and use their gifts effectively. When they do, they can expect a positive divine response as well as heightened responsibility: "For those who live in the confidence that God is trustworthy and generous, they find more and more of that generosity; but for those who run and hide under the bed from a bad, mean, and scolding God, they condemn

41. For one scholar's view, see Barbara E. Reid, "Violent Endings in Matthew's Parables and Christian Nonviolence," *CBQ* 66 (2004): 237–55.

themselves to a life spent under the bed alone, quivering in needless fear."[42] Discipleship is not a spectator sport but, rather, should be approached like an entrepreneur who looks for situations that are favorable. The best way to avoid spiritual bankruptcy, it would appear, is to make a long series of wise investments in the kingdom of God, remembering that in *this* economy, risk is always rewarded.

42. Long, *Matthew*, 283.

Conclusion

Debtor's Prison

WE RECALL THAT back in 2 Kings 4 there is a scene with a widow in distress. In the midst of her desperate plight, she cries out to Elisha the prophet for help: "Your servant my husband died, and you know that your servant feared the Lord, but the creditor is coming to take my two boys for himself as slaves!" (v. 1). She is rescued from this crisis when the prophet delivers a miraculous flow of oil that she can sell to her neighbors, and this intervention prevents her sons from being handed over to the creditor. Nevertheless, this scene underscores the seriousness of debt and credit problems, and the consequences of not being able to pay one's creditor. Slavery often awaits those in dire financial straits, and the impoverished are particularly vulnerable.

Our final parable features a situation where *debt* is a key issue. In this short conclusion we will explore an episode where the central character accumulates an unbelievable amount of debt and then has to face the king to give an account of his conduct. There are several interesting elements in *the parable of the unmerciful servant* found in Matthew 18:21–35, including an exotic setting in a foreign court with royalty and gargantuan sums of money. In essence, the parable is about two debtors, each of whom has a vastly different experience with a creditor. Woven throughout the parable is a tapestry of forgiveness, which emerges as the main theme of the parable. As we might expect, there is a plot twist in this parable. But in this case, it reveals a dark side of our main character, and at the climax of the story, his brooding malevolence is unmasked. Altogether, this concluding parable in our study points not only to the need for mercy but also to the obligation to extend mercy to others.

Rolling a Seven

Matthew 18 begins with the disciples as a group coming to Jesus and asking about who is the greatest in the kingdom of heaven. As an illustration, Jesus brings a child into their midst and declares firmly: "Unless you change and become like little children, you will never enter the kingdom of heaven" (18:3). This continues a lengthy exchange about the values of the kingdom versus the typical values of the world and indicates how the disciples need to rewire their thinking to be in tune with this new economy. Near the midpoint of the chapter, another question is posed to Jesus, this time by Peter, and it will soon prompt a parable in response.

> 21Then Peter came to Jesus and asked, "Lord, how many times shall I forgive my brother or sister who sins against me? Up to seven times?"
> 22Jesus answered, "I tell you, not seven times, but seventy-seven times."

Arguably the highest profile member of the twelve disciples, Peter is often the one who speaks on behalf of the whole group. Here he raises the topic of forgiveness and, more specifically, is asking Jesus how many times he should forgive a fellow disciple who sins against him. The audience is not sure whether Peter asks this question in order to showcase his own willingness to be a person of forgiveness, but his reference to "seven times" implies that he would be an exemplary disciple indeed. But if Peter is expecting a compliment from his master, he is disappointed because he is instead given the much loftier goal of exponentially more forgiveness.

Numerical formulas including the numbers seventy and seven appear earlier in biblical narratives. In Genesis 4:24 a character named Lamech boasts to his wives about murdering a young man and alludes to the earlier murder by Cain: "If Cain's revenge is sevenfold, then Lamech's is seventy-sevenfold" (ESV).[1] Lamech uses poetic speech, but without a doubt he is

1. Sylvia C. Keesmaat discusses the biblical significance of the number seven in terms of "sabbath" and the history of God's people: "An emphasis on 'seventy times seven,' therefore, would evoke the sabbatical forgiveness of Israel's past" ("Strange Neighbors and Risky Care [Matt.

bragging about his brutality. At this early point in Genesis, patterns are set in motion that are repeated throughout the following story, and Lamech's words foreshadow the grim cycle of violence to come in Genesis and beyond. It is likely that Jesus alludes to this ancient episode of viciousness in order to subvert it and to demonstrate how the kingdom of God can transform every approach to daily life. But how on earth can someone forgive instead of plotting revenge for harm done to them?[2] Where can forgiveness come from? The parable that now follows is designed not only to answer Peter's question but also to draw attention to the quite different mode of calculation used in the economy of grace.

Accounts Payable

"The simplest meaning of Jesus' seventy-seven," notes one commentator, "is 'never give up on anyone.'"[3] Still, replacing the desire for revenge with an attitude of openhanded forgiveness—especially in the case of grievous offense—sounds much easier in principle than in actual practice. Surely this is the reason why Jesus illustrates the radical overhaul brought in by the kingdom of God by means of a parable, a dramatic example of canceling a debt (and the lack thereof) that unfolds a mind-blowing image of what divine forgiveness really feels like. Keeping in mind that the parable in Matthew 18 stems from Peter's question, we will return to the subject of Peter at the end, as he is someone who will certainly need forgiveness before the larger story is over.

> [23]Therefore, the kingdom of heaven is like a king who wanted to settle accounts with his servants. [24]As he began the settlement, a man who owed him ten thousand bags of gold was brought to him. [25]Since he was not able to pay, the master ordered that he and his wife and his children and all that he had be sold to repay the debt.

18:21–35; Luke 14:7–14; Luke 10:25–37]," in R. Longenecker, *Challenge of Jesus' Parables*, 266). See also Richard B. Hays, *Echoes of Scripture in the Gospels* (Waco: Baylor University Press, 2016), 156: "'Seventy times seven' (or 'seventy-seven times'—whichever it is) should certainly be heard as an echoic reversal of the chest-thumping boast of Lamech."

2. On the community dimension of forgiveness and other references in Matthew, see Margaret Davies, *Matthew* (Sheffield: JSOT Press, 1993), 129.

3. Frederick Dale Bruner, *Matthew: A Commentary*, rev. ed., 2 vols. (Grand Rapids: Eerdmans, 2004), 2:579, quoting the sixteenth-century work of John Calvin.

Very little description is given about this king—the first figure mentioned in the parable—other than his orders to call his servants to provide an account of their commercial activities. In the case of the shrewd manager, the Oil Baron boss calls him to account because he has heard rumors of misconduct. In *the parable of the talents*, the property owner calls his slaves to give reports on how they used their bags of gold after he returns from a long journey. Whether this king has returned from a trip or heard rumors, he likewise summons his servants for interviews. We noted previously that ten talents is an enormous sum of money, but that amount is to be eclipsed here in this parable. Moreover, if we thought that seventy times seven was a large number, it too will be exceeded.

On several occasions in the Bible, big money is part of the story. For example, King David donates three thousand talents of gold and seven thousand talents of silver toward the construction of the Jerusalem temple in 1 Chronicles 29:3–4. More maliciously, Haman the Agagite pledges ten thousand talents of silver if King Xerxes is willing to destroy a "certain people group" in Esther 3:9. But these amounts appear to be surpassed by the *myriad* talents owed to the king by the servant in this parable. The term is usually translated as "ten thousand" and points to an astronomically high number. The servant is not given much description either, but the trillion-dollar question is: How does the servant possibly waste this amount of money?

Scholars have speculated that the servant must be a highly placed royal official or a government minister responsible for tax revenues and the king's treasury.[4] Otherwise, how would he have access to such exorbitant amounts of ready cash? In the absence of any details, the audience has to be flabbergasted by this spending spree. The shrewd manager squandered the Oil Baron's property, and the younger son dissipated his father's inheritance, but the volume of money here sets a new record for wastefulness in our financial parables. Extreme profligacy on this scale cannot be tolerated by the king, we assume, hence the command that the servant and his family "be sold." With echoes of 2 Kings 4 and the widow's desperation, it appears that the entire family is bound for the auction block as slaves. Selling the servant (along with his wife and children) as slaves would barely recoup even a small portion of the king's losses, so this action should

4. Richard T. France, *The Gospel of Matthew*, TNTC (Grand Rapids: Eerdmans, 2007), 636.

probably be interpreted as a consequence of the king's disappointment or a warning to others.[5] The servant gets what he deserves, and his family is also forced to pay the price.

Limitless

Business theorists might argue that the most infamous cases of fraud—whether in a financial company, a bank, an energy corporation, or the entertainment industry—usually have an unscrupulous rogue at the center. However, this parable gives no indication about how the servant squanders so much money; it only stresses the enormity of his debt. Most of us must have some awareness of our bank balance, so we must wonder if this servant was worried about his mounting debt. Did he not expect to be called before the king, his "creditor"? Regardless, after the king sentences him to be sold into slavery, the debt-ridden servant opts to cry out for mercy. Similarly, the prodigal son, as he was feeding the pigs and starving to death, came to his senses and decided to cast himself on his father's kindness. Whether the servant in this parable has reason to think that the king will show pity is unknown, but at this point he has no other option.

> 26At this the servant fell on his knees before him. "Be patient with me," he begged, "and I will pay back everything." 27The servant's master took pity on him, canceled the debt and let him go.

The posture of falling down and prostrating oneself is also seen in Matthew 2:11, when the Magi arrive in Bethlehem and fall down in worship in the presence of the child Jesus. Similarly, in Matthew 8:1–3 a leprous person bows down before Jesus and asks for healing: "'Lord, if you choose, you can make me clean.' He stretched out his hand and touched him, saying, 'I do choose. Be made clean!' Immediately his leprosy was cleansed" (NRSV). Similarly, when the servant in this parable falls down before the king, he signals his complete deference to the king's authority and his acknowledgment of dependence on the king. These actions are completely understandable, but the servant then follows up by asking

5. W. D. Davies and Dale C. Allison Jr., *A Critical and Exegetical Commentary on the Gospel According to St. Matthew*, vol. 2, *8–18*, ICC (Edinburgh: T&T Clark, 1991), 799.

the king for patience, as he promises to pay back *everything*.[6] Really? In today's currency the servant owes untold billions of dollars. It is scarcely possible that he could pay off even a portion of the debt. Perhaps he is just being polite, but his request for patience while he works to repay the king is utterly absurd.

As ridiculous as the servant's proposal sounds, the king's reaction is even more outlandish: He releases the servant (presumably from some sort of prison or place of confinement as he waits to be sold) and forgives the debt! The key term—one we have seen previously in our study—is the response of pity, being moved with compassion. When the Samaritan sees the wounded victim at the side of the road, and when the father catches a glimpse of his rebellious younger son, they are both moved with compassion (σπλαγχνίζομαι), the exact same word used for the king in response to his fortune-wasting servant. By means of this reaction, the audience is able to access the heart of the parable: We are given a picture of divine grace and how it is extended to human beings. Note that in the story, the guilty servant asks the king for patience but does not get what he asks for. Instead, he receives total forgiveness of his debt, exponentially more than he ever could have imagined. As one commentator writes, the servant is someone who "owed the king more money than was even in circulation in the whole country at the time! This is yet another example of dramatic hyperbole, and it makes a Kingdom point—the sin debt we owe God is unrepayable since it is so enormous."[7]

Pay It Forward?

It might further be suggested that in this parable *sin* is pictured as a debt. What does that mean? Through the parable we realize that human beings have accumulated a mountain of debt against God, probably through some combination of ingratitude, squandering divine gifts, cruelty to one another, and living in a manner that's oblivious to God's goodness as creator and worthiness to be worshiped. Such debt is crippling, and how can it be paid?[8] The straightforward reality is that it cannot. However, despite our

6. Cf. Ulrich Luz, *Matthew: A Commentary*, 3 vols., trans. James E. Crouch, Hermeneia (Minneapolis: Fortress, 2001–7), 2:472.

7. Ben Witherington III, *Matthew* (Macon, GA: Smyth & Helwys, 2006), 353–54.

8. For an insightful discussion of this imagery, see Gary A. Anderson, *Sin: A History* (New Haven: Yale University Press, 2009).

massive amount of sin, God seems willing forgive those who ask, which is demonstrated in this parable when the king cancels the debt (or more precisely, absorbs the loss and pays the bill on behalf of the debtor).

On the one hand, this is probably not the most comfortable truth for our ears: "The New Testament message works hard to give us an assessment of the human condition that we don't usually hear; outside the New Testament we are rarely reported as being anywhere near as problematic as 'zillions.' The gospel tells human beings the truth about themselves."[9] But on the other hand, the king is moved with compassion and extends total forgiveness toward the undeserving sinner who asks for mercy. Receiving this divine gift of mercy then opens the door to a completely new way to live. When the audience hears this parable alongside other parables, they should now grasp that our capacity to forgive the offenses of other people flows from the divine forgiveness that has been extended to each of us. Earlier in Matthew's Gospel is the famous "Lord's Prayer." A central line in that prayer is frequently translated as "forgive us our debts, as we also have forgiven our debtors" (Matt. 6:12).[10] It might be suggested that this parable illustrates and enhances that previous teaching.

Flashing back for a moment to *the parable of the good Samaritan* who has pity on the half dead victim of robbers. We recall that the context of this parable is a dialogue between Jesus and a lawyer who asks some barbed questions, such as, "Who is my neighbor?" (Luke 10:29). After the parable, Jesus in turn asks the lawyer, "Which of these three do you think was a neighbor to the man?" When the lawyer answers, "The one who had mercy on him," Jesus then challenges him to "go and do likewise" (10:36–37). At the conclusion of *the parable of the good Samaritan*, Jesus invites the lawyer—and all other hearers by implication—to respond accordingly. A similar dynamic occurs in the parable in Matthew 18, and it is embedded within the story itself: Readers might expect that the servant who has been forgiven the massive debt will live differently in light of his forgiveness. Indeed, since an unpayable debt has just been canceled by royal decree, it is reasonable to think that the servant should experience a sense of relief and an overwhelming gratitude that results in seeing the world in a fresh way. The audience doesn't know much about this servant other than that

9. Bruner, *Matthew*, 2:267.

10. On the larger structure, see James N. Neumann, "Thy Will Be Done: Jesus's Passion in the Lord's Prayer," *JBL* 138 (2019): 161–82.

he racks up an exponential credit card bill, but against all odds, the loss is absorbed by the king. In the next scenes of the parable, however, more will be learned about the servant, and none of it is pleasant.

> [28]"But when that servant went out, he found one of his fellow servants who owed him a hundred silver coins. He grabbed him and began to choke him. "Pay back what you owe me!" he demanded. [29]His fellow servant fell to his knees and begged him, "Be patient with me, and I will pay it back." [30]But he refused. Instead, he went off and had the man thrown into prison until he could pay the debt. [31]When the other servants saw what had happened, they were outraged and went and told their master everything that had happened.

"Antiheroes" have been gradually trending of late in novels and the cinema; these are main characters who lack the traditional qualities, such as courage, sacrifice, and a moral compass, that typically identify a hero.[11] Despite possessing a certain ambiguity or self-interest, the antihero in some stories is actually someone who contributes to an overall redemptive storyline. But at the pivotal moment in this parable, the main character emerges as much less of an antihero and much more of an outright villain. There is no explicit indication of a time frame, but maybe quite soon after the servant's debt relief he finds a fellow servant who owes him money. The relative amount of the debt should be clarified: The NIV translates the amount as "a hundred silver coins," and the margin note of some translations explains that this was "just a few dollars." But in fact *a hundred silver coins* (one hundred denarii) is rather more than a few dollars. We recall that a denarius is a day's wage, so one hundred denarii is closer to four months of wages, or in our world, the price of a compact car (give or take). While this is considerable value, it is only a mere fraction of what the servant himself had just been forgiven. He has just been let off the hook and lavished with grace, not to mention that his family has been released from a grim fate. Sure, the colleague owes him four months of wages, but the parable is gradually unfolding an alternative perspective on our debts: "In the light of an immense forgiveness a human being should be able to put up with almost anything," because

11. E.g., Margrethe Bruun Vaage, *The Antihero in American Television* (New York: Routledge, 2016).

our "guilt before God is unendingly greater than any other person's guilt can be before us."[12]

After being forgiven, the servant "went out" and "found" his colleague. It is slightly unclear if we are dealing with a random encounter here. Given that the other guy owes him money, it is quite conceivable that the king's servant is calling in the loan: Now that he's out of prison, he needs something to live on (having recently burned through gazillions in cash). Rather than a chance meeting, then, it could be that the servant seeks out his debtor in order to collect the sum, even though he's just had a sky-high debt canceled by the king. Furthermore, in stunning contrast to the king's mercy, this servant instantly opts for physical violence, grabbing his colleague by the throat and demanding immediate payment. Somehow the debtor manages to speak despite being throttled and begs for mercy using language that is nearly identical to what the servant used before the king: a plea for patience and a promise of repayment. Within the larger biblical tradition, this same idea of patience is often used for God's "long-suffering" toward the people of Israel.[13] Exactly what God shows toward Israel—and what the king shows toward the debt-ridden servant—is now withheld from the colleague who owes a very small amount of money in comparison.

The mirrored language of patience and the promise of repayment really should have reminded the servant how much he had so recently been forgiven. Yet he does not listen. Moments earlier he fell to the ground before the king, but now he ignores the pleas of his colleague, who falls to the ground before him. The servant threw himself on the king's mercy, but now he throws his fellow servant into the equivalent of debtor's prison and does not respond to the plea for mercy. As far as scholars can tell, a person couldn't have earned money in debtor's prison, so the debtor would be reliant on somebody else paying the debt on his behalf.[14] The servant's viciousness is an inverted parody of his own experience of unmerited royal favor, and this causes deep distress among all who witness such behavior. The other colleagues have no doubt followed the story of his soaring debt

12. Bruner, *Matthew*, 2:269, quoting Julius Schniewind, *Das Evangelium nach Matthäus* (1935; repr., Göttingen: Vandenhoeck & Ruprecht, 1962), 202.

13. Grant R. Osborne, *Matthew*, ZECNT (Grand Rapids: Zondervan, 2010), 695.

14. Craig L. Blomberg, *Interpreting the Parables*, 2nd ed. (Downers Grove, IL: InterVarsity, 2012), 318.

and radical forgiveness, and upon seeing his treatment of the debtor, they are "greatly distressed" (NRSV). From this distress, they are motivated to make a report to the king. Altogether, it would have been better if the story concluded earlier, on the happy note of astonishing grace. But the final scenes continue this dark turn, with the king making another appearance as the parable moves to a conclusion.

Measure for Measure

Returning briefly to the party we attended in Luke 7 at the house of Simon the Pharisee, through the short parable that occurs around the dinner table we discovered that forgiveness should evoke a certain response of gratitude. While the reader doesn't know much about the woman or any details of her scandalous past, it is clear that she risks public embarrassment by weeping and anointing the feet of Jesus with expensive perfume. Simon has doubts about Jesus—and is perhaps concerned for his own reputation as well—but by means of *the parable of the moneylender* in Luke 7:41–42, Jesus underscores that the more someone is forgiven, the greater their sense of thankfulness should be: "The brief parable of the two debtors ensnares Simon in a recognition of the difference between his behavior toward Jesus and that of the woman. Her behavior is that of a person who has been forgiven."[15] The dinner host is challenged to rethink the whole matter of debt relief and the implications for daily life.

In our parable in Matthew 18:23–35, the fellow servants must have been expecting that the guilty servant would live differently in light of his incalculable forgiveness. Having seen how the man who owed the money was throttled and thrown into debtor's prison—forced now to wait for someone else to pay his debt—the colleagues are filled with distress and have little choice but to report this outrage to the same king who earlier showed such outrageous mercy. These servants must have thought that

15. Fred B. Craddock, *Luke*, Interpretation (Louisville: John Knox, 1990), 148. Note also the reminder to assess the Pharisees in a fair way: "Furthermore, for Jesus to eat with tax collectors and sinners and refuse table fellowship with Pharisees would have made him as guilty of reverse prejudice as some of us who discover in our zeal to right wrongs we develop prejudices against the prejudiced, a condition that places us in the camp of those we charge with standing in the way of God's reign on earth" (147). David B. Gowler strongly emphasizes that his study is about "the *Lukan* Pharisees, not the *historical* Pharisees." Gowler, "'At His Gate Lay a Poor Man': A Dialogic Reading of Luke 16:19–31," *PRSt* 32 (2005): 252.

such forgiveness would prompt a deep appreciation and would guide the former debtor into a radically new lifestyle. But that did not happen, so once more the guilty servant hears the words of the king:

> [32]Then the master called the servant in. "You wicked servant," he said, "I canceled all that debt of yours because you begged me to. [33]Shouldn't you have had mercy on your fellow servant just as I had on you?" [34]In anger his master handed him over to the jailers to be tortured, until he should pay back all he owed. [35]This is how my heavenly Father will treat each of you unless you forgive your brother or sister from your heart.

Up to this point in the parable, the audience has not actually heard the voice of the king. Earlier in verse 24 the king summoned his servants to give accounts of their actions, and it is revealed that one rogue servant squandered ten thousand bags of gold. The king orders that the servant and his family be sold as slaves, but when the guilty servant cries out for patience, royal compassion is extended and the debt is canceled. The servant isn't reprimanded or publicly shamed, and there are no labels attached (that is, he's not called wicked or anything else). Instead of a plan for repayment of debt or a series of conditions, the king simply extends an olive branch after this servant has wasted a fortune.

But now it has been reported to him that the guilty servant strangles his colleague and throws him into prison, and so the king refers to this scoundrel as a "wicked" servant. Other translations render the same term as "evil," as in the Lord's Prayer: "Lead us not into temptation, but deliver us from evil" (Matt. 6:13 ESV). The king reminds this servant how his infinite debt was canceled when he asked for mercy, and then he asks if he shouldn't have shown mercy as a result. As it stands, the king was more than "willing to forgive a debt the slave could never have paid, but will not forgive his refusal of an act of generosity which was within his power."[16] The king must have expected that his pardoned servant would be amazed by the grace he received and is understandably shocked when he hears the report of the entitled and arrogant treatment of this fellow servant.

Is it an accident that the king orders that the servant be thrown into prison? Presumably the jailers who inflict the torture are not overly inclined

16. France, *Matthew*, 639.

to show compassion.[17] On the previous occasion, the king ordered the servant and his family to be sold (as slaves). It would appear that the king opts for a measure-for-measure punishment this time: The servant threw his colleague into prison, and now he ends up in a similar place. Having been handed over to the jailers until he has paid back all he owes, this servant needs someone to step up and pay the debt on his behalf, but there is little chance that anyone he knows has this kind of money, and most would be hesitant to rush to the aid of someone who has annoyed the king twice.[18] Given this indefinite sentence, the audience is left to wonder if he'll ever get out. Presumably, his only hope for release is to beg the king for mercy once more.

Theater of Redemption

Lest the audience's ire be solely directed at the guilty servant, Jesus quickly turns the matter into a more direct application for all who hear the parable, with a caution about similar consequences for "each of you unless you forgive your brother or sister from your heart" (Matt. 18:35). Not only is this an acute challenge for every listener in general, but Jesus's summary statement on forgiveness brings us back to Peter specifically. As we noticed, the parable is unfurled in response to Peter's question about what to do when people let us down or, worse, utterly betray us. Rather than simply giving a number of times that we should forgive others, Jesus narrates this parable of an unmerciful servant to illustrate the source of a genuine attitude of mercy and debt cancellation.

Peter is a prominent character in all four Gospels, and a few scenes in the Gospel of John help us gain a broader perspective on how Peter occupies an important position within the landscape of forgiveness. From the outset it should be emphasized that Peter does not lack enthusiasm.[19]

17. Witherington, *Matthew*, 354.

18. Craig S. Keener, *A Commentary on the Gospel of Matthew* (Grand Rapids: Eerdmans, 1999), 461: "Yet who would be so politically naive as to come to the rescue of one who had obviously fallen from the king's favor? The magnitude of the debt was simply unpayable by any means, and the man would *never* escape the torturers."

19. For biographical discussions, see Martin Hengel, *Saint Peter: The Underestimated Apostle*, trans. Thomas H. Trapp (Grand Rapids: Eerdmans, 2010); and Markus Bockmuehl, *Simon Peter in Scripture and Memory: The New Testament Apostle in the Early Church* (Grand Rapids: Baker Academic, 2012).

In John 13:37–39, for instance, he declares to Jesus that he's willing to lay down his life for him; that is, he is willing to die if necessary. But the response to this bold declaration needs to be kept in mind: "Then Jesus answered, 'Will you really lay down your life for me? Very truly I tell you, before the rooster crows, you will disown me three times!'" The reader is unsure about Peter's reaction, but a short time later a mob dispatched by the authorities—replete with soldiers and led by Judas Iscariot—come to arrest Jesus in John 18. Peter soon draws his sword and starts swinging (vv. 10–11), but Jesus commands him to put his weapon away.[20] Yet amid this aggression, the earlier words about Peter's denial linger in the reader's ear. After Jesus is arrested and led to the chambers of the high priest for interrogation, the scene focuses on Peter and a colleague on this dark night:

> [15]Simon Peter followed Jesus, and so did another disciple. Since that disciple was known to the high priest, he entered with Jesus into the courtyard of the high priest, [16]but Peter stood outside at the door. So the other disciple, who was known to the high priest, went out and spoke to the servant girl who kept watch at the door, and brought Peter in. [17]The servant girl at the door said to Peter, "You also are not one of this man's disciples, are you?" He said, "I am not." [18]Now the servants and officers had made a charcoal fire, because it was cold, and they were standing and warming themselves. Peter also was with them, standing and warming himself. (ESV)

The key word here is "charcoal fire," a term that occurs only one other place in the entire New Testament, as we will soon discover. Meanwhile, after Jesus is questioned, the scene switches back to Peter outside in the courtyard, as he remains near that same charcoal fire. In verse 25 those standing near him ask him again if he is a disciple, and for the second time Peter denies it. Right afterward, there is a further inquiry followed by Peter's final declaration in verses 26–27:

> [26]One of the high priest's servants, a relative of the man whose ear Peter had cut off, challenged him, "Didn't I see you with him in the garden?" [27]Again Peter denied it, and at that moment a rooster began to crow.

20. Note the study of Michael Labahn, "Simon Peter: An Ambiguous Character and His Narrative Career," in *Character Studies in the Fourth Gospel: Narrative Approaches to Seventy Figures in John*, ed. Steven A. Hunt, D. Francis Tolmie, and Ruben Zimmermann (Grand Rapids: Eerdmans, 2016), 151–67.

To emphasize, all four of the Gospels include the account of Peter's threefold denial, each with its own unique angle.[21] For example, in Matthew 26:75 Peter remembers the words that Jesus spoke the moment he hears the rooster crow. Matthew then tells us that Peter goes out and weeps bitterly, perhaps stressing the sense of isolation in the aftermath of betrayal.

But the Gospel of John records no reaction from Peter, and so the reader is left to ponder Peter's response in silence. The lack of any reaction, however, does provide a transition to the next events in the story, which take place after the resurrection of Jesus. Of course, the reader is aware that Jesus rises on the third day after his crucifixion, but the disciples don't seem to perceive the full impact of the empty tomb at this point, despite Jesus's several post-resurrection appearances. At the beginning of John 21, Peter announces that he is going fishing, though whether he is prompted by despair or some other reason is not stated. Several other disciples join him. It is a fruitless night, and they catch nothing, but just as dawn is breaking a mysterious stranger on the beach asks them whether they've caught anything. Hearing their negative reply, the visitor instructs them: "Throw your net on the right side of the boat and you will find some" (John 21:6). They do so and are "unable to haul the net in because of the large number of fish." In due course they recognize the Lord Jesus, who has prepared a morning meal on the beach:

> [9]When they got out on land, they saw a charcoal fire in place, with fish laid out on it, and bread. [10]Jesus said to them, "Bring some of the fish that you have just caught." [11]So Simon Peter went aboard and hauled the net ashore, full of large fish, 153 of them. And although there were so many, the net was not torn. [12]Jesus said to them, "Come and have breakfast." (ESV)

After breakfast, Jesus and Peter have a special conversation, and most interpreters note the threefold restoration that takes place: Just as Peter denies Jesus three times, so he is restored three times in this conversation, with Jesus also encouraging him to go and "feed my sheep," pointing to Peter's leadership in the emerging Christian community. The conversation takes place with the embers of the charcoal fire in the background, evoking

21. Cf. Robert H. Gundry, *Matthew: A Commentary on His Literary and Theological Art* (Grand Rapids: Eerdmans, 1982), 551.

an ambiance of forgiveness for the earlier denials.[22] In Matthew 18 we just studied a parable that describes a king who cancels an exorbitant debt, and now with Peter's failures in the Gospel of John, the reader witnesses astonishing forgiveness in action. In John's story there is a multidimensional picture of restoration and empowerment, and when Peter is called to "feed the flock," this no doubt includes encouraging the followers of Jesus to be agents of forgiveness in a debt-ridden world. Presumably, every listener is likewise invited to experience a similar kind of reconciliation and move forward to a quite different kind of future.

On this note of debts and their cancellation, we draw our study to close, while inviting the reader to continue to ponder these and the rest of the parables in the Gospels. The parables are an accessible point of entry to the world of the New Testament, and the goal of this short book has been to provide some exposure to these compact and quite captivating stories of Jesus. The reader can continue analyzing the parables while also considering these anecdotes within the context of the various Gospels and the rest of the biblical writings. In fact, reading the parables in light of the whole biblical story provides further insight into the drama of redemption that unfolds. Fittingly for us, "redemption" itself is a financial term with an expansive use in the Bible. It is used to describe God's work to rescue the Israelites from Egyptian slavery and also to depict the reconnection of humanity as part of an inclusive divine community. Reading the parables absorbs us in the larger biblical drama and reminds us to keep an eye out for treasure hidden in a field.

22. Markus Bockmuehl, *The Remembered Peter in Ancient Reception and Modern Debate*, WUNT 262 (Tübingen: Mohr Siebeck, 2010), 203: "This of course has long been a favourite topic of preachers and exegetes. And the link between the two scenes seems strikingly underscored even by the intriguing detail that the Greek word ἀνθρακιά used for the warming coal fire in high priest's courtyard (18.18) recurs only once more in the entire Old or New Testaments—namely to denote Jesus' coal fire by the sea of Galilee (21.9). Having thrice denied and thrice 'turned' from that denial, Peter is ready to share his master's task and his master's fate."

Abbreviations

General

AT	author translation	e.g.	*exempli gratia*, for example
BCE	before the Common Era	esp.	especially
CE	Common Era	v.	verse
cf.	*confer*, compare	vv.	verses

Bible Versions

ESV	English Standard Version
NIV	New International Version
NRSV	New Revised Standard Version

Secondary Sources

AB	Anchor Bible
ABD	*Anchor Bible Dictionary*. Edited by David Noel Freedman. 6 vols. New York: Doubleday, 1992
AGJU	Arbeiten zur Geschichte des antiken Judentums und des Urchristentums
ASBT	Acadia Studies in Bible and Theology
AYBRL	Anchor Yale Bible Reference Library
BBR	*Bulletin for Biblical Research*
BECNT	Baker Exegetical Commentary on the New Testament
BibInt	*Biblical Interpretation*
BIS	Biblical Interpretation Series
BR	*Biblical Research*
BRLJ	Brill Reference Library of Judaism
BTB	*Biblical Theology Bulletin*
BTCB	Brazos Theological Commentary on the Bible
BZNW	Beihefte zur Zeitschrift für die neutestamentliche Wissenschaft
CBQ	*Catholic Biblical Quarterly*
CBQMS	Catholic Biblical Quarterly Monograph Series
ECC	Eerdmans Critical Commentary

ECL Early Christianity and Its Literature
EDB *Eerdmans Dictionary of the Bible*. Edited by David Noel Freedman. Grand Rapids: Eerdmans, 2000
HBT *Horizons in Biblical Theology*
ICC International Critical Commentary
Int *Interpretation*
JBL *Journal of Biblical Literature*
JCPS Jewish and Christian Perspectives Series
JETS *Journal of the Evangelical Theological Society*
JSHJ *Journal for the Study of the Historical Jesus*
JSNT *Journal for the Study of the New Testament*
JSNTSup Journal for the Study of the New Testament Supplement Series
JSOTSup Journal for the Study of the Old Testament Supplement Series
JTI *Journal of Theological Interpretation*
LNTS Library of New Testament Studies
SNTSMS Society for New Testament Studies Monograph Series
NIB *The New Interpreter's Bible*. Edited by Leander E. Keck. 12 vols. Nashville, Abingdon, 1994–2004
NICNT New International Commentary on the New Testament
NICOT New International Commentary on the Old Testament
NIGTC New International Greek Testament Commentary
NovT *Novum Testamentum*
NovTSup Supplements to *Novum Testamentum*
NTL New Testament Library
NTS *New Testament Studies*
OECS Oxford Early Christian Studies
OTT Old Testament Theology
PNTC Pillar New Testament Commentary
PRSt *Perspectives in Religious Studies*
ResQ *Restoration Quarterly*
RevExp *Review & Expositor*
TNTC Tyndale New Testament Commentaries
TynBul *Tyndale Bulletin*
VT *Vetus Testamentum*
WBBC Wiley Blackwell Bible Commentaries
WBC Word Biblical Commentary
WUNT Wissenschaftliche Untersuchungen zum Neuen Testament
ZECNT Zondervan Exegetical Commentary on the New Testament

Bibliography

Allen, O. Wesley, Jr. *Matthew*. Minneapolis: Fortress, 2013.

Allison, Dale C., Jr. "Matthew." In *The Oxford Bible Commentary*, edited by John Barton and John Muddiman, 844–86. Oxford: Oxford University Press, 2001.

Alter, Robert. *The Five Books of Moses: A Translation with Commentary*. New York: Norton, 2008.

Anderson, Garwood P. "Parables." In Green, Brown, and Perrin, *Dictionary of Jesus and the Gospels*, 2nd ed., 651–63.

Anderson, Gary A. *Sin: A History*. New Haven: Yale University Press, 2009.

Anselmo, Anna, ed. *Twentieth-Century Poets: A Selection with Notes*. Milan: EduCatt, 2011.

Baasland, Ernst. *Parables and Rhetoric in the Sermon on the Mount: New Approaches to a Classical Text*. WUNT 351. Tübingen: Mohr Siebeck, 2015.

Bailey, Kenneth E. *Jacob and the Prodigal: How Jesus Retold Israel's Story*. Downers Grove, IL: InterVarsity, 2003.

———. *Poet and Peasant: A Literary-Cultural Approach to the Parables in Luke*. Grand Rapids: Eerdmans, 1976.

Baker, Peter. "The Prodigal Returns? Karl Barth's Christological Interpretation of Luke 15:11–32." *JTI* 16 (2022): 57–73.

Balentine, Samuel E. "Prayer." In Freedman, *Eerdmans Dictionary of the Bible*, 1077–79.

Bamberger, Michael. *The Man Who Heard Voices: Or, How M. Night Shyamalan Risked His Career on a Fairy Tale*. New York: Penguin Books, 2006.

Banning, Edward B. "Towers." In Freedman, *Anchor Bible Dictionary*, 6:622–24.

Barnes, Julian. "What Are *You* Looking At?" *New York Review of Books*, May 12, 2022, 16–18.

Barrett, C. K. *A Critical and Exegetical Commentary on the Acts of the Apostles*. Vol. 2, *Introduction and Commentary on Acts 15–28*. ICC. Edinburgh: T&T Clark, 1998.

Bauckham, Richard. "The Rich Man and Lazarus: The Parable and the Parallels." *NTS* 37 (1991): 225–46.

Beavis, Mary Ann. "The Power of Jesus' Parables: Were They Polemical or Irenic?" *JSNT* 82 (2001): 3–30.

Bennema, Cornelis. "The Rich Are the Bad Guys: Lukan Characters and Wealth Ethics." In *Characters and Characterization in Luke-Acts*, edited by Frank E. Dicken and Julia A. Snyder, 95–108. LNTS 548. London: T&T Clark, 2016.

Bird, Michael F. *Evangelical Theology: A Biblical and Systematic Introduction*, 2nd ed. Grand Rapids: Zondervan, 2020.

Blake, Jenny. *Pivot: The Only Move That Matters Is Your Next One*. New York: Penguin Random House, 2016.

Blomberg, Craig L. *Interpreting the Parables*. 2nd ed. Downers Grove, IL: InterVarsity, 2012.

———. "Interpreting the Parables: Where Do We Go from Here?" *CBQ* 53 (1991): 50–78.

———. "Poetic Fiction, Subversive Speech, and Proportional Analogy in the Parables." *HBT* 18 (1996): 115–32.

Bock, Darrell L. *Luke*. 2 vols. Grand Rapids: Baker, 1994–96.

Bockmuehl, Markus. *The Remembered Peter in Ancient Reception and Modern Debate*. WUNT 262. Tübingen: Mohr Siebeck, 2010.

———. "Resurrection." In *The Cambridge Companion to Jesus*, edited by Markus Bockmuehl, 102–18. Cambridge: Cambridge University Press, 2001.

———. *Simon Peter in Scripture and Memory: The New Testament Apostle in the Early Church*. Grand Rapids: Baker Academic, 2012.

Bonhoeffer, Dietrich. *The Cost of Discipleship*. Translated by R. H. Fuller. 1937. Repr., New York: Macmillan, 1979.

Boomershine, Thomas E. "Audience Address and Purpose in the Performance of Mark." In *Mark as Story: Retrospect and Prospect*, edited by Kelly R. Iverson and Christopher W. Skinner, 115–42. Atlanta: Society of Biblical Literature, 2011.

Boring, M. Eugene. *Mark: A Commentary*. NTL. Louisville: Westminster John Knox, 2006.

Borsch, Frederick Houk. "Parables of Jesus: Told and Enacted." In *Earliest Christianity Within the Boundaries of Judaism: Essays in Honor of Bruce Chilton*, edited by Alan J. Avery-Peck, Craig A. Evans, and Jacob Neusner, 255–66. BRLJ 49. Leiden: Brill, 2016.

Botton, Alain de. *Status Anxiety*. New York: Penguin Books, 2004.

Boucher, Madeleine. *The Mysterious Parable*. CBQMS 6. Washington, DC: Catholic Biblical Association of America, 1977.

Bovon, François. *Luke 2: A Commentary on the Gospel of Luke 9:51–19:27*. Hermeneia. Minneapolis: Fortress, 2013.

Boxall, Ian. *Matthew Through the Centuries*. WBBC. Oxford: Wiley-Blackwell, 2019.

Bredenhof, Reuben. *Failure and Prospect: Lazarus and the Rich Man (Luke 16:19–31) in the Context of Luke-Acts*. LNTS 603. London: T&T Clark, 2019.

Briggs, Richard S. *The Lord Is My Shepherd: Psalm 23 for the Life of the Church*. Touchstone Texts. Grand Rapids: Baker Academic, 2021.

Brown, Jeannine K. *Matthew*. Teach the Text Commentary Series. Grand Rapids: Baker Books, 2015.

Brown, Jeannine K., and Kazuhiko Yamazaki-Ransom. "The Parable of the Good Samaritan and the Narrative Portrayal of Samaritans in Luke-Acts." *JTI* 15 (2021): 233–46.

Brown, Raymond E. *An Introduction to the New Testament: The Abridged Edition*, edited and abridged by Marion L. Soards. AYBRL. New Haven: Yale University Press, 2016.

Bruner, Frederick Dale. *Matthew: A Commentary*. Rev. ed. 2 vols. Grand Rapids: Eerdmans, 2004.

Burke, Trevor L. "The Parable of the Prodigal Father: An Interpretative Key to the Third Gospel (Luke 15:11–32)." *TynBul* 64 (2013): 217–38.

Burkett, Delbert. "The Parable of the Unrighteous Steward (Luke 16.1–9): A Prudent Use of Mammon." *NTS* 64 (2018): 326–42.

Callon, Callie. "*Adulescentes* and *Meretrices*: The Correlation Between Squandered Patrimony and Prostitutes in the Parable of the Prodigal Son." *CBQ* 75 (2013): 259–78.

Carroll, John T. *Luke: A Commentary*. NTL. Louisville: Westminster John Knox, 2012.

Chalmers, Matthew. "Rethinking Luke 10: The Parable of the Good Samaritan Israelite." *JBL* 139 (2020): 543–66.

Christian, Ed. "The Rich Man and Lazarus, Abraham's Bosom, and the Biblical Penalty *KARET* ('Cut Off')." *JETS* 61 (2018): 513–23.

Cole, R. Dennis. "Vine, Vineyard." In Freedman, *Eerdmans Dictionary of the Bible*, 1356–57.

Coleman, Rachel L. *The Lukan Lens on Wealth and Possessions: A Perspective Shaped by the Themes of Reversal and Right Response*. BIS 180. Leiden: Brill, 2019.

Collins, Adela Yarbro. *Mark*. Hermeneia. Minneapolis: Fortress, 2007.

Cotter, Wendy J. "The Parable of the Feisty Widow and the Threatened Judge (Luke 18:1–8)." *NTS* 51 (2005): 328–43.

Craddock, Fred B. *Luke*. Interpretation. Louisville: John Knox, 1990.

Crossan, John Dominic. "Parable." In Freedman, *Anchor Bible Dictionary*, 5:146–52.

Cuddon, J. A. *The Penguin Dictionary of Literary Terms and Literary Theory*. Revised by C. E. Preston. London: Penguin Books, 1999.

Culler, Jonathan. *Literary Theory: A Very Short Introduction*. Oxford: Oxford University Press, 1997.

Culpepper, R. Alan. "The Gospel of Luke." In *The New Interpreter's Bible*, vol. 8, *Luke and John*, edited by Leander E. Keck, 3–490. Nashville: Abingdon, 2003.

———. *John, the Son of Zebedee: The Life of a Legend*. Columbia: University of South Carolina Press, 1994.

———. *Matthew*. NTL. Louisville: Westminster John Knox, 2021.

Damm, Alex. "Gandhi and the Parable of the Prodigal Son." *BibInt* 29 (2021): 90–105.

Davies, Margaret. *Matthew*. Sheffield: JSOT Press, 1993.

Davies, W. D., and Dale C. Allison Jr. *A Critical and Exegetical Commentary on the Gospel According to St. Matthew*. Vol. 2, *8–18*. ICC. Edinburgh: T&T Clark, 1991.

Dinkler, Michal Beth. *Literary Theory and the New Testament*. AYBRL. New Haven: Yale University Press, 2019.

Dodd, C. H. *The Parables of the Kingdom*. London: Collins, 1961.

Donahue, John R., S. J. *The Gospel in Parable: Metaphor, Narrative, and Theology in the Synoptic Gospels*. Philadelphia: Fortress, 1988.

———. "Tax Collector." In Freedman, *Anchor Bible Dictionary*, 6:337–38.

Edwards, James R. *The Gospel According to Luke*. PNTC. Grand Rapids: Eerdmans, 2015.

Esser, Hans-Helmut. "Grace, Spiritual Gifts." In *The New International Dictionary of New Testament Theology*, edited by Colin Brown, 2:115–23. Grand Rapids: Zondervan, 1975–78.

Eubank, Nathan. "What Does Matthew Say About Divine Recompense? On the Misuse of the Parable of the Workers in the Vineyard (20.1–16)." *JSNT* 35 (2013): 242–62.

Evans, Craig A. *Jesus and His Contemporaries: Comparative Studies*. AGJU 25. Leiden: Brill, 1995.

———. *To See and Not Perceive: Isaiah 6:9–10 in Early Jewish and Christian Interpretation*. JSOTSup 64. Sheffield: Sheffield Academic Press, 1989.

Fitzmyer, Joseph A. *The Gospel According to Luke*. 2 vols. Garden City, NY: Doubleday, 1981–85.

Forbes, Greg W. *The God of Old: The Role of the Lukan Parables in the Purpose of Luke's Gospel*. JSNTSup 198. Sheffield: Sheffield Academic Press, 2000.

Fox, Michael V. "Wisdom in the Joseph Story." *VT* 51 (2001): 26–41.

France, Richard T. *The Gospel of Matthew*. TNTC. Grand Rapids: Eerdmans, 2007.

———. "On Being Ready (Matthew 25:1–46)." In R. Longenecker, *Challenge of Jesus' Parables*, 177–95.

Freedman, David Noel, ed. *The Anchor Bible Dictionary*. 6 vols. New York: Doubleday, 1992.

———, ed. *Eerdmans Dictionary of the Bible*. Grand Rapids: Eerdmans, 2000.

Garland, David E. *Luke*. ZECNT. Grand Rapids: Zondervan, 2011.

———. *Reading Matthew: A Literary and Theological Commentary on the First Gospel*. Reading the New Testament. Macon, GA: Smyth & Helwys, 2001.

Gathercole, Simon. *Defending Substitution: An Essay on Atonement in Paul*. ASBT. Grand Rapids: Baker Academic, 2015.

Ghosh, Amitav. *The Nutmeg's Curse: Parables for a Planet in Crisis*. Chicago: University of Chicago Press, 2021.

Giambrone, Anthony. "A Note on Luke's Parable of the Minas and the Ancient Practice of Burying Coin Hoards." *NTS* 65 (2019): 589–97.

Gnanavaram, M. "'Dalit Theology' and the Parable of the Good Samaritan." *JSNT* 50 (1993): 59–83.

Goldingay, John, and Tom Wright. *The Bible for Everyone: A New Translation*. London: SPCK, 2018.

Gourgues, Michel. "The Priest, the Levite, and the Samaritan Revisited: A Critical Note on Luke 10:31–35." *JBL* 117 (1998): 709–13.

Gowler, David B. "'At His Gate Lay a Poor Man': A Dialogic Reading of Luke 16:19–31." *PRSt* 32 (2005): 249–65.

———. *The Parables After Jesus: Their Imaginative Receptions Across Two Millennia*. Grand Rapids: Baker Academic, 2017.

———. *What Are They Saying About the Parables?* New York: Paulist Press, 2000.

Green, Joel B. *The Gospel of Luke*. NICNT. Grand Rapids: Eerdmans, 1997.

Green, Joel B., Jeannine K. Brown, and Nicholas Perrin. *Dictionary of Jesus and the Gospels*. 2nd ed. Downers Grove, IL: InterVarsity, 2013.

Green, Michael. *The Message of Matthew*. Downers Grove, IL: InterVarsity, 2000.

Guelich, Robert A. *Mark 1:1–8:26*. WBC. Dallas: Word, 1989.

Gundry, Robert H. *Matthew: A Commentary on His Literary and Theological Art*. Grand Rapids: Eerdmans, 1982.

Hagner, Donald A. *Matthew*. 2 vols. WBC. Dallas: Word, 1993–95.

Halberstam, Chaya. "Law in Biblical Israel." In *The Cambridge Companion to Judaism and Law*, edited by Christine Hayes, 19–47. New York: Cambridge University Press, 2017.

Hauerwas, Stanley. *Matthew*. BTCB. Grand Rapids: Brazos, 2006.

Hays, Richard B. *Echoes of Scripture in the Gospels*. Waco: Baylor University Press, 2016.

———. "Knowing Jesus: Story, History and the Question of Truth." In *Jesus, Paul, and the People of God: A Theological Dialogue with N. T. Wright*, edited by Nicholas Perrin and Richard B. Hays, 41–61. Downers Grove, IL: InterVarsity, 2011.

Hedrick, Charles W. *Many Things in Parables: Jesus and His Modern Critics*. Louisville: Westminster John Knox, 2004.

———. "Parables." In Freedman, *Eerdmans Dictionary of the Bible*, 1006–8.

———. *Parabolic Figures or Narrative Fictions? Seminal Essays on the Stories of Jesus*. Eugene, OR: Cascade Books, 2016.

Hengel, Martin. *Saint Peter: The Underestimated Apostle*. Translated by Thomas H. Trapp. Grand Rapids: Eerdmans, 2010.

Hershman, Evan. *Jesus as Teacher in the Gospel of Mark: The Function of a Motif*. LNTS 626. London: T&T Clark, 2021.

Hicks, John Mark. "The Parable of the Persistent Widow (Luke 18:1–8)." *ResQ* 33 (1991): 209–23.

Hultgren, Arland J. *The Parables of Jesus: A Commentary*. Grand Rapids: Eerdmans, 2000.

Jack, Alison M. *The Prodigal Son in English and American Literature: Five Hundred Years of Literary Homecomings*. Oxford: Oxford University Press, 2019.

Jenson, Robert W. *Systematic Theology*. Vol. 1, *The Triune God*. New York: Oxford University Press, 1997.

Jeremias, Joachim. *The Parables of Jesus*. 2nd rev. ed. New York: Scribner's, 1972.

Johnson, Luke Timothy. *The Gospel of Luke*. Collegeville, MN: Liturgical Press, 1991.

Jokinen, Heidi. "New Wineskin of Conflict Resolution: Conditions of Change in the Parable on Wineskin." *BTB* 50 (2020): 22–34.

Jordan, Jillian, and David Rand. "Are You 'Virtue Signaling'?" *New York Times*, March 30, 2019.

Keddie, G. Anthony. "'Who Is My Neighbor?' Ethnic Boundaries and the Samaritan Other in Luke 10:25–37." *BibInt* 28 (2020): 246–71.

Keener, Craig S. *A Commentary on the Gospel of Matthew*. Grand Rapids: Eerdmans, 1999.

Keesmaat, Sylvia C. "Strange Neighbors and Risky Care (Matt. 18:21–35; Luke 14:7–14; Luke 10:25–37)." In R. Longenecker, *Challenge of Jesus' Parables*, 263–85.

King, Fergus J. "A Funny Thing Happened on the Way to the Parable: The Steward, Tricksters and (Non)sense in Luke 16:1–8." *BTB* 48 (2018): 18–25.

Knoppers, Gary N. *Jews and Samaritans: The Origins and History of Their Early Relations*. Oxford: Oxford University Press, 2013.

Knowles, Michael P. "What Was the Victim Wearing? Literary, Economic, and Social Contexts for the Parable of the Good Samaritan." *BibInt* 12, no. 2 (2004): 145–74.

Kselman, John S. "Grace." In Freedman, *Anchor Bible Dictionary*, 2:1085–86.

Labahn, Michael. "Simon Peter: An Ambiguous Character and His Narrative Career." In *Character Studies in the Fourth Gospel: Narrative Approaches to Seventy Figures in John*, edited by Steven A. Hunt, D. Francis Tolmie, and Ruben Zimmermann, 151–67. Grand Rapids: Eerdmans, 2016.

LaHurd, Carol. "Rediscovering the Lost Women in Luke 15." *BTB* 24 (1994): 66–76.

Lehtipuu, Outi. *The Afterlife Imagery in Luke's Story of the Rich Man and Lazarus*. NovTSup 123. Leiden: Brill, 2007.

———. *Debates over the Resurrection of the Dead: Constructing Early Christian Identity*. OECS. Oxford: Oxford University Press, 2015.

Leim, Joshua Eugene. "To Inherit Eternal Life: Jesus, the Lawyer, and Luke's Soteriological Grammar." *BBR* 31 (2021): 167–90.

Leveen, Adriane. "Becoming Israel in the Wilderness of Numbers." In *The Oxford Handbook of Biblical Narrative*, edited by Danna Nolan Fewell, 147–56. New York: Oxford University Press, 2015.

Levine, Amy-Jill. *Short Stories by Jesus: The Enigmatic Parables of a Controversial Rabbi*. San Francisco: HarperOne, 2014.

Lewis, Linda M. *Dickens, His Parables, and His Reader*. Columbia: University of Missouri Press, 2011.

Löhr, Hermut. "Luke-Acts as a Source for the History of the Pharisees." In *The Pharisees*, edited by Joseph Sievers and Amy-Jill Levine, 170–84. Grand Rapids: Eerdmans, 2021.

Long, Thomas G. *Matthew*. Louisville: Westminster John Knox, 1997.

Longenecker, Bruce W. "The Story of the Samaritan and the Innkeeper (Luke 10:30–35): A Study in Character Rehabilitation." *BibInt* 17 (2009): 422–47.

Longenecker, Richard N., ed. *The Challenge of Jesus' Parables*. Grand Rapids: Eerdmans, 2000.

Longman, Tremper, III. *Proverbs*. Grand Rapids: Baker Academic, 2006.

Luz, Ulrich. *Matthew: A Commentary*. 3 vols. Translated by James E. Crouch. Hermeneia. Minneapolis: Fortress, 2001–7.

Malbon, Elizabeth Struthers. *Mark's Jesus: Characterization as Narrative Christology*. Waco: Baylor University Press, 2009.

Maloney, Linda. "'Swept Under the Rug': Feminist Homiletical Reflections on the Parable of the Lost Coin (Lk. 15.8–9)." In *The Lost Coin: Parables of Women, Work and Wisdom*, edited by Mary Ann Beavis, 34–38. The Biblical Seminar 86. London: Sheffield Academic Press, 2002.

Marcus, Joel. *Mark 1–8: A New Translation with Introduction and Commentary*. AB 27. New York: Doubleday, 2000.

———. *Mark 8–16: A New Translation with Introduction and Commentary*. AB 27a. New Haven: Yale University Press, 2009.

Marshall, I. Howard. *The Gospel of Luke: A Commentary on the Greek Text*. Grand Rapids: Eerdmans, 1978.

———. *New Testament Theology: Many Witnesses, One Gospel*. Downers Grove, IL: InterVarsity, 2004.

Mason, Steve. "Pharisees." In Freedman, *Eerdmans Dictionary of the Bible*, 1043–44.

Matthews, Mary W., Carter Shelley, and Barbara Scheele. "Proclaiming the Parable of the Persistent Widow (Lk. 18.2–5)." In *The Lost Coin: Parables of Women, Work and Wisdom*, edited by Mary Ann Beavis, 46–70. The Biblical Seminar 86. London: Sheffield Academic Press, 2002.

Meier, John P. *A Marginal Jew: Rethinking the Historical Jesus*. Vol. 5, *Probing the Authenticity of the Parables*. AYBRL. New Haven: Yale University Press, 2016.

Metzger, James A. *Consumption and Wealth in Luke's Travel Narrative*. BIS 88. Leiden: Brill, 2007.

Moberly, R. W. L. *The Theology of the Book of Genesis*. OTT. Cambridge: Cambridge University Press, 2009.

Neumann, James N. "Thy Will Be Done: Jesus's Passion in the Lord's Prayer." *JBL* 138 (2019): 161–82.

Niditch, Susan. *Ethics in the Hebrew Bible and Beyond*. New York: Oxford University Press, 2024.

Nolland, John. *The Gospel of Matthew: A Commentary on the Greek Text*. NIGTC. Grand Rapids: Eerdmans, 2005.

Oden, Thomas C., ed. *Parables of Kierkegaard*. Princeton: Princeton University Press, 1978.

Olmstead, Wesley G. *Matthew's Trilogy of Parables: The Nation, the Nations and the Reader in Matthew 21.28–22.14*. SNTSMS 127. Cambridge: Cambridge University Press, 2003.

Oppong-Kumi, Peter Yaw. *Matthean Sets of Parables*. WUNT 2/340. Tübingen: Mohr Siebeck, 2013.

Osborne, Grant R. *Matthew*. ZECNT. Grand Rapids: Zondervan, 2010.

Parrott, Douglas M. "The Dishonest Steward (Luke 16:1–8a) and Luke's Special Parable Collection." *NTS* 37 (1991): 499–515.

Parsons, Mikeal C. "The Character of the Good Samaritan: A Christological Reading." In *Let the Reader Understand: Studies in Honor of Elizabeth Struthers Malbon*, edited by Edwin K. Broadhead, 123–34. LNTS 583. London: T&T Clark, 2018.

Patte, Daniel. "Bringing Out of the Gospel-Treasure What Is New and What Is Old: Two Parables in Matthew 18–23." *Quarterly Review* 10 (1990): 79–108.

Perrin, Nicholas. *Luke: An Introduction and Commentary*. TNTC 3. Downers Grove, IL: InterVarsity, 2022.

Peterson, Eugene H. *Tell It Slant: A Conversation on the Language of Jesus in His Stories and Prayers*. Grand Rapids: Eerdmans, 2008.

Polzin, Robert. *David and the Deuteronomist*. Bloomington: Indiana University Press, 1993.

Proctor, Mark A. "'Who Is My Neighbor?' Recontextualizing Luke's Good Samaritan (Luke 10:25–37)." *JBL* 138 (2019): 203–19.

Reid, Barbara E. "A Godly Widow Persistently Pursuing Justice: Luke 18:1–8." *BR* 45 (2000): 25–33.

———. *The Gospel According to Matthew*. Collegeville, MN: Liturgical Press, 2005.

———. *Parables for Preachers, Year C*. Collegeville, MN: Liturgical Press, 2000.

———. "Violent Endings in Matthew's Parables and Christian Nonviolence." *CBQ* 66 (2004): 237–55.

Resseguie, James L. *Narrative Criticism of the New Testament: An Introduction*. Grand Rapids: Baker Academic, 2005.

———. "The Woman Who Crashed Simon's Party: A Reader-Response Approach to Luke 7:36–50." In *Characters and Characterization in Luke-Acts*, edited by Frank E. Dicken and Julia A. Snyder, 7–22. LNTS 548. London: T&T Clark, 2016.

Ridlehoover, Charles Nathan. *The Lord's Prayer and Sermon on the Mount in Matthew's Gospel*. LNTS 616. London: T&T Clark, 2020.

Rindge, Matthew S. *Jesus' Parable of the Rich Fool: Luke 12:13–34 Among Ancient Conversations on Death and Possessions*. ECL. Atlanta: Society of Biblical Literature, 2011.

———. "Luke's Artistic Parables: Narratives of Subversion, Imagination, and Transformation." *Int* 68, no. 4 (2014): 403–15.

Rowe, C. Kavin. *Early Narrative Christology: The Lord in the Gospel of Luke*. BZNW 139. Berlin: de Gruyter, 2006.

Saldarini, Anthony J. "Pharisees." In Freedman, *Anchor Bible Dictionary*, 5:289–303.

Samkutty, V. J. *The Samaritan Mission in Acts*. LNTS 338. London: T&T Clark, 2006.

Schellenberg, Ryan S. "Which Master? Whose Steward? Metalepsis and Lordship in the Parable of the Prudent Steward (Lk. 16.1–13)." *JSNT* 30, no. 3 (2008): 263–88.

Schipper, Jeremy. *Parables and Conflict in the Hebrew Bible*. New York: Cambridge University Press, 2007.

Schnabel, Eckhard J. *Mark*. TNTC. Downers Grove, IL: InterVarsity, 2017.

———. *New Testament Theology*. Grand Rapids: Baker Academic, 2023.

Schniewind, Julius. *Das Evangelium nach Matthäus*. 1935. Repr., Göttingen: Vandenhoeck & Ruprecht, 1962.

Schreiner, Thomas R. "Luke." In *ESV Expository Commentary*. Vol. 8, *Matthew–Luke*, edited by Iain M. Duguid, James M. Hamilton Jr., and Jay Sklar, 703–1106. Wheaton: Crossway, 2021.

———. *New Testament Theology: Magnifying God in Christ*. Grand Rapids: Baker Academic, 2008.

Schumacher, R. Daniel. "Saving Like a Fool and Spending Like It Isn't Yours: Reading the Parable of the Unjust Steward (Luke 16:1–8a) in Light of the Parable of the Rich Fool (Luke 12:16–20)." *RevExp* 109 (2012): 269–76.

Scott, Bernard Brandon. *Hear Then the Parable: A Commentary on the Parables of Jesus*. Minneapolis: Fortress, 1989.

Sellew, Philip. "Interior Monologue as a Narrative Device in the Parables of Luke." *JBL* 111 (1992): 239–53.

Sievers, Joseph, and Amy-Jill Levine, eds. *The Pharisees*. Grand Rapids: Eerdmans, 2021.

Smith, Abraham. "A Prodigal Sings the Blues: The Characterization of Harriett Williams in Langston Hughes's 'Not Without Laughter.'" In *Yet with a Steady Beat: Contemporary U.S. Afrocentric Biblical Interpretation*, edited by Randall C. Bailey, 145–58. Atlanta: SBL, 2002.

Snodgrass, Klyne R. "Are the Parables Still the Bedrock of the Jesus Tradition?" *JSHJ* 15 (2017): 131–46.

———. “From Allegorizing to Allegorizing: A History of the Interpretation of the Parables of Jesus.” In R. Longenecker, *Challenge of Jesus’ Parables*, 3–29.

———. *Stories with Intent: A Comprehensive Guide to the Parables of Jesus*, 2nd ed. Grand Rapids: Eerdmans, 2018.

Somov, Alexey, and Vitaly Voinov. “‘Abraham’s Bosom’ (Luke 16:22–23) as a Key Metaphor in the Overall Composition of the Parable of the Rich Man and Lazarus.” *CBQ* 79 (2017): 615–33.

Spencer, Nick. *The Political Samaritan: How Power Hijacked a Parable*. New York: Bloomsbury, 2018.

Spencer, Patrick E. *Rhetorical Texture and Narrative Trajectories of the Lukan Galilean Ministry Speeches: Hermeneutical Appropriation by Authorial Readers of Luke-Acts*. LNTS 341. London: T&T Clark, 2007.

Stigall, Josh. “‘They Have Moses and the Prophets’: The Enduring Demand of the Law and Prophets in the Parable of the Rich Man and Lazarus.” *RevExp* 112 (2015): 542–54.

Strauss, Mark L. *Mark*. ZECNT. Grand Rapids: Zondervan, 2014.

Strong, Justin David. “Lazarus and the Dogs: The Diagnosis and Treatment.” *NTS* 64 (2018): 178–93.

Stuhlmacher, Peter. *Biblical Theology of the New Testament*. Translated and edited by Daniel P. Bailey. Grand Rapids: Eerdmans, 2018.

Sweet, Leonard. *The Bad Habits of Jesus: Showing Us the Way to Live Right in a World Gone Wrong*. Carol Stream, IL: Tyndale, 2016.

Talbert, Charles H. *Matthew*. Paideia Commentaries on the New Testament. Grand Rapids: Baker Academic, 2010.

Tannehill, Robert C. *The Shape of Luke’s Story: Essays on Luke-Acts*. Eugene, OR: Wipf & Stock, 2005.

———. “Should We Love Simon the Pharisee? Hermeneutical Reflections on the Pharisees in Luke.” *Currents in Theology and Mission* 21 (1994): 424–33.

Teugels, Lieve M. “Talking Animals in Parables: A *Contradictio in terminis*?” In *Parables in Changing Contexts: Essays on the Study of Parables in Christianity, Judaism, Islam, and Buddhism*, edited by Eric Ottenheijm and Marcel Poorthuis, 129–48. JCPS 35. Leiden: Brill, 2020.

Thurén, Lauri. *Parables Unplugged: Reading the Lukan Parables in Their Rhetorical Context*. Minneapolis: Fortress, 2014.

Tosi, Justin, and Brandon Warmke. *Grandstanding: The Use and Abuse of Moral Talk*. New York: Oxford University Press, 2020.

Turner, David L. *Matthew*. BECNT. Grand Rapids: Baker, 2008.

Udoh, Fabian E. “The Tale of an Unrighteous Slave (Luke 16:1–8 [13]).” *JBL* 128 (2009): 311–35.

Ulmer, Gregory L. “Post-Criticism: Conceptual Takes.” In *The Routledge Companion to Experimental Literature*, edited by Joe Bray, Alison Gibbons, and Brian McHale, 267–78. New York: Routledge, 2012.

Vaage, Margrethe Bruun. *The Antihero in American Television*. New York: Routledge, 2016.

Vanhoozer, Kevin J. *The Drama of Doctrine: A Canonical-Linguistic Approach to Theology*. Louisville: Westminster John Knox, 2005.

Vayntrub, Jacqueline. “‘To Take Up a Parable’: The History of Translating a Biblical Idiom.” *VT* 66 (2016): 627–45.

Vearncombe, Erin K. “Redistribution and Reciprocity: A Socio-Economic Interpretation of the Parable of the Labourers in the Vineyard (Matthew 20.1–15).” *JSHJ* 8 (2010): 199–236.

Waetjen, Herman C. “The Subversion of ‘World’ by the Parable of the Friend at Midnight.” *JBL* 120 (2001): 703–21.

Wailes, Stephen L. *Medieval Allegories of Jesus’ Parables*. Berkeley: University of California Press, 1987.

Waltke, Bruce K. *The Book of Proverbs, Chapters 15–31*. NICOT. Grand Rapids: Eerdmans, 2005.

Weaver, Dorothy Jean. "Luke 18:1–8." *Int* 56 (2002): 317–19.

Webster, Douglas D. *The Parables: Jesus's Friendly Subversive Speech*. Grand Rapids: Kregel Academic, 2021.

Wenkel, David H. *Coins as Cultural Texts in the World of the New Testament*. London: T&T Clark, 2017.

Wierzbicka, Anna. *What Did Jesus Mean? Explaining the Sermon on the Mount and the Parables in Simple and Universal Human Concepts*. New York: Oxford University Press, 2001.

Wilder, Amos. *The Language of the Gospel: Early Christian Rhetoric*. Rev. ed. New York: Harper & Row, 1971.

Wilkins, Michael J. *Matthew*. Grand Rapids: Zondervan, 2004.

Wilson, Frances. *How to Survive the Titanic: The Sinking of J. Bruce Ismay*. London: Bloomsbury, 2011.

Wilson, Walter T. *The Gospel of Matthew*. Vol. 2, *Matthew 14–28*. ECC. Grand Rapids: Eerdmans, 2022.

Witherington, Ben, III. *Matthew*. Macon, GA: Smyth & Helwys, 2006.

Wolter, Michael. *The Gospel According to Luke*. Vol. 2, *Luke 9:51–24*. Translated by Wayne Coppins and Christoph Heilig. Waco: Baylor University Press, 2017.

Wright, N. T. *Jesus and the Victory of God*. Minneapolis: Fortress, 1996.

Wright, N. T., and Michael F. Bird. *The New Testament in Its World: An Introduction to the History, Literature, and Theology of the First Christians*. Grand Rapids: Zondervan, 2019.

Wright, Stephen I. "Parables on Poverty and Riches (Luke 12:13–21; 16:1–13; 16:19–31)." In R. Longenecker, *Challenge of Jesus' Parables*, 217–39.

Yoder, Keith L. "In the Bosom of Abraham: The Name and Role of Poor Lazarus in Luke 16:19–31." *NovT* 62 (2020): 2–24.

Zimmermann, Ruben. "Are There Parables in John? It Is Time to Revisit the Question." *JSHJ* 9 (2011): 243–76.

———. *Puzzling the Parables of Jesus: Methods and Interpretation*. Minneapolis: Fortress, 2015.

Name Index